# About This Book

## Why Is This Topic Important?

From Twitter and Facebook to YouTube, blogs, smartphones, and tablet PCs, employees' access to the web—and employers' exposure to potentially costly and protracted risks—is greater today than ever before. Social media and other web 2.0 applications dramatically increase organizations' risks of workplace lawsuits, regulatory fines, security breaches, mismanaged business records, productivity drains, public relations nightmares, and other electronic disasters.

Your business cannot afford to ignore social media risks and rules. Even if your organization does not currently operate a business blog, have a corporate presence on public social networking sites, or collaborate internally via private enterprise-grade social media, you must act now to manage behavior, mitigate risks, and maximize compliance through the implementation of a strategic social media policy and compliance management program—or face the possibility of seven-figure lawsuits, multimillion-dollar regulatory fines, and other electronic disasters that can sink companies and shatter careers.

## What Can You Achieve with This Book?

A comprehensive risk and compliance management toolkit, *The Social Media Handbook* takes employers step-by-step through the process of developing and implementing effective social media policy and compliance management programs that are designed to minimize—and in some case prevent—social networking and web 2.0 risks. Written to help employers of all sizes and industries navigate safely through the social networking universe, this book provides organizations with the must-have tips and tools necessary to effectively manage social media risks, records, content, use, policies, and procedures.

## How Is This Book Organized?

*The Social Media Handbook* provides employers with a clear-eyed, comprehensive review of the legal, regulatory, security, reputation, and other risks inherent in employees' social media use and content. It then reveals how organizations can help minimize risks and maximize compliance through the implementation of best practices–based policies, supported by comprehensive employee education, and enforced by proven-effective technology tools. The book provides a seven-step action plan for compliance management success, reveals how and why to conduct a social media policy audit, and shares the secrets of effective policy writing. The book also emphasizes the important role that employee education plays when it comes to legal, regulatory, and organizational compliance. Sample policies are provided for employers who are looking for help developing effective, well-written social media, blog, and related rules and policies.

To get the most from *The Social Media Handbook*, it is not necessary to read the book from cover to cover. Feel free to jump around, reading the content that best addresses your legal, regulatory, records, e-discovery, privacy, security, policy, reputation management, training, and technology questions, concerns, and challenges.

# About Pfeiffer

Pfeiffer serves the professional development and hands-on resource needs of training and human resource practitioners and gives them products to do their jobs better. We deliver proven ideas and solutions from experts in HR development and HR management, and we offer effective and customizable tools to improve workplace performance. From novice to seasoned professional, Pfeiffer is the source you can trust to make yourself and your organization more successful.

**Essential Knowledge** Pfeiffer produces insightful, practical, and comprehensive materials on topics that matter the most to training and HR professionals. Our Essential Knowledge resources translate the expertise of seasoned professionals into practical, how-to guidance on critical workplace issues and problems. These resources are supported by case studies, worksheets, and job aids and are frequently supplemented with CD-ROMs, websites, and other means of making the content easier to read, understand, and use.

**Essential Tools** Pfeiffer's Essential Tools resources save time and expense by offering proven, ready-to-use materials—including exercises, activities, games, instruments, and assessments—for use during a training or team-learning event. These resources are frequently offered in looseleaf or CD-ROM format to facilitate copying and customization of the material.

Pfeiffer also recognizes the remarkable power of new technologies in expanding the reach and effectiveness of training. While e-hype has often created whizbang solutions in search of a problem, we are dedicated to bringing convenience and enhancements to proven training solutions. All our e-tools comply with rigorous functionality standards. The most appropriate technology wrapped around essential content yields the perfect solution for today's on-the-go trainers and human resource professionals.

**Pfeiffer**
www.pfeiffer.com

*Essential resources for training and HR professionals*

# THE SOCIAL MEDIA HANDBOOK

# THE SOCIAL MEDIA HANDBOOK

## POLICIES AND BEST PRACTICES TO EFFECTIVELY MANAGE YOUR ORGANIZATION'S SOCIAL MEDIA PRESENCE, POSTS, AND POTENTIAL RISKS

Nancy Flynn
Author of *The e-Policy Handbook, Blog Rules, Writing Effective E-Mail*, and *The ePolicy Toolkit*

**Pfeiffer**
A Wiley Imprint
www.pfeiffer.com

Published by Pfeiffer An Imprint of Wiley One Montgomery Street, Suite 1200, San Francisco, CA 94104-4594 www.pfeiffer.com

For additional copies/bulk purchases of this book in the U.S. please contact 800–274–4434. Pfeiffer books and products are available through most bookstores. To contact Pfeiffer directly call our Customer Care Department within the U.S. at 800-274-4434, outside the U.S. at 317-572-3985, fax 317-572-4002, or visit www.pfeiffer.com.

Pfeiffer publishes in a variety of print and electronic formats and by print-on-demand. Some material included with standard print versions of this book may not be included in e-books or in print-on-demand. If this book refers to media such as a CD or DVD that is not included in the version you purchased, you may download this material at http://booksupport.wiley.com. For more information about Wiley products, visit www.wiley.com.

*Library of Congress Cataloging-in-Publication Data*

Flynn, Nancy.
    The social media handbook : policies and best practices to effectively manage your organization's social media presence, posts, and potential risks / Nancy Flynn.
        p.   cm.
    Includes bibliographical references and index.
    ISBN 978-1-118-08462-5 (cloth)
        1.  Social media—Economic aspects.   I.  Title.
    HM742.F58   2012
    302.23'1—dc23
                                                                            2011046013

| | |
|---|---|
| Acquiring Editor: | Matthew Davis |
| Director of Development: | Kathleen Dolan Davies |
| Production Editor: | Dawn Kilgore |
| Editor: | Donna Weinson |
| Editorial Assistant: | Michael Zelenko |
| Manufacturing Supervisor: | Becky Morgan |

Printed in the United States of America

HB Printing       10   9   8   7   6   5   4   3   2   1
PB Printing       10   9   8   7   6   5   4   3   2   1

# CONTENTS

# CONTENTS
# OF THE WEB

The following materials are available for download from
www.pfeiffer.com/go/flynn
password: professional

*To Truman*

# ABOUT THE AUTHOR

Nancy Flynn is founder and executive director of The ePolicy Institute™, an organization dedicated to reducing electronic risks, including litigation, through the development and implementation of effective policies and training programs.

An in-demand speaker and trainer, she is the author of twelve books published in six languages. Her titles include *The e-Policy Handbook*, *Blog Rules*, *E-Mail Rules*, *Instant Messaging Rules*, *Writing Effective E-Mail*, *E-Mail Management*, and *The ePolicy Toolkit*.

Through The ePolicy Institute, Flynn offers training, policy writing, expert witness services, surveys, and content development for clients worldwide.

Flynn is a popular media source who has been featured in *Fortune*, *Time*, *Newsweek*, *USA Today*, *Reader's Digest*, *US News & World Report*, *The Wall Street Journal*, *BusinessWeek*, and *The New York Times*, as well as on CBS, ABC, NBC, CNN, CNBC, MSNBC, BBC, NPR, and other media outlets.

To schedule a training seminar, book a consultation, or conduct a media interview, contact:

*Nancy Flynn*
*Founder and Executive Director*
*The ePolicy Institute*
614-451-3200
nancy@epolicyinstitute.com
www.ePolicyInstitute.com

# INTRODUCTION

## GETTING THE MOST FROM THIS RESOURCE

*The Social Media Handbook: Policies and Best Practices to Effectively Manage Your Organization's Social Media Presence, Posts, and Potential Risks* is a best practices–based guide for safe, effective, and compliant electronic business communication in the age of social networking, two-way conversations, and real-time collaboration, both within your office walls and without. *The Social Media Handbook* is written for human resource (HR) professionals, information technology (IT) managers, legal professionals, compliance officers, records managers, training professionals, business owners, and others with a need to manage twenty-first-century technology tools with twenty-first-century employment rules.

## SOCIAL MEDIA POSE POTENTIALLY COSTLY RISKS TO BUSINESS

Just like email and the Internet, social media and other web 2.0 applications are fraught with potentially costly and protracted risks for business, including workplace lawsuits, regulatory audits and fines, exposure of company secrets, loss of confidential data, mismanaged and misplaced business records, public relations nightmares, security breaches, and lost productivity, among others.

To clarify, *web 2.0* is the umbrella term that is used to describe the type of interactive, Internet-based communication tools and technologies that facilitate online conversations, collaboration, and customization. Web 2.0 applications include social networking sites like Facebook, blogs like *The Huffington Post,* microblogs like Twitter, wikis like Wikipedia, photo-sharing sites like Flickr, and video-sharing sites like YouTube.

Web 2.0 is all about the creation and exchange of open, honest, and transparent user-generated content, content that makes social networking so appealing to individuals and so potentially risky for business. When used appropriately and lawfully, social media can deliver undeniable communication and collaboration, sales and service, marketing and publicity benefits to business. Left unmanaged, however, social media and other web 2.0 applications can open organizations of all sizes and types to potentially costly and protracted risks.

*The Social Media Handbook* provides employers with a clear-eyed, comprehensive review of the risks inherent in employees' social media use and content. It then reveals how organizations can help manage behavior, mitigate risks, and maximize compliance through the implementation of strategic social media compliance management programs, combining written policies, supported by comprehensive employee education, and enforced by proven-effective technology tools.

## *Your Business Cannot Afford to Ignore Social Media*

Even if your organization doesn't currently operate a business blog, have a corporate presence on public social networking sites like Facebook and Twitter, or communicate and collaborate via private enterprise-grade social networking sites like Yammer, employers cannot afford to ignore social networking. Fail to provide the must-have, in-demand social media applications of the day, and your employees (particularly younger employees who expect ready access to social media) will bring web 2.0 in through the back door, creating potential legal, regulatory, security, and productivity nightmares for your business.

Fortunately, through the strategic implementation of a comprehensive social media compliance management program that combines policy, training, and technology—as detailed in the pages of this book—employers can minimize their legal, regulatory, and organizational risks while maximizing compliance with internal rules and external requirements.

### Policy Is at the Heart of Successful Social Media Compliance Management

Regardless of your organization's industry, size, or status as a public or private entity, best practices call for the establishment and enforcement of written social media policies. An effective social media policy will help protect your organization from risks triggered by employees' authorized (and unauthorized) use of your systems, accounts, sites, and devices. Carefully crafted, clearly written policies also will help protect your organization and its individual employees from liabilities triggered by using their own personal social media accounts and private electronic devices, both after hours and at the office, as well.

## WHAT *THE SOCIAL MEDIA HANDBOOK* OFFERS READERS

Far from an "emerging" technology that doesn't yet warrant employers' time, attention, or IT dollars, social networking already has changed the shape of business (and personal) communication. Social media sites have revolutionized the ways in which organizations do business by facilitating speedy, public, free, interactive electronic conversations and information sharing among employees and job applicants, customers and prospects, executives and staff, physicians and patients, faculty and students, the media and decision makers, investors and the public, and just about every other type of internal and external audience your organization may want to engage—within your organization, locally in your own community, or halfway around the globe.

As of 2011, Facebook boasted more than 800 million active users, each of whom averaged 130 online "friends." More than 350 million of those active users accessed Facebook through smartphones, cell phones, tablets, and other mobile devices.[1]

According to the Human Capital Institute, 49 percent of organizations currently use private enterprise-grade, or in-house, social networking sites like Yammer or Socialtext for secure communication among workers, as well as public sites like Twitter and Facebook for interactive discussions with external parties.[2]

One new blog, the "original" social networking tool, is created every second.[3] Among small- to medium-sized companies, 69 percent use Facebook for business; 44 percent have a corporate presence on Twitter; 32 percent share videos on YouTube; and 23 percent connect via LinkedIn, according to Panda Security's *Social Media Risk Index for Small to Medium Sized Businesses*.[4]

Industry analyst Gartner, Inc. predicts that by 2014 social networking will have replaced corporate email as the primary form of business communication for 20 percent of users.[5]

It's safe to assume that the social networking phenomenon will continue its ascent as the electronic communications tool of choice for business and personal users. Consequently, ever-increasing numbers of employers (and employees) will be in need of the type of proven, reliable, expert advice on social media policies, practices, and procedures that is contained in *The Social Media Handbook*.

## What Distinguishes The Social Media Handbook from Other Books?

Written primarily for business readers, *The Social Media Handbook* focuses on managing social media risks and maximizing employee and organizational compliance—not building brands, following friends, creating connections, or positioning products online.

If you are an entrepreneur or business owner looking for advice or strategies to help grow an Internet business via social media channels, then *The Social Media Handbook* is not for you. If you are a brand manager or marketing professional eager to establish a reputation, position a product, or dominate a market via Facebook, Twitter, or YouTube, then *The Social Media Handbook* is not for you. If you are an individual or organization looking for help getting your social media profile up and running in order to enhance business communication, marketing, and networking, then *The Social Media Handbook* is not for you, either.

*The Social Media Handbook* is an entirely different book, aimed at entirely different audience needs. A comprehensive risk and compliance management toolkit, *The Social Media Handbook* takes employers step-by-step through the process of developing and implementing effective social media policy and compliance management programs that are designed to minimize—and in some cases prevent—social networking and web 2.0 risks and other electronic disasters.

## WHAT YOU WILL FIND IN *THE SOCIAL MEDIA HANDBOOK*

*The Social Media Handbook* provides employers with best practices–based guidelines for developing and implementing effective policies and procedures designed to help manage employee behavior, mitigate organizational risks, and maximize compliance with the law, regulatory guidelines, and organizational rules. Written to help employers of all sizes and industries navigate safely through the social networking universe, this book provides the must-have tips and tools necessary to manage social media risks, records, content, use, policies, and procedures.

### Summary of Contents

Following are brief summaries of each chapter.

#### Chapter One. Why Every Organization Needs a Social Media Policy and Compliance Management Program.

This chapter introduces readers to the dangers of social media, including but not limited to workplace lawsuits, regulatory investigations and fines, data security breaches, compromised customer and company information, negative publicity, damaged business and personal reputations, lost revenues, productivity slowdowns, and employee terminations, among other risks. Chapter One sets the stage for strategic social media compliance management, spelling out why—and how—organizations should take immediate action to proactively manage social media use and content, records and risks.

## Chapter Two. Social Media and the Law: What Every Organization Needs to Know About Legal Compliance.

Chapter Two addresses the importance of keeping social media use and content lawful, civil, and business-appropriate. This chapter includes a comprehensive review of the legal risks that are inherent in using social media as a business communication tool, from vicarious liability and copyright infringement, to harassment and discrimination claims, defamation suits, and other potentially costly and protracted legal risks. In addition, Chapter Two provides employers with best practices–based guidelines to help ensure that employees' social media use, business and personal, is compliant with the laws of every jurisdiction in which you operate, employ workers, or litigate workplace lawsuits.

## Chapter Three. Social Networking Creates Legal Evidence: How to Manage Records and E-Discovery Compliantly.

Whether in the form of blog posts, Facebook walls, LinkedIn profiles, YouTube videos, Twitter tweets, Flickr photos, text messages, or "good-old-fashioned" email, all online content has the potential to create electronic business records. The electronic equivalent of DNA evidence, business records may be subpoenaed and used to support (or sink) your organization in the event of litigation. As detailed in Chapter Three, all organizations are required—for legal, regulatory, and business reasons—to manage their electronic business records in a compliant fashion.

"Discovery" is the phase of litigation during which the court orders all parties to a lawsuit to produce documents that are relevant to the case. Increasingly, those documents are electronic and may include blog posts, tweets, text messages, email attachments, history of

Internet surfing, and other forms of electronically stored information (ESI). When electronic evidence is subpoenaed during discovery and produced for review by opposing legal counsel, that process is called "e-discovery."

In the United States, federal and state courts alike take e-discovery seriously. Failure to produce subpoenaed ESI during e-discovery can result in multimillion-dollar court sanctions and other penalties. Read Chapter Three for best practices–based guidelines to help ensure the legally compliant preservation, protection, and production of social media content and other ESI.

### Chapter Four. Regulatory Compliance: Government and Industry Watchdogs Keep an Eye on the Social Web.

For regulated companies operating in the age of social networking, it is essential to determine exactly how social media use, content, and records fit into your organization's regulatory mix. Whether you operate in the financial services arena, health care profession, or another regulated industry, knowledge of regulatory risks and compliance with regulators' rules governing electronic use, content, and records are essential business tasks.

As detailed in Chapter Three, social media content often rises to the level of an electronic business record, which may be subpoenaed and might be used as evidence in the course of regulatory investigations. Unmanaged social media content and mismanaged ESI can put your organization at risk of regulatory violations, monetary fines, and negative publicity.

Chapter Four provides an overview of the risks facing regulated companies whose employees use social media either to collaborate and converse on the job or communicate at home. Readers will leave this chapter with a clear understanding of how a social media compliance management program, combining policy, training, and technology, can help reduce (and in some cases eliminate) potentially devastating regulatory risks.

## Chapter Five. Privacy, Security, and Social Media: What Every Employer—and User—Should Know.

Employers are obligated—for legal, regulatory, and business reasons—to protect corporate secrets, safeguard customers' personal and financial data, and secure patients' electronic protected health records from loss, theft, or exposure to unauthorized parties via social media. The pervasive use of smartphones and other mobile devices to communicate with customers and conduct company business ramps up the security risks inherent in all forms of electronic business communication, social media included. Readers will benefit from a review of potential security concerns and a discussion about the ways in which a comprehensive social media policy and compliance management program can help organizations manage (and in some cases minimize) threats to confidential company and consumer data.

Chapter Five also makes it clear that there is no privacy on the public web. Employers and prospective employers, customers and coworkers, law enforcement personnel and the courts, regulators and the media—all are likely to access users' business and personal blogs, Facebook profiles, tweets, photos, videos, and other online content. Employees in the United States have no reasonable expectation of privacy when using the company's computer system. Private sector employers regularly terminate employees for inappropriate or otherwise offensive blog posts and social media content. Many organizations review job applicants' social media presence and blog posts as a means of uncovering the "real" person hiding behind a résumé.

From employer monitoring to social media background checks, this chapter makes clear the realities of online privacy—and spells out what employees should, and should not, do online if they hope to land a position, keep a job, or advance a career in the age of blogging and social networking.

## Chapter Six. Blog Risks and Compliance Rules.

The "original" social networking application, blogs remain a hugely popular interactive communications platform for businesses, professionals, and individuals alike. As Chapter Six makes clear, the creation of your organization's social media policy and compliance management program is the ideal time to review your organization's blog policy for employees, as well as your community blogging guidelines for third-party commenters.

### Chapter Seven. Mobile Devices Drive Social Media Risks.

In the age of social media, the use of mobile devices has shifted into high gear. From smartphones and BlackBerries to cell phones, iPhones, tablet PCs, and iPads, employees increasingly are using mobile gadgets to conduct both company and personal business. With growing numbers of employees clamoring to bring their ever-present and increasingly sophisticated smartphones to the office, savvy employers are advised to adopt policies and procedures to satisfy workforce demands while managing workplace risks. Chapter Seven reviews the mobile device–related legal, regulatory, security, business record, and productivity risks facing employers and employees alike. It also provides best practices–based guidelines for creating and enforcing effective mobile device policies.

### Chapter Eight. Seven-Step Action Plan for Successful Social Media Policy and Compliance Management.

Business and personal social media use is fraught with potentially costly risks that are best managed through a formal social media policy and compliance management program. To help ensure the success of your organization's social media program, best practices call for adherence to the seven steps spelled out in Chapter Eight: (1) form a social media policy team; (2) develop a strategic social media policy and compliance management plan; (3) conduct comprehensive social media policy audits among managers and staff; (4) write effective social media policy and related acceptable use policies (AUPs); (5) educate employees about risks and rules, policies and procedures; (6) manage written policies with disciplinary action; and (7) enforce policy and help ensure compliance with technology tools designed to monitor, filter, block, and otherwise manage use, content, and records.

## Chapter Nine. Conduct a Social Media Policy Audit.

Before committing your organization's formal social media policy (and related AUPs) to writing, you'll want to conduct a clear-eyed, comprehensive review all of the social networking–related risks and challenges, laws and regulations, opportunities and benefits facing your business, employees, customers, prospects, and other audiences with whom you currently communicate and collaborate—or hope to reach—via external social networking sites, internal enterprise-grade networking and collaboration tools, and mobile devices.

Chapter Nine takes readers step-by-step through the process of conducting social media policy audits of executives, managers, and staff in order to determine the shape that the organization's workplace social media policy and compliance management program should take, along with the risks and rules effective social media policies should address.

## Chapter Ten. Writing Effective Social Media Policies.

While online technologies and electronic devices continue to evolve, one fact of strategic compliance management will never change. Best practices always have—and always will—called for the establishment and enforcement of acceptable use policies—including social media policy, blog policy, and mobile device policy, among others—designed to maximize compliance with legal, regulatory, security, and organizational rules while minimizing the risks facing businesses and individual users.

Chapter Ten shares the secrets of successful policy writing and teaches readers how to create effective social media policies (and other types of employment policies) that accomplish three important goals: (1) communicating organizational, legal, and regulatory rules to employees, executives, independent contractors, and others working on behalf of the organization; (2) providing employees with a clear understanding of what constitutes appropriate, acceptable, and lawful business behavior; and (3) helping employers demonstrate to courts, regulators, employees, customers, investors, and other important audiences that the organization is committed to operating a business environment that is civil, compliant, and otherwise correct.

**Chapter Eleven. Content Rules Are Critical to Compliance.**

As Chapter Eleven makes clear, the easiest way to control social media risks is to control published content. As a best practice, employers are advised to use content, language, and netiquette rules and policies to remind employees that online content must be 100 percent lawful, civil, and business-appropriate, as well as compliant with all of the organization's employment policies and guidelines. Support content rules with training, so that employees know what type of language and content is allowed and what is banned. Enforce content rules with technology tools designed to spot and stop inappropriate content from being transmitted, accessed, viewed, acquired, uploaded, downloaded, copied, printed, or otherwise communicated via your organization's systems, accounts, or devices.

**Chapter Twelve. Enforce Policy Compliance with Education.**

You cannot expect an untrained workforce to be a compliant workforce. Best practices call for the education of everyone—from interns and part-timers to full-time professionals and C-level executives—about social media risks and rules, policies and procedures, records and regulations, and other important issues.

Chapter Twelve spells out why (and how) employers should combine formal employee education with disciplinary action to help motivate employees to comply with social media policy (as well as all other acceptable use policies and employment guidelines), whether working at the office, at home, or on the road.

**Chapter Thirteen. Reputation Management: Responding to and Recovering from a Social Networking Nightmare.**

Social networking and blogging can (and regularly do) trigger public relations nightmares. Is your organization capable of responding quickly and effectively if bloggers or social networkers were to post inaccurate, embarrassing, or potentially harmful information about your company, its people, products, or services?

When it comes to social networking nightmares, cybersmears, and blog attacks, the best defense is a good offense. This chapter lays out rules, policies, and procedures that can be implemented to help prevent ruined reputations, bashed brands, and other social media PR disasters from happening. Included is a discussion of how a proactive social media disaster response plan can help you respond immediately, minimizing damage to your organization's reputation and revenues, business, and brand should you come under fire in the blogosphere or on Facebook, Twitter, YouTube, or any other social networking site.

## Chapter Fourteen. Sample Policies: Social Media, Blogs, and Related AUPs.

Looking for help writing policy documents? This chapter offers sample policies governing social networking; blogging; video sharing; texting; smartphones; mobile devices; email in the age of social media; Internet in the age of social media; sexual harassment and discrimination in the age of social media; community guidelines for social media and blogs; and electronic code of conduct.

You will find sample policies in several categories. Feel free to use these sample policies, under the direction of experienced legal counsel, to develop and implement effective social media policies and related acceptable use policies and employment policies for your organization.

## Chapter Fifteen. Glossary of Social Media, Legal, Regulatory, and Technology Terms.

The glossary of terms is intended to help all readers navigate easily through this book, regardless of their awareness and understanding of social media, legal, regulatory, or technology terms. In addition, employers are encouraged to incorporate these terms and definitions into written policies and employee training programs, to help ensure that individual users and the organization as a whole are 100 percent in sync when it comes to social media and web 2.0 risks and rules, records and regulations, policies and procedures, and definitions and terms.

# USE THIS BOOK TO HELP MANAGE YOUR ORGANIZATION'S SOCIAL MEDIA PRESENCE, POSTS, AND POTENTIAL RISKS

An unstoppable phenomenon, social networking has quickly and forever changed the face of online communication, conversations, and collaboration. Add the ever-present smartphone to the social media mix and voilà, you have a recipe for legal, regulatory, security, and organizational disasters.

Social networking tools and technologies are still developing, along with laws and regulations governing their use, content, and records. Consequently, employers and employees alike are grappling with a broad range of social media–related challenges and concerns, questions, and issues.

Given the emerging and evolving nature of social networking and web 2.0, *The Social Media Handbook* does not always offer hard-and-fast dictates. Rather, this book strives to provide best practices–based information and recommendations designed to help employers manage social media use and content, risks and records, policies and procedures, and legal and regulatory compliance.

*The Social Media Handbook* is sold as a general best practices guide. It does not provide advice on legal, regulatory, privacy, security, technology, or other issues. The author did not and could not contemplate every issue, challenge, or situation that may arise when using social media tools and technologies to communicate, collaborate, or converse for business or personal reasons. Some organizations and industries may be required to comply with different or additional laws and regulations, rules, and procedures from those addressed in *The Social Media Handbook*.

Before acting on any policy, procedure, recommendation, best practice, or other issue addressed in *The Social Media Handbook,* readers are advised to seek the counsel of competent professionals—including but not limited to legal, regulatory, records management, IT, security, privacy, human resources, public relations, and other experts—with the experience necessary to review the issues in question.

To get the most out of *The Social Media Handbook,* it is not necessary to read linearly from cover to cover. Feel free to jump around, reading the content that best addresses your legal, regulatory, records, e-discovery, privacy, security, policy, public relations, training, and technology questions, concerns, and challenges.

Here's to safe and secure, clear and communicative, civil and compliant social networking—at work, at home, and on the road.

# WHY EVERY ORGANIZATION NEEDS A SOCIAL MEDIA POLICY AND COMPLIANCE MANAGEMENT PROGRAM

From Twitter and Facebook to YouTube, blogs, smartphones, and tablet PCs, employees' access to the web—and employers' exposure to potentially costly and protracted risks—is greater today than ever before. Whether responding to customer inquiries via Twitter, posting coupons on Facebook, building brand awareness on blogs, or conducting product demonstrations on YouTube, the business community's ever-growing social media use dramatically increases organizations' exposure to potential lawsuits, regulatory violations, security breaches, mismanaged business records, productivity drains, netiquette nightmares, public relations disasters, and other electronic risks.

When employed strategically, there's no denying that business blogs, corporate Facebook pages, instructional YouTube videos, private enterprise-grade social networking platforms, and other social media and web 2.0 tools can facilitate speedy and successful two-way communication with customers, as well as creative and constructive collaboration with colleagues.

Workplace use of social networking sites and web 2.0 technologies increased dramatically between 2007 and 2010, growing from just 11 percent to over 66 percent in a three-year span. Over 90 percent of organizations believe web 2.0 technologies are effective at increasing brand awareness, and another 89 percent consider these communication and collaboration tools essential when it comes to generating new business or supporting customer service. That's according to Clearswift's 2010 report, *Web 2.0 in the Workplace Today*.[1]

Similarly, when managed properly, employees' personal use of social media (via company accounts and systems as well as users' own personal sites and devices) can enhance workers' overall satisfaction with and commitment to their jobs. In fact, one-fifth of the group that the Clearswift report labels "Generation Standby" workers (younger employees who never fully switch off from the Internet at work or home) say that they would turn down employment if the boss did not allow them to access social networking sites or personal email during working hours.[2]

In the age of social media, employers must perform a balancing act. On the one hand, you want to provide enough social web access to keep your business thriving and maintain consideration for some level of personal usage. On the other hand, you are obligated to manage social media use effectively in order to protect your organization's assets, reputation, and future.

The most effective way to accomplish both goals is to implement social media policies, also known as acceptable use policies (AUPs), supported by comprehensive employee training, and enforced by best-in-class technology tools.

## TEST YOUR SOCIAL MEDIA COMPLIANCE MANAGEMENT KNOW-HOW

When it comes to communicating and collaborating with internal and external audiences, employees today enjoy a broad range of electronic options. From tweeting and blogging to surfing, Skyping, texting, and talking via mobile devices, twenty-first-century communication tools and technologies facilitate speedy interactions between organizations and their important audiences, including customers, prospects, investors, the media, decision makers, and the public.

Given the comprehensive mix of electronic business communication tools now available to companies and users, compliance management—more than ever—is a critical business skill. Take this brief quiz to determine your social media compliance management know-how.

1. As of 2011, social networking had surpassed email as the electronic communication tool of choice for most business users.
   ☐ True     ☐ False

2. Because computers have been workplace staples for so long, most employers today are fully aware of—and adept at managing—electronic risks including potentially costly litigation, regulatory fines, security breaches, productivity drains, and public relations nightmares.
   ☐ True     ☐ False

3. In the United States, federal and state laws governing the use, content, records, privacy, and security of electronic information have changed very little since the year 1995.
   ☐ True     ☐ False

4. Government and industry regulations governing the use, content, records, privacy, and security of email and other forms of electronic business communication basically are the same today as they were in 2001.
   ☐ True     ☐ False

5. The Federal Rules of Civil Procedure, which govern e-discovery, are mirrored by the rules of civil procedures in all 50 states.

☐ True ☐ False

6. Text messaging is completely different from email. Consequently, email risks and rules do not apply to text messaging.

☐ True ☐ False

7. In accordance with best practices, Acceptable Use Policies (AUPs) governing social media, blogs, email, mobile devices, and other electronic business communication tools and technologies should be reviewed and updated once every decade.

☐ True ☐ False

## THE NEED FOR STRATEGIC COMPLIANCE MANAGEMENT HAS NEVER BEEN GREATER

If you answered "true" to any of these seven statements, then it's time to brush up on your knowledge of social media compliance management—and electronic compliance management in general.

Effective compliance management is a priority for any organization—large or small, public or private, regulated or unregulated—that is eager to adhere to legal, regulatory, and organizational rules, while mitigating potentially costly risks. Effective compliance management, of course, begins with formal rules and written policies.

### Social networking is risky business

By now, most people are familiar with the type of high-profile, well-publicized email gaffes and Internet disasters that tarnish corporate reputations, savage stock valuations, launch million-dollar lawsuits, derail careers, and trigger media feeding frenzies. Thanks to social media—and the widespread use of mobile devices to access social networking sites day and night—employers' exposure to electronic risks is greater than ever.

### Inappropriate tweets and posts trigger lawsuits and regulatory audits

Anyone with Internet access can establish a Twitter presence, Facebook page, or LinkedIn account and start sharing negative, critical, defamatory, or otherwise harmful comments about your organization's people, products, financials, and future. Given the potentially costly and protracted risks inherent in social networking, it's essential for organizations to establish social media rules and written policies governing the type of content that employees may—and may not—post on business—and personal—social networking sites.

### Unauthorized photos and videos cause humiliation and crush credibility

Armed with nothing more than a smartphone, your employees, disgruntled ex-employees, and office visitors can capture, upload, and post embarrassing or otherwise damaging photos and videos of executives, staff, clients, company secrets, facilities, and operations, or even themselves. With more than 350 million active users accessing Facebook through mobile devices,[3] it's essential for organizations to establish formal rules and policies governing the use of BlackBerries, smartphones, cell phones, tablet PCs, and other mobile devices.

### Leaked secrets sink companies and sabotage careers

Should dissatisfied workers or angry ex-employees post confidential company information or disclose customers' personal financial data on social networking sites or blogs, the devastating results can range from negative publicity and public scrutiny to regulatory investigations, litigation, and declining stock valuations.

A quarter of employees surveyed in 2010 said they had sent regrettable content via social networks and email, according to Clearswift's *Web 2.0 in the Workplace Today report*.[4] One year earlier, 14 percent of employees admitted to emailing confidential company information to third parties; 6 percent emailed customers' credit card data and Social Security numbers to outsiders; and another 6 percent emailed patients' protected health information to third parties, reveals the *2009 Electronic Business Communication Policies and Procedures Survey* from American Management Association and The ePolicy Institute.[5]

Social media use increases the likelihood that employees will expose confidential internal data and customers' private (and legally protected) information to outside parties, triggering regulatory audits and lawsuits in the process. Concern about confidentiality breaches has prompted professional football teams to ban Twitter. Hollywood studios now insert legal clauses in actors' contracts forbidding them to write about films in mid-production on any social networking site or blog. Most of the household-name companies on Germany's DAX 30 stock market index have outlawed the use of Facebook and Twitter over concerns about industrial espionage and lost productivity.

## Courts and regulators view tweets and posts as electronic business records

Just like email, social media can create business records, or electronically stored information (ESI). If employees use the company system to tweet on Twitter, network on Facebook, post on business blogs, or upload videos to YouTube, that content may be subpoenaed, must be produced, and could be used as evidence in lawsuits and regulatory investigations. Employers are responsible for the legally compliant preservation, protection, and production of social media content, as well as email and other ESI.

## Social media create productivity drains

Although 87 percent of employees lack a clear business reason to use Facebook, some use it as much as two hours a day while at work, according to Nucleus Research.[6] Add to that the fact that 52 percent of employees spend up to two hours a day on email, and another 20 percent devote four or more hours to email, according to American Management Association/ePolicy Institute research,[7] and that equals a lot of wasted time and money. Best practices call for the implementation of personal use rules to help manage employees' social media use—and misuse.

## Social networking puts employees at risk

Social networking can lead to not working. In 2009, 2 percent of bosses fired workers for content posted on personal social networking sites; 1 percent dismissed employees for posts on their personal blogs; 1 percent terminated workers for misuse of the corporate blog; and another 1 percent fired employees for videos posted on YouTube, according to American Management/ePolicy Institute research.[8] We can expect those numbers to rise as employees' use of social media grows.

## Social media can be a barrier to employment

Forty-five percent of organizations review job applicants' personal Facebook profiles as part of the interview process. Another 35 percent of employers have rejected job applicants on the basis of the content posted on Facebook, according to a CareerBuilder survey.[9] Unfortunately, as detailed in Chapter Five, social media background checks can backfire for employers, putting companies at risk of discrimination claims by rejected job candidates.

## Compliance management begins with social media policy

In the twenty-first century, it is essential for all companies to develop and enforce written policies governing social media use, content, and business records. Even if your organization does not currently have a social media presence, you cannot afford to turn a blind eye to the communications phenomenon that is social networking. Don't wait for a social media disaster to strike. Put a strategic social media policy and compliance management program to work immediately to help reduce (and in some cases prevent) disasters triggered by employees' business and personal use of online communication and collaboration tools.

## SOCIAL MEDIA BEST PRACTICES: POLICY IS ESSENTIAL TO COMPLIANCE MANAGEMENT

1. Social media and web 2.0 content, use, and records create increased exposures to legal, regulatory, security, productivity, records management, public relations, and other potentially costly risks.
2. When managed strategically, social networking and web 2.0 tools can facilitate speedy and successful two-way communication with customers, as well as creative and constructive collaboration with coworkers.
3. When managed effectively, employees' personal use of social media can enhance workers' overall satisfaction with and commitment to their jobs.
4. The most effective way to manage social media risks is to implement social media rules and policies, supported by comprehensive employee training, and enforced by best-in-class technology tools.

# SOCIAL MEDIA AND THE LAW

## WHAT EVERY ORGANIZATION NEEDS TO KNOW ABOUT LEGAL COMPLIANCE

Ever-growing social media use, combined with an overall increase in business and personal online activity, has ushered in a "new era" of Internet-related litigation. No longer are work-related lawsuits restricted to inappropriate email content or unmanaged web surfing. Employees today are using smartphones to transmit "sext" messages, including obscene photos and off-color text, to coworkers, customers, and the online community as a whole. Angry workers are using Twitter and blogs to defame suppliers, criticize customers, and malign managers. Resentful employees and poorly trained staff are using YouTube and Facebook to reveal company secrets, gossip about patients, and expose consumer data. Still others are using LinkedIn, blogs, Flickr, email, instant messenger, and other electronic communication tools to post, publish, transmit, access, acquire, upload, download, view, copy, print, and otherwise communicate inappropriate, unlawful, or otherwise objectionable content—accidentally or intentionally.

Consequently, employers face increased exposure to workplace lawsuits, ranging from hostile work environment claims and sexual harassment allegations to defamation suits, copyright infringement claims, invasion of privacy lawsuits, and emotional distress claims, along with other potentially costly and protracted legal actions.

## SOCIAL MEDIA MAXIMIZE ELECTRONIC EXPOSURES

Along with "good, old-fashioned" email messages and attachments, the content employees post on Facebook, Twitter, LinkedIn, Flickr, YouTube, blogs, and other social networking and web 2.0 sites creates a treasure trove of potential evidence that could be used for or against an employer in the event of a civil lawsuit or criminal proceeding. As detailed in Chapter Three, more and more attorneys are regularly scanning more and more social media sites in search of more and more potential evidence to help support (or sink) legal claims.

For example, if a company supervisor were to post sexually charged comments about a business subordinate on a personal Twitter account, public Facebook wall, or private in-house wiki, those remarks potentially could provide evidentiary fodder in a hostile work environment claim or sexual harassment lawsuit filed against the company.

If a member of your corporate board of directors were to jump the gun and blog about top-secret merger plans or anticipated quarterly financial results, those posts could potentially put the company at odds with government and industry regulators, the law, and the Wall Street investment community.

If a distracted employee-driver were to cause a car crash during business hours while busy talking or texting, blogging or emailing, posting or surfing on a mobile device, the organization might be held liable—regardless of whether the employee was driving a company-owned vehicle and using a company-provided smartphone or operating a private car and communicating via a personal electronic tablet.

## POLICY HELPS MINIMIZE LEGAL RISKS AND MAXIMIZE COMPLIANCE

When it comes to minimizing legal risks and maximizing legal compliance, best practices call for the development and implementation of formal acceptable use policies (AUPs) that incorporate clear and consistent rules governing employees' business and personal use of social media, web 2.0, smartphones, cell phones, electronic tablets, email, instant messenger, the Internet, the Intranet, text messaging, and all other electronic communication tools and technologies—old, new, and emerging.

Effective policy should couple clear usage rules with comprehensive content guidelines designed to minimize (and ideally prevent) the posting and publishing of written text, photos, videos, art, or any other content that potentially could trigger legal claims or serve as smoking-gun evidence of wrongdoing. To learn more about content management and the important role that content rules play when it comes to legal, regulatory, and organizational compliance, see Chapter Eleven.

## SOCIAL MEDIA AND THE LAW: RISK MANAGEMENT 101

Employees' use of business and personal social networking sites, blogs, and other web 2.0 applications can increase employers' exposure to a wide variety of legal claims. What follows is a recap of some of the most common and potentially costly legal risks facing employers, along with best practice–based tips to help mitigate social media risks and manage employees' online behavior while maximizing organizational and individual compliance with the law.

### Vicarious liability: The boss is legally responsible for employees' behavior—good or bad

Vicarious liability (and the related legal concept of *respondeat superior*) is the legal term that is used when an organization is held legally (and financially) responsible for the unlawful, offensive, or otherwise inappropriate actions of its employees. Vicarious liability applies regardless of whether the offending employee's violation was accidental or intentional. It also may apply regardless of whether the employee commits the offense at the office using company-owned computer resources, at home using personal devices and private accounts, or on the road using either business or personal accounts, sites, tools, and technologies.

In other words, thanks to vicarious liability, an employer might be held legally responsible for the obscene, harassing, discriminatory, or otherwise illegal or objectionable blog posts, tweets, Facebook comments, or YouTube videos of a rogue employee—regardless of where, when, or how the offending content was created, transmitted, posted, or published.

---

**REAL-LIFE MYSPACE DISASTER STORY: A CAUTIONARY SOCIAL MEDIA TALE FOR EMPLOYERS AND EMPLOYEES ALIKE**

After a night of heavy drinking, a 20-year-old employee of a Pennsylvania company awoke at six in the morning, stepped into his company-owned van, and started driving to work. On his way to the office, with alcohol still in his system, the employee fell asleep at the wheel, striking and killing a cyclist in the process.

During the e-discovery (evidence-gathering) phase of litigation, the lawyer representing the victim's family (the plaintiffs) uncovered a MySpace profile, on which the employee had written, "I'm an alcoholic and I work for [insert name] company." The plaintiffs' lawyer argued that, because the employee's history as an alcoholic was posted on the web and accessible to the public, the company should have been aware of it and was therefore liable for putting an alcoholic behind the wheel of a company vehicle. Faced with the employees' public admission, the company (the defendant) had no choice but to settle the case out of court.[1]

This sad story is a prime example of why employers must proactively manage employees' business and personal social media use.

## Seven best practices to help battle vicarious liability and other legal risks

For employers, there is no escaping vicarious liability. If, in the course of business, employees (or independent contractors working on behalf of your organization) behave inappropriately, negligently, or illegally, there is a good chance that your organization will be held legally responsible. That's the bad news.

The good news: a clear and comprehensive social media policy (and related AUPs and employment rules), supported by formal employee education, may give you some defense from liability. The courts tend to appreciate and respond positively to organizations that make an effort to manage risk, behavior, and compliance through the combination of written rules and effective training.

Although there is no way to ensure a workplace that is 100 percent free from online missteps or misuse, employers who are eager to reduce vicarious liability risks (and other legal actions) are advised to adhere to the following best practices:

1. Establish—and annually update—clear and comprehensive written policies governing social media, blogs, web 2.0, mobile devices, email, the Internet, and all other electronic communication tools. (See Chapter Ten.)
2. Conduct a formal, ongoing training program, designed to educate employees about social media (and other electronic) legal and regulatory risks, business record management, security, privacy, policy, and compliance, among other important issues. (See Chapter Twelve.)
3. In the course of training, notify employees that social media policy (and all of the organization's other acceptable use policies and employment rules, codes, and guidelines) apply 24 hours a day, seven days a week, 365 days a year, at the office, at home, and on the road.
4. If you are a U.S.-based employer, exercise your legal right to monitor all content, transmissions, and use of your computer system, sites, accounts, and electronic devices including desktops, laptops, and mobile tools. (See Chapter Five.)

5. If you operate internationally, assign experienced legal counsel the task of researching the privacy laws and monitoring rules impacting your organization and its employees in every jurisdiction in which you operate or have workers. Based on those findings, take appropriate legal action to protect your organization's assets, reputation, and future.

6. Take advantage of the fact that content posted on employees' personal blogs and public social networking sites is available for everyone (including you) to access, read, view, comment upon, or otherwise interact with. Use technology tools and human resources to monitor employees' public and personal posts on a regular basis.

7. If a policy violation or other red flag is discovered, take swift and appropriate action. In other words, discipline policy violators in accordance with your organization's social media policy and other employment guidelines and policies. In the event of a lawsuit, your organization may be in a stronger legal position if you can demonstrate to the court that you have established clear, comprehensive, current policies that are enforced through a combination of disciplinary action and technology tools. Without education and enforcement, you cannot expect employees to fully understand or comply with policy.

## THIRD PARTIES CREATE LEGAL RISKS FOR BUSINESS BLOGS

Once you begin accepting commentary from customers and other third parties on your business blogs, your organization may be deemed a publisher in the eyes of the law. As an online publisher, your company potentially could be held liable—legally and financially—for defamation, slander, libel, and other legal claims triggered by inappropriate (and potentially unlawful) comments posted by outsiders eager to express their thoughts and opinions in the comment sections of your business blogs.

Fortunately, there are effective ways to minimize the potentially costly legal risks associated with the publication of visitors' blog comments. Specifically, consider taking these four steps to help ensure legal compliance in the blogosphere:

## 1. Establish community blogging guidelines for third parties

Take the advice offered in Chapter Six. If you are going to accept commentary from customers and other outside parties on your business blogs, then you should create and post a clear and comprehensive policy for visitors who choose to comment on your sites.

Your "community blogging guidelines" document is separate from your blog policy for employees. The purpose of your community blogging guidelines is to help ensure that the third-party comments and conversations that are published on your organization's business blogs are as polite, productive, focused, and friendly as possible. Most important, your published guidelines will help keep visitors' comments compliant with the law, regulatory guidelines, and organizational rules governing language, content, netiquette, copyright, intellectual property, harassment, discrimination, bullying, and ethics, among other issues.

## 2. Require visitors to register before commenting on your blog

Establish a brief, readable, mandatory registration form for any outside party who wants to post comments on your business blogs. As part of the formal electronic registration process, inform blog visitors that they must read and agree to the company's community blogging guidelines before they will be permitted to post any comments on your site.

Use your community blogging guidelines to notify visitors that all comments will be reviewed by the company's chief compliance officer (or another authorized employee) prior to posting. Clearly spell out your language, content, netiquette, copyright, intellectual property, and other comment-related rules. Let visitors know exactly what type of commentary they are prohibited from posting. Make it clear that any comments found to be in violation of the company's community blogging guidelines (or any other company policy, guideline, code, or rule) will be excluded from publication. (See Chapter Fourteen for examples of community blogging guidelines.)

### 3. Review third-party comments prepublication

You can't control what visitors to your blogs and other social network-ing sites write, but you can determine whether or not their comments ever see the light of day. As an online blog publisher, you wield absolute editorial control over published content. Take advantage of your position and power by reviewing all third-party comments prior to publication on your business blogs. Yes, it will slow down the blogging process and somewhat diminish the "transparent" nature of blogging, but what's the alternative? You can't afford to take chances with inappropriate comments that could offend readers, trigger lawsuits, violate regula-tors' rules, ignite public relations firestorms, or crush your company's credibility. Assign a responsible party—a lawyer, compliance officer, or member of the social media policy team (see Chapter Eight)—to review, reject, or approve every reader comment before publishing it online for all the world to read.

In spite of the risk-management benefits that editing offers, it's important to note that the formal review, editing, and possible exclusion of third-party comments may open your organization to criticism by your readers and the blogosphere in general. Some people may accuse your organization of sanitizing its business blogs, cleansing them of the type of honest, unvarnished content that helps distinguish blogs from other forms of communication, electronic or traditional. So be it. The rebuke of a few would-be commenters may sting a bit, but it can't compare to the devastating impact a high-profile lawsuit would have on your company's reputation, financials, and future, were you to post an inflammatory, illegal, or otherwise "wrong" comment on an "official" business blog.

### 4. Deactivate your blog's comment function

If you want to minimize legal risks and gaffes, but don't want to devote the human, technology, or financial resources necessary to review every comment written by every visitor prepublication, then you may want to consider deactivating the comment function on your business blogs. Doing so is likely to reduce your legal and regulatory compliance risks significantly.

Remember, just because the blog makes interactive communication possible, that does not obligate you to participate in two-party conversations. Feel free to restrict your business blogs to business-related posts written by approved business bloggers, charged with the task of communicating the organization's official positions, policies, opinions, and insights.

## COPYRIGHT VIOLATIONS ON THE SOCIAL WEB

If you publish a visitor's comments on your business blog, corporate Facebook page, or other social networking site—and that content happens to be protected by another person's copyright—your organization could be held vicariously liable for copyright infringement. In other words, regardless of whether a visitor accidentally or intentionally violates the law by posting copyright-protected comments or content on your business blogs and social sites, it's possible that your organization, as an online publisher, could be held legally responsible for the violation.

To help reduce the chance of copyright infringement, use your community blogging guidelines to educate third parties about intellectual property laws in general and the company's copyright rules in particular. Also require visitors to complete a formal registration process before posting comments on your site. As part of the registration process, require users to agree that, in their comments, they will not infringe on another party's copyright or other intellectual property including, for example, trademarks, confidential data, trade secrets, and proprietary information.

### Take advantage of Digital Millennium Copyright act protections

As detailed in Chapter Six, if deemed to be a third-party copyright infringer, your organization could be subject to treble damages—unless you have followed the procedures necessary to ensure "safe harbor" protection from liability through the Digital Millennium Copyright Act (DMCA).

Under DMCA, your organization is safe from liability even if it has inadvertently fed copyright-protected content into syndication and created a scenario in which the infringed-upon material is available in the blogosphere long after your organization has removed it as required by law.

To qualify for DMCA safe harbor protection from third-party liability for copyright infringement, your organization must follow three steps: (1) designate a DMCA agent with the Library of Congress; (2) list your DMCA agent on your company website; and (3) establish a formal plan to handle complaints in compliance with DMCA requirements.[2] Also on your website, recap the DMCA-mandated protocols that your organization follows when responding to allegations of third-party copyright infringement.

Do have your legal counsel review all DMCA policies, procedures, and requirements to ensure that your organization has taken all the necessary steps to ensure compliance and safe harbor protection. Do not solicit or post comments by customers or other third parties until your DMCA registration process has been completed and approved by a legal expert.

## DEFAMATION CLAIMS ON THE SOCIAL WEB

Defamation is defined as a false statement of fact, versus an opinion. When a defamatory statement appears in writing (such as a tweet), it's known as "libel." A defamatory statement that is made orally (on a YouTube video, for example) is "slander." An employer may be held liable for defamatory statements made by an employee, if the employee possesses "apparent authority" from the company to speak on its behalf.

In addition, if an employee were to use an employer's company blog, social networking site, photo-sharing site, or video-sharing site to post a doctored image that falsely depicts a third party engaged in a crime, then both the employee and employer might be slapped with a "false light" defamation claim, filed by the third party who was injured by the phony photo.

# INVASION OF PRIVACY CLAIMS ON THE SOCIAL WEB

What if an employee were to intercept an email message or other document belonging to an individual outside the organization (a third party), and then post that improperly acquired content to one of the company's business blogs or social networking sites? What if the offending employee used private, home-based computer resources (laptop, Internet account, personal blog, or social media account) to acquire or post the pilfered document? In either case, whether the employee has used business or personal resources, the employer could face an invasion-of-privacy lawsuit, if a reasonable person could assume that the employer was aware of the employee's actions. (For a detailed discussion about privacy and social media, see Chapter Five.)

# EMPLOYMENT LAW: THINK TWICE BEFORE USING SOCIAL MEDIA TO SCREEN JOB APPLICANTS

Using social media to screen job candidates is an increasingly common practice. According to the *2009 Electronic Business Communication Policies and Procedures Survey* from American Management Association and The ePolicy Institute, 13 percent of employers turn to social media for help recruiting and evaluating prospective employees. Another 3 percent have rejected job applicants on the basis of personal blogs or private social networking accounts.[3] Expect those numbers to grow as the use of social media as "go-to" electronic business communication tools increases.

Although social media may provide a quick and easy source of information about job hunters, employers must be careful about using the results of those searches. Recruiters and human resource professionals can open their organizations to legal risks when they rely on applicants' personal blogs and private social networking sites as part of the employment screening process.

## Social searches may trigger discrimination claims

In the United States, federal antidiscrimination law prohibits employers from harassing or discriminating against "protected classes" of individuals on the grounds of race, color, religion, gender, national origin, age, sex, familial status, sexual orientation, gender identity, disability, veteran status, or genetic information. When employers use social media to help research, recruit, or refuse job applicants, they may be opening themselves up to the possibility of discrimination claims.[4]

Imagine, for example, a scenario in which a human resources manager, eager to gain some insight into a job applicant's "real" personality and professionalism, takes a peek at the applicant's personal blog, private Facebook profile, or personal Twitter presence. In so doing, the HR manager discovers a photo, video, or other personal information that the company might not otherwise have been privy to.

For example, the HR manager (whose knowledge of the applicant previously was limited to facts on a printed résumé) might now uncover information about the applicant's age, sex, race, ethnicity, disability, or other characteristic that falls under the "protected class" umbrella. If management decides against hiring that job candidate on the basis of the information gleaned from the HR manager's peek at a personal social networking site or blog, then there is a chance that the rejected applicant might file a discrimination claim, alleging that the organization made its hiring decision based on a protected class.

The lesson: social media sites give employers access to the type of personal information (political opinions, lifestyle choices, and hobbies, for example) that a job applicant might otherwise prefer to keep under wraps. Think twice before using social media to help speed the selection and screening of prospective employees—unless you don't mind the prospect of battling a legal claim based on your company's violation of Title VII of the Civil Rights Act, Fair Credit Reporting Act, Age Discrimination in Employment Act, Americans with Disabilities Act, or another federal or state law designed to protect against discrimination and harassment in the workplace.

### Mistaken identities abound online

Another risk that employers face when they rely heavily on the Internet to research job candidates: you may inadvertently investigate the wrong person. Consider a scenario in which your company receives an intriguing (and unsolicited) résumé from someone who, on paper, looks like a good fit for your organization. Before investing time and energy on a face-to-face interview, you decide to conduct a bit of preliminary online research on the candidate. You start with a Google search of the applicant's name, and then follow the online trail, which may include a personal blog, Twitter presence, LinkedIn account, Facebook page, and YouTube videos.

Thanks to the social web, you're quickly armed with a wealth of information (favorable or unfavorable) about the job applicant. Or so you think. In actuality, your hiring manager inadvertently has been cyber-trailing the right name, but the wrong person. If you've made any negative assumptions based on the misguided information uncovered online, a viable job candidate's career prospects with your company may be ruined.

Lesson learned: be absolutely certain you are reviewing the right information about the right person any time you use social media sites or other web resources to conduct research about job applicants, or any other business-related people or matters.

## SMARTPHONES IMPACT WAGE AND HOUR LAWS

Smartphones, tablet PCs, and laptops can open the organization up to overtime claims by nonexempt employees and other employees claiming they have been encouraged to work off-the-clock and without pay, via smartphone or other mobile tools. To reduce the likelihood of these claims, use policy to prohibit nonexempt employees from performing any work outside of their normal schedule unless specifically authorized to do so. Also, require employees who perform work outside their normal working hours to record and report it immediately.

As part of your organization's social media policy and compliance management program, have an employment law expert research—and address through a combination of formal policy and employee education—wage and hour risks facing the company in the age of social media and smartphones.

# MOBILE DEVICES HELP DRIVE LEGAL RISKS

Email has long provided a quick and easy way for employees to remove confidential data, trade secrets, and proprietary information from company systems—accidentally or intentionally. Thanks to Black-Berries, smartphones, iPhones, iPads, electronic tablets, and other mobile devices, confidential information today is at greater risk of exposure than ever before. Fully 56 percent of U.S. companies report being "highly concerned" that confidential information will be transmitted out of the system via email sent on mobile devices, according to Proofpoint's survey, *Outbound Email and Data Loss Prevention in Today's Enterprise, 2010.*[5]

Employers have good reason for concern. The Proofpoint survey reveals that one in five companies in 2010 investigated the exposure of confidential, sensitive, or private information via lost or stolen mobile devices.[6]

In addition to the security risks associated with lost and stolen data, organizations' legal risks increase when employees engage in text messaging, blogging, social networking, web surfing, emailing, and other forms of electronic communication via smartphones and other mobile devices, regardless of whether they are using company-provided or personally owned tools.

Mobile device use and content pose risks that extend beyond the digital sphere into the "real world." For example, under the legal principle of vicarious liability, your organization may be held legally responsible if an employee causes a traffic accident while texting or talking, blogging or posting, emailing or surfing via a mobile device. It doesn't matter whether the employee is driving a company-owned vehicle or a personal car at the time of the crash. It makes no difference whether the distracted employee is using a personal smartphone or a company-provided tablet to converse or communicate. Your organization could be held legally and financially responsible for any accidents, injuries, or deaths caused by distracted employees driving during business hours.

**REAL-LIFE MOBILE DEVICE DISASTER STORIES**

Need convincing of the risks associated with on-the-job mobile device use? A trucking company paid $18 million to a victim who was left in a permanent vegetative state after being struck by an 18-wheeler driven by an employee who was checking text messages at time of the accident.[7] A lumber company paid $16.2 million to a pedestrian who was struck and disabled by an on-duty salesman who was distracted by his mobile device while driving.[8]

Could your organization survive a multimillion-dollar legal settlement triggered by an employee-driver distracted by mobile blogging, networking, talking, texting, surfing, or emailing?

Accident-related litigation is just one potentially costly risk posed by mobile device use. Defamation claims, harassment suits, regulatory fines, data security breaches, business record mismanagement, lost productivity, and public relations nightmares round out the list of smartphone and mobile device-related disasters facing employers.

To help minimize legal risks and maximize compliance, 30 percent of organizations in 2009 established formal policies governing texting use and content, with another 26 percent banning texting while driving, according to the *2009 Electronic Business Communication Policies and Procedures Survey* from American Management Association and The ePolicy Institute.[9] Follow their lead. Establish formal rules and written policies today to help reduce the risk of legal claims tomorrow.

## SOCIAL MEDIA BEST PRACTICES: LEGAL COMPLIANCE

1. Social networking touches nearly every aspect of the law including criminal and corporate cases, employment law, harassment and discrimination, copyright infringement, defamation—and the list goes on and on.

2. Case law has not kept pace with social media technology. In other words, many legal issues related to social networking have not reached the higher courts or been resolved yet.

3. Formal social media policy that is supported by company-wide employee education may provide your organization with some defense from liability in the event of a workplace lawsuit. The courts tend to appreciate consistency. So, if a company establishes social media policy (and other formal acceptable use policies and employment policies), and effectively communicates policy to users, then the law is likely to presume that the company has done the right thing. In other words, policy can help protect the employer from liability.

4. Vicarious liability is the legal term that is used when an organization is held legally (and financially) responsible for the unlawful, offensive, or otherwise inappropriate actions of its employees. Vicarious liability applies, regardless of whether the offending employee's violation was accidental or intentional. Thanks to vicarious liability, an employer might be held legally responsible for the obscene, harassing, discriminatory, or otherwise illegal or objectionable blog posts, tweets, or Facebook comments of a rogue employee—on the organization's business blogs, public social networking sites, private enterprise-grade wikis and social networking tools, or possibly on the employee's personal, home-based blogs and social media accounts.

5. Once you begin accepting commentary from third parties on your business blogs, your organization may be deemed an online publisher and could be held liable for defamation or other legal claims triggered by inappropriate (and potentially unlawful) comments posted by outsiders in the comment sections of your business blogs.

   Reduce blog-related legal risks by posting community blogging guidelines; requiring visitors to register before commenting; reviewing all comments prepublication; rejecting any comments that violate your community blogging guidelines or other company policies; or deactivating the comment function on your business blogs.

6. The social web and blogosphere require an ongoing supply of thought-provoking, intelligent, insightful, entertaining, informational, and educational content. Unfortunately, not all posters, bloggers, and commenters are blessed with originality. If an employee or third party were to accidentally or intentionally violate the law by posting copyright-protected content on a business blog or social networking site, it's possible that your organization could be held legally responsible. Help protect your organization from liability through a combination of policy, training, and the Digital Millennium Copyright Act (DMCA).

7. Exercise caution when using public social media sites to recruit or research job applicants. Misguided or mismanaged online research could result in a discrimination claim against your company.

8. Smartphones and other mobile devices can open the organization up to overtime claims by nonexempt employees and other employees claiming they have been encouraged to work off-the-clock and without pay. Be sure to have an employment law expert research—and address through a combination of formal policy and employee education—wage and hour risks facing the company in the age of social media and smartphones.

9. Under the legal principle of vicarious liability, employee-drivers who cause car crashes when distracted by mobile devices can create liability concerns for employees. However, accident-related litigation is just one potentially costly risk posed by mobile device use. Defamation claims, harassment suits, regulatory fines, data security breaches, business record mismanagement, lost productivity, and public relations nightmares round out the list of smartphone and mobile device-related disasters facing employers. Use written policy (social media policy and mobile device policy), supported by formal employee education, to help reduce legal risks, manage employee behavior behind-the-wheel, and increase compliance with organizational rules and the law. See Chapter Seven for additional information about smartphone, cell phone, and mobile device risks and rules, policies, and procedures.

# SOCIAL NETWORKING CREATES LEGAL EVIDENCE

## HOW TO MANAGE RECORDS AND E-DISCOVERY COMPLIANTLY

Just like email messages and attachments that are written, transmitted, acquired, and stored on the company system, social media content—including blog posts, third-party blog comments, tweets, Facebook profiles, LinkedIn comments, Flickr photos, YouTube videos, and other forms of social networking—has the potential to create electronic business records.

What is an electronic business record? Essentially, a business record is the electronic equivalent of DNA evidence. Should your company become embroiled in civil litigation (a workplace lawsuit, in other words) or a criminal investigation (related to an employee's distracted driving, perhaps) on the federal, state, or local level, electronic business records may be subpoenaed by the court, must be produced on time and in the format requested by the court, and are likely to be used to support (or sink) your organization's legal position.

**SELF-ASSESSMENT: WHERE DO YOU STAND WHEN IT COMES TO E-DISCOVERY, RECORD RETENTION, AND POLICY COMPLIANCE?**

1. Do you have in place a social media policy that is clear, comprehensive, and current? In other words, has your social media policy (and related policies governing mobile devices and blogs, for example) been reviewed and updated within the past 12 months?

   ☐ Yes   ☐ No   ☐ Don't Know

2. Have you created a record retention policy to govern the retention and disposition of your organization's electronic business records (including social media records) and help ensure legal compliance with e-discovery obligations?

   ☐ Yes   ☐ No   ☐ Don't Know

3. Have you provided all users (full- and part-time employees, executives, board members, consultants, students, faculty, independent contractors, and all other authorized users) with your organization's formal, written definition of "business record"?

   ☐ Yes   ☐ No   ☐ Don't Know

4. Do your users know the difference between business-critical records that must be retained and archived for legal and regulatory compliance versus personal email and otherwise insignificant electronic content that may be deleted in the ordinary course of business?

   ☐ Yes   ☐ No   ☐ Don't Know

5. Do you support your organization's written retention policy with archiving technology?

   ☐ Yes   ☐ No   ☐ Don't Know

6. Does your organization's social media policy (and all other acceptable use policies governing email, text messaging, blogging, and mobile devices, for example) incorporate clear rules governing written content?

☐ Yes ☐ No ☐ Don't Know

7. Does your organization's social media policy (and all other acceptable use policies governing email, text messaging, blogging, and mobile devices, for example) incorporate clear rules governing personal use of the company's computer resources, as well as employees' private devices and accounts?

☐ Yes ☐ No ☐ Don't Know

8. Is your organization's email archive a potentially dangerous mix of rules-based professional correspondence and off-the-cuff personal conversations that could potentially embarrass your users or sabotage your legal position?

☐ Yes ☐ No ☐ Don't Know

9. Could you quickly search, locate, and produce legally compliant electronic business records in response to a subpoena from a court or regulator, or a public records request from a taxpayer or reporter?

☐ Yes ☐ No ☐ Don't Know

10. If you are a U.S.-based business, do you know, understand, and adhere to the amended Federal Rules of Civil Procedure (FRCP), as well as the state rules of civil procedure and e-discovery guidelines of all of the states in which you operate, have employees, or litigate lawsuits?

☐ Yes ☐ No ☐ Don't Know

11. If you operate a government agency, school system, or other public entity, could you quickly search, locate, and produce legally compliant electronic business records in response to a federal Freedom of Information Act (FOIA) request or a state public records request from a citizen or member of the media?

☐ Yes ☐ No ☐ Don't Know

If you answered no to any of these questions, then your ability to manage social media content and other electronic business records in a legally compliant manner is suspect. You are not alone, however. Many organizations are challenged by the dual task of effectively managing business records and successfully meeting e-discovery obligations.

Unfortunately, legal compliance is not an option. You must manage and maintain electronic business records in a legally compliant manner. You must produce electronic business records when ordered to do so by courts, regulators, or taxpayers. This chapter is devoted to helping employers better understand and achieve those critical compliance goals.

## POSTS, BLOGS, TWEETS, TEXTS, PROFILES, AND COMMENTS CREATE LEGAL EXPOSURES AND EVIDENCE

During the discovery stage of litigation, the court orders all parties to a lawsuit to produce documents relevant to the case. In the twenty-first century, relevant documents are almost certain to include email messages and attachments, text messages, instant messages, blog posts, third-party blog comments, tweets, Facebook profiles, YouTube videos, history of Internet surfing, and other forms of electronically stored information (ESI). The process of searching, locating, and producing subpoenaed ESI during discovery is called "e-discovery."

Regardless of the industry in which your company operates, its size, or its status as a private or public entity, your ability to formally define, effectively retain, successfully manage, and promptly produce electronic business records in response to a court order or FOIA request is one of the most important tasks your organization can undertake. Unfortunately, thanks to the rapid-fire growth of social networking, the preservation, protection, and production of ESI is becoming increasingly challenging for many organizations, especially those companies that are still struggling to manage email compliantly—in spite of email's long-standing position as the business community's primary form of electronic communication.

## What constitutes an electronic business record?

In an ideal world, there would be a one-size-fits-all definition of "business record," which all organizations could apply to the management of company data. In the real world, however, nearly every organization must determine for itself what type of ESI—including social media content, email messages, and all other types of electronically produced, transmitted, and stored information—rises to the level of a business record.

The only exceptions to that rule are regulated businesses, for which government and industry overseers provide clear guidelines on what constitutes a business record, how electronic business records are to be managed, and for how long business records must be retained.

If your organization is not regulated, then you will need to create your own definition of "business record," either on a company-wide or department-by-department basis. You also will need to formulate an effective record retention policy for your company and institute procedures for the compliant management of electronic business records within your organization.

### How to spot a business record

In general, business records, whether in the form of electronic documents or traditional hard-copy materials, provide evidence of an organization's business-related people, processes, activities, events, transactions, revenues, and other business-related matters. Retained according to their ongoing business, legal, regulatory, operational, and historic value to the organization, business records would include documents that address or discuss company financials and accounting matters, personnel and human resources issues, marketing plans and customer lists, research and development activities, consumer activities and accounts, or other business-specific documents.

It's important to note that not every email message that enters or leaves your company's system is a business record. Not every tweet that an employee publishes on Twitter constitutes a business record. Not every employee post or third-party comment on your business blog rises to the level of a business record. Consequently, effective records management can be a daunting task.

## KNOW AND ADHERE TO THE FEDERAL RULES OF CIVIL PROCEDURE

For companies operating in the United States, the amended Federal Rules of Civil Procedure (FRCP) are at the heart of e-discovery. The nation's federal court system raised the bar on electronic compliance management in 2006, when the long-anticipated amendments to the Federal Rules of Civil Procedure were announced. As of 2011, discussions about possible e-discovery changes to the FRCP were under way by a subcommittee of the Judicial Conference of the United States. However, official changes to U.S. federal e-discovery guidelines are not likely until 2013 at the earliest.[1] For now, the Federal Rules of Civil Procedure make clear the following:

1. Electronically stored information (ESI)—including social media content, blog posts, email messages, text messages, instant messages, attachments, photos, videos, and all other forms of electronically produced, acquired, transmitted, and stored content—is discoverable. In other words, social networking conversations, comments, and content may be used as evidence for or against your organization in the course of harassment and discrimination claims or other workplace lawsuits filed in federal court.

2. Social media content and all other forms of ESI related to current, pending, or potential litigation must be effectively retained, professionally managed, and promptly produced in a legally compliant fashion during e-discovery, or the evidence-gathering phase of litigation.

3. In spite of legal e-discovery obligations, employers are allowed to routinely purge their electronic archives of data—as long as those records are not relevant to ongoing litigation, pending cases, or suits that you suspect may be filed against your company at some future time.

   When it comes to e-discovery, employers are required to be a bit psychic. If, for example, you suspect that a particularly disgruntled employee is likely to file a discrimination suit against your company at some future date, then you are obligated today to retain all of the business records related to that individual in anticipation of a possible lawsuit tomorrow. Failure to do so could be costly.

Consider, for example, the discrimination claim that ex-employee Laura Zubulake filed against her one-time employer, investment bank UBS. In the course of litigation, it was discovered that corporate email messages related to Zubulake were missing, along with UBS backup tapes.

Writing that "almost everyone associated with Zubulake recognized the possibility that she might sue" (given her complaints about discriminatory treatment during her tenure with the company), the judge ruled that UBS should have predicted that the email would one day be used as evidence, and that the company had violated its own retention policy by deleting the missing email.

Instructed by the judge to "infer that the [missing] evidence would have been unfavorable to UBS," the jury awarded Zubulake $29.3 million. Following a threatened appeal by UBS, Zubulake and the company reached a confidential settlement in 2005.[2]

4. Many organizations rely on backup tape, rather than archiving technology, to store their valuable electronic records and other information. Bad idea. In the first place, backup simply provides the mass storage of data and the recovery of information in the event of a hurricane, system crash, or other natural or man-made disaster. Backup is not a substitute for archiving technology, which facilitates the strategic storage, search, and production of exactly the records you need, precisely when you need them.

Second, according to the Federal Rules of Civil Procedure, writing over backup tape once litigation is under way may be viewed as "virtual shredding," which could result in allegations of spoliation, or the illegal destruction of electronic evidence. If the court determines you are guilty of altering or destroying evidence, accidentally or intentionally, you face potentially steep penalties (known as court sanctions), ranging from multimillion-dollar fines to instructions to the jury to assume that your organization has something to hide.

---

**BEST PRACTICE RECOMMENDATION**

If your organization is eager to ensure legal compliance, then be sure to adopt a proven-effective automatic archiving solution, rather than relying on backup tape to maintain and manage all-important electronic business records.

---

5. Not all electronic business records are viewed equally in the eyes of the law. To be accepted as valid legal evidence, social networking content, blogs posts, email messages, and other forms of ESI must be preserved and produced in a trustworthy, authentic, and tamperproof manner. That's why organizations that are eager to protect electronic business records are advised to turn to archiving technology. Archiving helps ensure forensic compliance. For example, by instantly encrypting and archiving a copy of every internal and external email sent or received across your organization, an archiving solution guarantees that your email is secure and tamperproof. Nothing in your archive can be deleted or altered. Everything in your archive is authentic and legally compliant.

6. FRCP's "99-day rule" requires all parties to a lawsuit to meet and discuss the scope and accessibility of ESI within 99 days of the initiation of a legal claim. Compliance with the 99-day rule requires employers to implement a record retention policy and archiving technology today—or face potentially costly court sanctions tomorrow.

Make no mistake. The courts take e-discovery seriously, and failure to produce ESI can be costly. For example, in 2010, the court sanctioned Qualcomm $8.5 million for a "massive discovery failure."[3] One year earlier, the court imposed more than $1 million in monetary sanctions against Onex Corp. after finding the company's behavior to be a "textbook case" of discovery abuse.[4]

Could your organization survive if mismanaged business records or mishandled e-discovery requests resulted in a multimillion-dollar sanction against your company? Prepare today for the inevitability of social media–related litigation tomorrow.

## E-DISCOVERY CAN BE COMPLEX AND TIME-CONSUMING

If your organization is hit with an e-discovery request, it's likely to focus on the ESI (including social networking content) generated by and about particular employees, containing specific information, or revolving around certain dates. For example, you could be required to search, locate, and turn over all of the email messages, instant messenger chat, text messages, blog posts, tweets, and other electronic content that was transmitted, acquired, posted, published, viewed, forwarded, copied, printed, downloaded, uploaded, or otherwise communicated by all individuals working in the HR, IT, and marketing departments of three separate offices during the first three months of your company's fiscal year. Could you successfully respond to that sort of e-discovery challenge? If not, now is the time to get your records management house in order.

Your organization's discovery obligations do not begin and end with employees' electronic conversations and correspondence, however. In addition, opposing legal counsel may want to examine your electronic policies and procedures, gain some insight into your organizational structure, or determine whether or not you have adhered to best practices when it comes to managing employees' online behavior, computer use, and legal compliance.

Depending on the nature of the lawsuit and the litigators' discovery goals, an e-discovery request could require you to produce large volumes of information, which then would be reviewed by numerous individuals including paralegals, lawyers, expert witnesses, computer forensic professionals, the court, jurors, the media, and the public, among others.

## *When it comes to e-discovery, it pays to be prepared*

To that end, here's a sampling of the type of documents that your organization might be ordered to produce during the e-discovery phase of civil litigation:

1. Written social media policies, email policies, Internet policies, mobile device policies, and other acceptable use policies, guidelines, rules, or codes governing employees' use of the company's computer systems, online accounts, Internet sites, computer resources, mobile devices, and electronic data. Any internal memos, letters, announcements, email messages, instant messages, text messages, blog posts, Internet posts, social networking comments, Intranet posts, meeting notes, calendar notations, or other formal or informal documents related to the subpoenaed policies and procedures.

2. Written record retention policies, record disposition schedules, record lifecycles, and record management procedures. Any internal memos, letters, announcements, email messages, instant messages, text messages, blog posts, Internet posts, social networking comments, Intranet posts, meeting notes, calendar notations, or other documents related to the subpoenaed policies and procedures.

3. Written litigation hold policies and procedures. Any internal memos, letters, announcements, email messages, instant messages, text messages, blog posts, Internet posts, social networking comments, Intranet posts, meeting notes, calendar notations, or other formal or informal documents related to those formal policies and procedures.

4. Written business policies, guidelines, rules, or codes governing, for example, harassment and discrimination, language and content, conduct and ethics, confidentiality and privacy, among other company employment policies. Any internal memos, letters, announcements, email messages, instant messages, text messages, blog posts, Internet posts, social networking comments, Intranet posts, meeting notes, or other formal or informal documents related to those policies, guidelines, rules, or codes.

5. Written policies and procedures governing computer security. Any internal memos, letters, announcements, email messages, instant messages, text messages, blog posts, Internet posts, social networking comments, Intranet posts, meeting notes, or other formal or informal documents related to the policies and procedures in question.

6. Written policies and procedures governing computer monitoring. Any internal memos, letters, announcements, email messages, instant messages, text messages, blog posts, Internet posts, social networking comments, Intranet posts, meeting notes, or other formal or informal documents related to the organization's monitoring and surveillance policies and procedures.

7. Formal organizational charts for specific departments including, for example, information technology, human resources, legal, compliance, training, and records management.

8. Organizational charts for your company's social media policy team, record retention policy team, litigation hold team, or other teams overseeing the development, implementation, and enforcement of AUPs or employment policies. Any internal memos, letters, announcements, email messages, instant messages, text messages, blog posts, Internet posts, social networking comments, Intranet posts, meeting notes, or other formal or informal documents related to the formation and activities of the policy teams in question.

9. Written social media policy audit questionnaires and other documents related to your social media policy audit or other AUP audits. Any internal memos, letters, announcements, email messages, instant messages, text messages, blog posts, Internet posts, social networking comments, Intranet posts, meeting notes, or other documents related to the development, implementation, and findings of your policy audit.

10. Records and materials related to your organization's social media policy training program and related electronic policy training programs. Might include instructors' training manuals, participants'

training workbooks, PowerPoint slides and scripts, handouts and fact sheets, sign-in sheets, certification quizzes, books, calendars, videotapes, audiotapes, online interactive training programs, and recorded webinars. Any internal memos, letters, announcements, email messages, instant messages, text messages, blog posts, Internet posts, social networking comments, Intranet posts, meeting notes, or other documents related to the development and implementation of your formal social media policy training program and any other epolicy-related training programs.

11. Written policies, procedures, and other information and materials related to the organization's computer assets and technology resources. Might include documents related to IT security protocols, encryption, passwords, software, hardware, desktops, laptops, mobile devices, hard drives, servers, files, and so on.

12. Written policies and procedures related to employees' personal use of the organization's computer assets for purely personal, non-business reasons. Any internal memos, letters, announcements, email messages, instant messages, text messages, blog posts, Internet posts, social networking comments, Intranet posts, meeting notes, or other documents related to personal use of the company's systems, accounts, sites, software, or devices.

13. Written policies and procedures related to employees' use of their own personal accounts, sites, and devices for business reasons. Any internal memos, letters, announcements, email messages, instant messages, text messages, blog posts, Internet posts, social networking comments, Intranet posts, meeting notes, or other documents related to employees' use of private tools and technologies to conduct company business at the office, at home, or on the road.

14. Documents related to the organization's relationships with technology vendors including cloud (or hosted) technology solutions, software providers, and hardware manufacturers or distributors among others. Could include, for example, contracts, letters of agreement, purchase orders, invoices, service agreements, and correspondence related to the organization's IT assets.

## STATE RULES OF CIVIL PROCEDURE AND STATE E-DISCOVERY GUIDELINES

In addition to complying with the Federal Rules of Civil Procedure, responding to federal subpoenas, and complying with federal e-discovery requests, U.S.-based organizations also must adhere to the e-discovery guidelines of every state in which they operate, have employees, or litigate legal claims. Unfortunately, state rules of civil procedure and state e-discovery guidelines are not as clear-cut as the federal rules. When it comes to electronic discovery, state rules continue to evolve. Some states mirror the Federal Rules of Civil Procedure precisely. Other states have yet to adopt rules based on the FRCP.

---

**BEST PRACTICE RECOMMENDATION**

*RESEARCH AND ADHERE TO STATE RULES AFFECTING YOUR COMPANY*

Assign your organization's legal counsel or compliance officer the task of researching and monitoring the ways in which each state in which you operate or litigate lawsuits handles e-discovery, electronic evidence, and record retention requirements. Once you have familiarized yourself with the rules, make sure you adhere completely and consistently to whatever state rules of civil procedure and state e-discovery guidelines impact your business. To help get your research project under way, here are the URLs for the state rules of civil procedure and e-discovery rules of all 50 states, plus the District of Columbia.

---

| | |
|---|---|
| **Alabama** | http://www.judicial.alabama.gov/library/rules_civ_procedure.cfm |
| **Alaska** | http://www.courts.alaska.gov/civ.htm |
| **Arizona** | http://www.azcourts.gov/rules/Home.aspx |
| **Arkansas** | http://courts.state.ar.us/rules/index.cfm |
| **California** | http://www.courts.ca.gov/rules.htm |

| Colorado | http://www.boulder-bar.org/bar_media_manual/evidence/13.11.html |
|---|---|
| Connecticut | http://www.jud.ct.gov/pb.htm |
| Delaware | http://courts.delaware.gov/forms/download.aspx?id=39348 |
| District of Columbia | http://www.dcsc.gov/dccourts/docs/SUPERIOR_COURT_RULES_OF_CIVIL_PROCEDURE_090707.pdf |
| Florida | http://www.floridabar.org/tfb/tfblegalres.nsf/d64b801203bc919485256709006a561c/e1a89a0dc5248d1785256b2f006cccee?opendocument |
| Georgia | http://www.georgiacourts.org/files/UNIFORM%20SUPERIOR%20COURT%20RULES_Updated_11_10.pdf |
| Hawaii | http://www.courts.state.hi.us/legal_references/rules/rulesOfCourt.html |
| Idaho | http://www.isc.idaho.gov/rules/Discovery_Rule306.htm |
| Illinois | http://www.ilga.gov/legislation/ilcs/ilcs3.asp?ActID=2017&ChapterID=56 |
| Indiana | http://www.in.gov/judiciary/orders/rule-amendments/2007/trial-091007.pdf |
| Iowa | http://www.iowacourtsonline.org/Court_Rules_and_Forms/Recent_Amendments__New_Rules/ |
| Kansas | http://www.kansasjudicialcouncil.org/Documents/Studies%20and%20Reports/2010%20Reports/Civil%20Code%20Time%20Computation%20Report.pdf |
| Kentucky | http://www.kybar.org/247 |
| Louisiana | http://www.legis.state.la.us/billdata/streamdocument.asp?did=447007 |
| Maine | http://www.courts.state.me.us/court_info/rules/rules.html |
| Maryland | http://www.courts.state.md.us/rules/reports/158thReport.pdf |

| | |
|---|---|
| **Massachusetts** | http://www.lawlib.state.ma.us/source/mass/rules/civil/index.html |
| **Michigan** | http://coa.courts.mi.gov/rules/documents/1chapter2civilprocedure.pdf |
| **Minnesota** | http://www.mncourts.gov/?page=511 |
| **Mississippi** | http://www.mssc.state.ms.us/rules/msrulesofcourt/rules_of_civil_procedure.pdf |
| **Missouri** | http://www.courts.mo.gov/courts/ClerkHandbooksP2RulesOnly.nsf/0/b83f5cbe4450f09686256ca60052134e?OpenDocument |
| **Montana** | http://courts.mt.gov/supreme/proposed_rules/civil-procedure.mcpx |
| **Nebraska** | http://www.supremecourt.ne.gov/rules/pdf/Ch6Art3.pdf |
| **Nevada** | http://www.leg.state.nv.us/courtrules/nrcp.html |
| **New Hampshire** | http://www.courts.state.nh.us/supreme/orders/ord20070118.pdf |
| **New Jersey** | http://www.judiciary.state.nj.us/rules/part4toc.htm |
| **New Mexico** | http://www.nmcompcomm.us/nmrules/nmruleset.aspx?rs=1 |
| **New York** | http://public.leginfo.state.ny.us/LAWSSEAF.cgi?QUERYTYPE=LAWS+&QUERYDATA=@LLCVP+&LIST=LAW+&BROWSER=BROWSER+&TOKEN=14959862+&TARGET=VIEW |
| **North Carolina** | http://www.ncbusinesscourt.net/new/localrules/ |
| **North Dakota** | http://www.ndcourts.gov/rules/civil/frameset.htm |
| **Ohio** | http://www.supremecourt.ohio.gov/LegalResources/Rules/civil/CivilProcedure.pdf |
| **Oklahoma** | http://www.oscn.net/applications/oscn/Index.asp?ftdb=STOKST12&level=1 |
| **Oregon** | http://www.leg.state.or.us/ors/orcpors.htm |
| **Pennsylvania** | http://www.pacode.com/secure/data/231/partItoc.html |
| **Rhode Island** | http://www.courts.ri.gov/default.aspx |

| South Carolina | http://www.judicial.state.sc.us/courtreg/indexADR.cfm |
| South Dakota | http://www.sdjudicial.com/ |
| Tennessee | http://www.tsc.state.tn.us/opinions/tsc/rules/tnrulesofcourt/02civp.htm |
| Texas | http://www.supreme.courts.state.tx.us/rules/trcp/rcp_all.pdf |
| Utah | http://www.utcourts.gov/resources/rules/urcp/ |
| Vermont | http://www.michie.com/vermont/lpext.dll?f=templates&fn=main-h.htm&cp=vtrules |
| Virginia | http://www.courts.state.va.us/courts/scv/rulesofcourt.pdf |
| Washington | http://www.courts.wa.gov/court_rules/ |
| West Virginia | http://www.state.wv.us/wvsca/rules/contents.htm |
| Wisconsin | http://nxt.legis.state.wi.us/nxt/gateway.dll?f=templates&fn=default.htm&d=stats&jd=ch.%20801 |
| Wyoming | http://www.courts.state.wy.us/CourtRules_Entities.aspx?RulesPage=CivilProcedure.xml |

## FOIA AND STATE SUNSHINE LAWS GRANT SUBPOENA POWER TO CITIZENS

Government agencies and municipalities, school systems, and universities—all public entities operating in the United States are under pressure to maintain the transparency and availability of social media content, email messages, text messages, and other electronic business records. The federal Freedom of Information Act (FOIA) and state sunshine laws (also known as open records laws) obligate public entities on the federal, state, county, and local levels to preserve and protect ESI while ensuring that electronic evidence can be produced promptly in response to a public records request. Fail to meet your electronic discovery obligations, and your public entity could suffer costly court sanctions—paid for with taxpayer dollars that might be needed (or better spent) elsewhere.

### REAL-LIFE OPEN RECORDS DISASTER STORIES

Government agencies, school systems, and other public entities are obligated to respond to records requests in a timely fashion. What type of records might you be required to produce? In one noteworthy case, a judge ordered the state of Kentucky to provide a man with copies of email correspondence transmitted between the man's wife, a state employee, and another state employee with whom the man suspected his wife was having an affair.[5]

In another case, the concerned father of a high school rower subpoenaed school records to uncover the reason why a winning coach, under whose guidance the girls' crew team had gained national prominence, was abruptly fired by high school administrators.

In 2010, an Ohio Appeals Court found the city of Cleveland to be in violation of open records law when the city took more than a "reasonable period of time" to satisfy a public records request from the Municipal Construction Equipment Operators' Labor Council. The city's delayed response, coupled with its failure to communicate with the union about the status of the request, led the 8th District Court of Appeals to award attorney's fees of $5,763.75 to the union.[6]

### BEST PRACTICE RECOMMENDATION

Do not allow unmanaged electronic records to undermine legal compliance. Prepare today for tomorrow's public records requests by reviewing and (as necessary) updating your organization's record retention policy, as well as your social media policy, email policy, and other acceptable use policies governing electronic business communication tools and technologies. Support written retention policy with an automated archiving solution to guarantee your ability to search, locate, and produce electronic business records in compliance with FOIA and state sunshine laws.

# HOW LONG SHOULD ESI BE RETAINED?

If you're struggling with this question, you're not alone. There are different schools of thought on business record retention periods. For some organizations, the retention and disposition of business records is governed by laws or regulations. In the financial sector, for example, the Securities and Exchange Commission (SEC) requires regulated broker-dealers to preserve and produce three years' worth of electronic records immediately upon request. The Employee Retirement Income Security Act (ERISA), on the other hand, requires the indefinite retention of email and other documents related to employee benefits. As detailed in Chapter Four, regulatory bodies all impose rules dictating electronic retention schedules.

That said, unless your organization's electronic business records are governed by law or regulations, you are free to determine your own retention policies and deletion schedules. Although the courts typically don't punish organizations for deleting email and other forms of ESI in the "ordinary course of business," many unregulated entities are opting to keep electronic business records for increasingly longer periods of time. Thanks to federal and state e-discovery rules, readily available technology solutions, and ever-decreasing storage costs, growing numbers of organizations are choosing the safety of long-term archiving over the convenience of deletion.

Yet, in spite of the growing evidentiary role that email, social media content, and other forms of ESI play, many organizations continue to engage in what is known as "destructive retention." Destructive retention calls for the preservation of email and other electronic records for a limited time, followed by its permanent deletion, manually or automatically, from the network. When it comes to destructive retention, preservation periods range from months to years. The most commonly applied retention period is seven years, according to ArcMail Technology.[7]

If you opt for destructive retention, bear in mind that email and other forms of electronic content never disappear completely. Employees, executives, independent contractors, and other users are likely to file, print, copy, forward, and otherwise retain their own personal stores of your organization's internal and external email, IM, text messages, posts, photos, videos, and other content. Outside parties may elect to retain incoming email messages and save blog posts, tweets, or other social networking content published by your employees. Thanks to links, permalinks, and content syndication, the comments, conversations, and content your employees post online is likely to remain accessible long after you purge your organization's system. Consequently, a retention policy that calls for the deletion of email and other forms of ESI at regular intervals (every 90 days, for example) could weaken your legal position, rendering you the only party to a lawsuit who lacks copies of your own business records.

## FORM A RECORDS MANAGEMENT TEAM AND ESTABLISH A RECORD RETENTION POLICY

Whether your organization is privately held or public, unmanaged ESI can trigger financial, productivity, legal, and public relations nightmares. The financial resources required to produce subpoenaed electronic records, retain experienced legal counsel, secure expert witnesses, fund a computer forensic investigation, mount a protracted legal battle, and cover the cost of jury awards and settlements would put many organizations out of business. Best practices call for a proactive approach to electronic record management and e-discovery compliance. As first steps, you will want to form a records management team and establish a formal record retention policy.

### Form a records management team

In addition to forming a social media policy team to oversee development and implementation of your organization's comprehensive policy and procedures (see Chapter Eight), best practices also call for the establishment of a team of experts charged with the task of creating and managing a formal record retention policy for your organization.

Records management team members should include a legal professional or compliance officer who is familiar with the amended Federal Rules of Civil Procedure and state e-discovery rules governing those jurisdictions in which you operate, employ workers, or litigate lawsuits. In addition to an experienced legal representative, your records management team should include a professional records manager (either an employee or consultant), as well as your IT director. Your team's responsibilities would include the following:

1. Define "business record" on a company-wide or department-by-department basis.
2. Research the e-discovery laws of every jurisdiction (domestic and international) in which you do business or litigate workplace lawsuits.
3. Research the record retention guidelines of any government or industry regulator that oversees your business.
4. Determine record lifecycles for all of your organization's ESI.
5. Establish a formal deletion schedule, spelling out which records are to be deleted when.
6. Write (or update) your organization's formal record retention policy and procedures.
7. Evaluate the organization's technology resources vis-à-vis your legal and regulatory compliance requirements. As necessary, update or purchase new technology solutions to help manage and maintain, preserve, and protect ESI in compliance with federal and state e-discovery rules and requirements, as well as the organization's customized record retention policy.
8. Educate all employees about the organization's e-discovery compliance obligations, record retention policy, and individual users' roles (if any) when it comes to the legally compliant retention and deletion of the company's email, social media content, and other electronic business records.
9. Regularly monitor legal updates, case law, and regulatory changes related to record retention and e-discovery on the state, federal, and (if appropriate) international levels. Update your retention policy

and procedures as necessary to reflect changes in the law or regulatory rules. Conduct continuing education programs to keep users up-to-date with policy revisions.

### Create litigation hold policy and procedures

In addition to establishing and enforcing record retention policy, your organization's record management team also should be charged with the task of developing and managing the company's litigation hold policy and procedures. Under the direction of experienced legal counsel, your litigation hold policy will help reduce the likelihood of spoliation (destruction of evidence) claims against the company. In the event of a lawsuit, your litigation hold policy is designed to stop the destruction of electronic business records that otherwise might be purged in the ordinary course of business. As soon as a lawsuit is filed or a regulatory audit is initiated, your records management team should implement and enforce the litigation hold policy. Remember, if you have even the slightest suspicion that a certain individual may one day file a lawsuit against the organization, you must stop destroying records and enforce your litigation hold policy immediately.

## SOCIAL MEDIA BEST PRACTICES: EFFECTIVE RECORDS MANAGEMENT AND E-DISCOVERY COMPLIANCE

1. Be proactive. Plan for the inevitability of e-discovery before it happens. The fact that your organization has never been the target of a civil lawsuit does not mean it never will be. We live in a litigious society. There is a good chance that your company will one day find itself battling a sexual harassment claim, hostile work environment allegation, or other workplace lawsuit on the federal or state level. Your ability to search, locate, and produce legally valid social networking content, email messages and attachments, and other forms of ESI can help make the difference between success and failure when that day comes.

2. Form a records management team made up of your legal counsel or compliance officer, records manager, and IT director.

3. Know and adhere to the amended Federal Rules of Civil Procedure (FRCP).

4. Research and comply with the state rules of civil procedure governing e-discovery and email retention in every state in which you operate, have employees, or litigate lawsuits.

5. If you manage a government agency, supervise a school district, or otherwise operate a public entity, you are obligated to comply with the federal Freedom of Information Act, as well as the open records laws of every state in which you operate or have employees or facilities.

6. If you operate in the health care arena, financial services industry, or any other regulated profession, you must research and adhere to the retention rules set forth by the government and industry regulatory bodies that oversee your business.

7. Assign your records management team the task of defining "business record" on a company-wide or department-by-department basis.

8. Ask your records management team to write or update the organization's formal record retention policy.

9. Under the direction of experience legal counsel, have your records management team draft a written litigation hold policy and establish procedures to halt the routine destruction of email records, social media content, and other ESI once litigation is under way or legal claims are anticipated.

10. Create an audit trail. Eliminate potential surprises by investigating your company's computer system, accounts, sites, and devices to determine exactly who has been doing precisely what on the system.

11. Take steps, through written social media policy, record retention policy, and an archiving technology solution to demonstrate that your electronic business records are authentic, reliable, and legally compliant. If you can demonstrate that your archiving solution is reliable, and your ESI is tamperproof, then your organization will be on more solid footing with courts and regulators in the event of a workplace lawsuit.

12. Educate all of your users (full-time and part-time, executives and employees, independent contractors and consultants, and anyone else who works on behalf of or for the benefit of your company). Don't expect users to understand business records—or their individual roles in electronic record management—without formal training. Address record-related legal, regulatory, and security risks facing the organization and its individual users; e-discovery risks and requirements; and the disciplinary action—up to and including termination—that awaits users who violate social media policy, record retention policy, and any other employment policy, law, or regulation. Communicate the organization's "business record" definition clearly and consistently to all users. Make sure everyone knows the difference between business records and non-records—and understands their individual roles (if any) in the preservation of electronic business records and the purging of non-records.

13. Automate the archiving process with technology to enhance productivity; reduce search costs; enforce retention policy compliance; ensure the legal validity of electronic evidence; meet e-discovery obligations; maximize legal and regulatory compliance; and minimize organizational risks.

# REGULATORY COMPLIANCE

## GOVERNMENT AND INDUSTRY WATCHDOGS KEEP AN EYE ON THE SOCIAL WEB

Government and industry regulators have long kept a watchful eye on the content created and business records generated by email messages and attachments. Thanks to the growing use of workplace social media, the bodies that are charged with overseeing heavily regulated industries, including health care and financial services, for example, have now turned their attention to social networking, blogging, and other web 2.0 applications. As a result, 37 percent of companies in the United States and United Kingdom were subjected to at least one regulatory proceeding in 2010, according to *Fulbright's Seventh Annual Litigation Trends Survey.*[1]

Regulated businesses cannot afford to take chances with compliance management. As a first step toward successful regulatory compliance, assign your organization's legal counsel or compliance officer the task of researching all of the regulatory risks and rules currently affecting your organization's electronic use, content, and records. Once you understand your regulatory compliance obligations, then it's time to get to work drafting policies and procedures to help ensure that your business and users are 100 percent compliant with the ever-increasing guidelines set forth by government and industry regulatory bodies.

## FINANCIAL SERVICES FIRMS FACE GROWING COMPLIANCE HURDLES

Financial services firms operating in the United States have long been mindful of the need for legal and regulatory compliance vis-à-vis email, instant messaging, and the Internet. In the age of social media and web 2.0, however, financial institutions and companies must expand their focus to include social networking, blogging, texting, and other forms of electronic business communication.

Whether your organization is public or private, a small business with a handful of employees, a mid-market firm with hundreds of users, or a large institution employing thousands of professionals, financial services companies simply cannot afford to play fast and loose with social media management. Compliance with all relevant regulations is mandatory, not an option. Fail to comply with industry rules and government regulations related to social media, email, and other electronic business communication tools, and you'll face potentially costly consequences including protracted regulatory audits, potentially stiff monetary fines, and reputation-shattering news coverage.

To survive and thrive in the twenty-first-century regulatory environment, financial services firms are advised to adopt the "three-e" approach to effective regulatory compliance: (1) establish written social media policy (and other acceptable use policies) to help increase compliance and decrease regulatory risks; (2) educate the workforce about regulatory risks and rules, as well as the company's policies and procedures; and (3) enforce social media policy with proven-effective technology solutions including archiving, encryption, anti-virus, URL blocks, and content control, among others. The combination of policy, training, and technology (the three-e approach) is the most efficient and effective way to manage regulatory risks and compliance.

As detailed below, among the regulatory guidelines and bodies with which the financial services industry must concern itself are the Gramm-Leach-Bliley Act (GLBA), Sarbanes-Oxley Act (SOX), Securities and Exchange Commission (SEC), Financial Industry Regulatory Authority (FINRA), New York Stock Exchange (NYSE), Payment Card Industry-Data Security Standard (PCI DSS), Office of the Comptroller of the Currency (OCC), Federal Deposit Insurance Corporation (FDIC), and the United States Patriot Act.

## Gramm-Leach-Bliley Act (GLBA) risks and regulations

Under GLBA, financial services firms are legally obligated to protect the privacy of consumers and their nonpublic personal financial information. If your company handles Social Security numbers, credit card data, debit card numbers, or other personal financial data belonging to customers, employees, students, or faculty, among others, then you must take steps to ensure GLBA compliance. Because security breaches, intercepted messages, corrupted files, and leaked, stolen, or lost data can put your organization at risk of noncompliance, effective social media management is fundamental to GLBA compliance.

In spite of Congress's attempts to protect customer privacy and regulate corporate accountability, many organizations remain challenged by GLBA. That's bad news for management. Under the legal principle of vicarious liability, the employer typically is held legally responsible for the wrong acts (accidental or intentional) of employees. Consequently, if a disgruntled employee were to intentionally post customers' credit card numbers on a blog, chances are the employer could be held liable. Similarly, if an executive accidentally attached a list of employees' Social Security numbers to a tweet, the company could be in regulatory hot water.

Financial industry regulators take compliance seriously, and business must do so as well. Failure to comply with GLBA could cost an employer up to 10 years in prison and a $1 million fine.

Employee education is essential to GLBA compliance. You cannot expect untrained employees to be familiar with regulatory rules, appreciate the importance of regulatory compliance, or understand their individual roles in the compliance process. Support the organization's social media policy and compliance management program with formal employee training. Be sure to stress the fact that regulatory compliance (strict adherence to GLBA as well as other rules and regulations) is not an option. It is 100 percent mandatory.

## Sarbanes-Oxley Act (SOX) risks and regulations

For public companies and registered public accounting firms, inadequate social media management and lax computer security can lead to SOX violations. Designed by the Securities and Exchange Commission (SEC) to thwart fraud in public companies, SOX requires regulated companies to implement internal controls for the gathering, processing, and reporting of accurate and reliable financial information. As with GLBA, the successful management of social media content, records, use, accounts, passwords, and sites is fundamental to SOX compliance.

Failure to retain electronic records related to audit work papers and financial controls for at least seven years as mandated by SOX can put your organization at risk of severe penalties for noncompliance. Knowingly altering or destroying electronic business records that are vital to an audit or investigation can net guilty parties 20 years in federal prison and fines of $15 million.

## SEC Regulation Fair Disclosure (FD)

Blogging, tweeting, posting, and other forms of social networking can put publicly traded companies in violation of the SEC's fair disclosure rule (Regulation FD), which is in place to govern the sharing of information between public companies and investors. Regulation FD is designed to prevent an issuer of stock from selectively disclosing (to family and friends, for example) material nonpublic information. Because Regulation FD predates social media, it does not specifically address the use of social media by public companies. Consequently,

**RECOMMENDED BEST PRACTICE**

Although SOX is vague about email and social media requirements and electronic record keeping, financial services firms
are advised to implement social media management programs
that address usage, content, security, retention, and archiving
as part of the organization's comprehensive electronic risk management and SOX compliance plan.

To help guarantee SOX compliance, review your organization's
social media management program to ensure that financial data
and related documents—including confidential internal memos,
revenue projections, or other content transmitted via email,
mobile devices, and other electronic tools and technologies—are
effectively protected from malware, viruses, and other malicious
intruders—and are preserved in a legally compliant manner.

all it takes is one inappropriate post, comment, tweet, or status update
to produce costly consequences for the company. Though a casual
tweet, for example, may seem harmless, the activity and response
sparked by an update could result in repercussions that could trigger an
SEC investigation and shareholder uproar.[2]

SEC compliance requires companies to determine whether the posting of information on a social networking site or company website
constitutes a "public" disclosure for purposes of Regulation FD. The

**RECOMMENDED BEST PRACTICE**

To help ensure compliance with Regulation FD, publicly traded
companies and their agents (certified public accountants, investor relations firms, or public relations consultants, for example)
should establish clear social media policies that specifically
address (perhaps limiting or forbidding) the disclosure of nonpublic information through blogs and social media.

SEC uses three criteria to help determine whether information posted on corporate websites is considered "public": (1) the company's website is a recognized channel of distribution; (2) information is posted, accessible, and disseminated in a manner calculated to reach investors; and (3) information is posted for a reasonable period, so it may be absorbed by investors.[3]

Without written social media policy and procedures in place, any employee who tweets, posts, or blogs about the company might be deemed to represent the company in an "official" communications role. Whether or not the employee officially represents the company is irrelevant. A violation of Regulation FD could stem from an employee's ill-timed Facebook post about a company secret, such as an upcoming product launch, a pending acquisition, or projected quarterly sales figures. Though the employee's Facebook page is on a public site, it nonetheless is limited to the employee's "friends." If a savvy friend were to take the post as a signal to buy or sell company stock, a charge of insider trading, social media style, could result.

The poster's intention is inconsequential. The SEC doesn't care whether or not the employee actually intended to pump up the company's stock. The violation revolves around the fact that the employee (privy to secret company information) chose to selectively disclose that secret information (which is not readily available to the public) to a limited number of friends on Facebook.

All it takes is one inappropriate post, comment, tweet, or status update to produce costly consequences for public companies. Social networking may be a wildly popular and pervasive communications tool, but that does not relinquish publicly held companies from their responsibility to communicate information to the public in an appropriate and lawful manner, in compliance with SEC guidelines.

## FINRA issues social media rules

The Financial Industry Regulatory Authority (FINRA) in 2010 issued guidance (Regulatory Notice 10–06) to securities firms and brokers regarding the use of public social networking sites (including Facebook,

**REAL-LIFE SEC DISASTER STORY: SOCIAL MEDIA POSTS TRIGGER INVESTIGATION, TARNISH BRAND**

In 2008, Whole Foods Market CEO John Mackey used social networking sites to anonymously post information about his company's stock and the stock of a competitor that happened to be a Whole Foods acquisition target. In his posts, Mackey disparaged the competitor's stock in an effort to weaken its market value and improve his company's acquisition position.

When his actions were discovered, Mackey was subjected to investigations by the SEC and an internal committee of Whole Foods. Ultimately, he was forced to issue a public apology. Though the SEC filed no charges against Mackey, both his public image and the Whole Foods brand were tarnished by the CEOs stock-related social networking.[4]

Twitter, LinkedIn, and blogs) to communicate with customers and the general public. The FINRA regulatory notice emphasizes the fact that each firm must develop its own set of social media policies and procedures. The goal of social media policies and procedures, according to FINRA, should be to ensure that regulated firms and their personnel comply with all applicable regulatory requirements when using social networking sites.[5]

## Wall Street blocks social sites

FINRA's social media rules have little impact on Goldman Sachs and other major Wall Street firms that automatically block access to social networking sites in an effort to reduce regulatory risks and security threats, while increasing productivity. In spite of the $500 million investment that Goldman and investor Digital Sky Technologies made in Facebook in 2011, employees of the brokerage firm cannot view the social site during working hours. They must wait until they get home to catch up on their Facebook friends—and their company's half-a-billion-dollar stake.[6]

## NYSE risks and regulations

Companies that are listed on the New York Stock Exchange (NYSE) must manage social media content, email, and other electronic content according to NYSE content and retention guidelines. They also are required to protect confidential business information and customers' personal data. Because much company and customer data is stored on computers and transmitted electronically, it is essential for NYSE-listed companies to put social media policies, procedures, and content security technology in place to protect confidential information from security breaches and other computer-related disasters.

## Payment Card Industry-Data Security Standard (PCI DSS)

PCI DSS establishes standards and technologies to protect consumer credit card data. Social media management and Internet security are essential to ensure data protection and regulatory compliance. Merchants, banks, credit card providers, and others that fail to comply with PCI DSS face potential fines of $500,000 per incident.

## Office of the Comptroller of the Currency (OCC) Advisory Letter: Electronic record keeping

The OCC Advisory requires banks to implement compliant electronic record retention systems to facilitate litigation, regulatory audits, and bank supervision. Banks' electronic record retention solutions should be designed to block external access to the system from third parties. In addition, the system should provide backup, internal controls, and record destruction, as well as the retention of social media content, email, and other electronic business records.

## FDIC Advisory: IT Risk Management Program (IT-RMP) new information technology

Under the 2005 FDIC Advisory, FDIC-supervised financial institutions must adhere to regulatory procedures governing risk assessment;

security and risk management; audits and independent reviews; and the encryption of electronic customer information while in transit or in storage on networks and systems to which unauthorized persons may have access.

## U.S. Patriot Act

The U.S. Patriot Act (314a) is designed to thwart and punish terrorist acts in the United States and around the world. To that end, the Patriot Act seeks to prevent, detect, and prosecute international money laundering and the financing of terrorism. The financial services industry is required to report potential money laundering and to search and produce electronic records as requested by federal law enforcement. A financial institution that receives a 314(a) request has two weeks to search their data stores and turn over requested electronic data. Failure to comply with the Patriot Act could net your financial institution 20 years in prison and a $1 million fine.

---

**BEST PRACTICE RECOMMENDATIONS FOR THE FINANCIAL SERVICES INDUSTRY**

To maximize SOX, GLBA, SEC, FINRA, NYSE, PCI DSS, OCC, FDIC, and Patriot Act compliance, public companies, financial services firms, and financial institutions must ensure that financial data, consumer information, electronic business records, and other regulated electronic documents are effectively protected from inappropriate exposure, unlawful disclosure, security breaches, or malicious intruders—and are preserved in a secure and legally compliant manner.

Combat risks and help ensure compliance through the combination of written social media policy and procedures, supported by employee education, and enforced by technology tools—proven-effective weapons in the battle against social media regulatory risks.

---

# THE IMPACT OF SOCIAL MEDIA ON HEALTH CARE COMPLIANCE

Social media, like email and other forms of electronic business communication, make health care concerns particularly vulnerable to regulatory risks, scrutiny, and penalties.

## *HIPAA compliance is mandatory*

Employee use of social media can open any health care company to regulatory investigations and fines should patients' electronic protected health information (EPHI) be accessed by unauthorized employees or shared with third parties. If your U.S.-based organization provides health care products, services, or insurance, then you are legally required to comply with the Health Insurance Portability and Accountability Act (HIPAA), which exists to protect the privacy of patient information.

HIPAA requires regulated organizations to safeguard electronic protected health information (EPHI) related to patients' health status, medical care, treatment plans, and payment issues. Failure to do so can result in regulatory fines, civil litigation, criminal charges, and jail time.

You cannot be present in every office on every floor of every facility every hour of every day. You cannot rely on managers and staff to exercise sound judgment and enforce rules and policies 100 percent of the time. And you should not discount the damage social networkers and bloggers pose to your health care company's people, patients, assets, future, reputation, and revenues.

## BEST PRACTICE RECOMMENDATIONS

Increasingly, medical professionals are seeking the security and privacy offered by private social networks like Sermo, Doximity, and PeerCase. Private, physician-only sites offer the benefits of clinical collaboration and conversations with professional colleagues in a secure online environment. Professionals can exchange HIPAA-secure messages and communicate about patient care and cases, without the regulatory and security risks associated with Facebook, LinkedIn, or other public social networking sites.

Regardless of whether you use public social media sites or private professionals-only networking sites, best practices call for the establishment of written social media policy, supported by formal employee education, and enforced by best-in-class technology solutions designed to monitor social media use, block access to off-limits blogs and social websites, manage content and language, and prevent data theft, confidentiality breaches, and other security threats. The strategic use of policy, training, and technology will help keep your health care organization HIPAA compliant.

## REAL-LIFE HIPAA DISASTER STORIES: CAUTIONARY TALES FOR HEALTH CARE COMPANIES

### UCLA Health System Settles HIPAA Violations for $865,000

In 2011, the University of California-Los Angeles (UCLA) Health System agreed to pay $865,000 as part of a settlement with federal regulators over allegations that UCLA hospital employees violated HIPAA by viewing celebrities' electronic health records without authorization. The agreement marked the U.S. Department of Health and Human Services' third-largest settlement involving HIPAA-violations.[7]

As devastating as UCLA's actual HIPAA violation and fine were, imagine the costs that the UCLA Health System might have incurred had the nosy employees added fuel to the regulatory fire by posting celebrities' EPHI on the social web, for hundreds, thousands, possibly millions of star-struck Twitter followers and Facebook friends to read.

**Oakwood Hospital Fires Employee for HIPAA Violation on Facebook**

In 2010, Michigan's Oakwood Hospital fired an employee for posting negative comments about a patient, in violation of HIPAA. Using her own computer on her own time, the employee announced that she had come face-to-face with a patient who was suspected of killing a local police officer, and she hoped he would rot in hell. Although the employee did not name the patient, discuss his condition, or identify her employer, she was terminated for violating HIPPA regulations by disseminating protected health information about a patient on a public forum and making disparaging and disrespectful remarks in violation of hospital policy.[8]

Best practices call for the enforcement of social media policy through training and disciplinary action. Although the termination of an otherwise valuable employee may be difficult for the organization and devastating for the worker, it is essential for employers to take policy enforcement and regulatory compliance seriously. Firing one policy-scofflaw today may prevent you from dismissing an entire department full of rule-breakers tomorrow.

## FTC RULES GOVERNING BLOGGING AND TWEETING

The United States Federal Trade Commission (FTC) in 2009 issued revised endorsement guidelines that affect blogging, tweeting, and posting on social networking sites. Specifically, the FTC "blogging rules" are aimed at bloggers, tweeters, and posters who accept payment or goods in exchange for written endorsements of companies' products or services.

The FTC rules require bloggers, tweeters, and other online posters to disclose any material connections between themselves and the products or services they discuss in their posts. In other words, product, service, or company endorsements must be honest and cannot be deceptive. Failure to comply with FTC endorsement guidelines could result in fines of up to $11,000 for individual bloggers. It might also create liability concerns for advertisers and bloggers.[9]

What does this mean for your business? Feel free to encourage employee bloggers, tweeters, and social networkers to promote the organization's products and services on their own personal blogs and social sites, but require them to disclose their affiliations with the company as part of their online profiles. Use your organization's written social media and blog policies and training programs to educate employees about the FTC's rules and to explain the compliance obligations facing the organization and individual bloggers, tweeters, and posters.

## SOCIAL MEDIA BEST PRACTICES: REGULATORY COMPLIANCE

1. Regulated businesses cannot afford to take chances with compliance management. As a first step toward successful regulatory compliance, assign your organization's legal counsel or compliance officer the task of researching all of the regulatory risks and rules currently affecting your organization's electronic use, content, and records.

2. Once you understand your company's regulatory compliance obligations, then it's time to get to work drafting policies and procedures to help ensure that your business and users are 100 percent compliant with the ever-increasing guidelines set forth by government and industry regulatory bodies.

3. Be mindful of the fact that, thanks to the growing use of workplace social media, the bodies that are charged with overseeing heavily regulated industries, including health care and financial services, have now turned their attention to social networking, blogging, and other web 2.0 applications.

4. To survive and thrive in the twenty-first century, regulated firms are advised to adopt the "three-e" approach to effective regulatory compliance: (1) establish written social media policy (and other acceptable use policies) to help increase compliance and decrease regulatory risks; (2) educate the workforce about regulatory risks

and rules, as well as the company's policies and procedures; and (3) enforce social media policy with proven-effective technology solutions including archiving, encryption, anti-virus, URL blocks, and content control, among others. The combination of policy, training, and technology (the three-e approach) is the most efficient and effective way to manage regulatory risks and compliance.

# PRIVACY, SECURITY, AND SOCIAL MEDIA

## WHAT EVERY EMPLOYER—AND USER—SHOULD KNOW

As everyone knows by now, there is no privacy on the public web. Nonetheless, employers are obligated—for legal, regulatory, and business reasons—to protect corporate secrets, safeguard consumers' personal data, and secure patients' private health information from loss, theft, or exposure to unauthorized parties via social media, email, or other electronic business communication tools.

Thanks to the pervasive use of web 2.0 and social media to communicate with customers, collaborate with coworkers, and conduct company business, the job of shoring up security risks is becoming increasingly challenging for business. No wonder 72 percent of information technology and security professionals surveyed by *SC Magazine* in 2010 report that their organizations are concerned about threats to their data from social networking sites.[1]

**REAL-LIFE SOCIAL MEDIA DISASTER STORY: PATIENT PRIVACY POACHED**

Consider, for example, the 2010 case in which five nurses employed by a California hospital were fired after posting patient information on Facebook. Although patient names, photos, or other identifying information was not posted, the nurses nonetheless violated hospital policy and HIPAA guidelines by using the social networking site to discuss hospital patients. The nurses' itch to gossip put the hospital at risk of a potentially costly and time-consuming Health and Human Services (HHS) regulatory investigation, not to mention the possibility of civil lawsuits filed by the victims of their secrecy-shattering posts.[2]

**BEST PRACTICES FOR EMPLOYERS**

Regulated or not, employers who want to protect individual privacy and keep business secrets under wraps are advised to combine written social media policy with formal employee education. When it comes to safeguarding confidential data, employee education is essential. Uninformed social networkers often are unaware of the security risks facing their employers, their families, and themselves. Forty percent of individuals who use social media at home admit that they have posted their full birthdates online, opening the door to identity thieves in the process. Twenty-six percent of Facebook users have published their children's names and photos on the popular public site, exposing their kids to risks from predators, according to Consumer Reports 2010 "State of the Net" survey.[3]

Don't take chances with security risks or compliance rules. Use policy and training to alert users to social media risks at the office, at home, and elsewhere. Once employees understand the risks, they are more likely to help management enforce the rules.

# EMPLOYEES HAVE NO EXPECTATION OF PRIVACY

In the United States, employees have no reasonable expectation of privacy when using the company's computer system, sites, accounts, or devices. The federal Electronic Communications Privacy Act (ECPA) makes it clear that the company's computer system is the property of the employer. The employer has the legal right to monitor employees' electronic use, content, activity, and transmissions.

While only two states, Delaware and Connecticut, require employers to notify employees that their computer use is being monitored, U.S. courts consistently have ruled that all employees should assume their online activity is being watched, even if the boss has given no indication that monitoring is taking place. Even in cases in which employees have been told that email entering and leaving the system is not being monitored, the courts have ruled that employees still should not expect privacy when using company-owned computer resources.

In 2011, the U.S. District Court for the Southern District of New York ruled that an employee does not have a reasonable expectation of privacy when communicating with a spouse through an employer's email system. Key to the court's decision was the fact that the employer, Reserve Management Co., Inc., had an email policy in place, notified employees that the email policy forbade personal communication, and warned employees that email messages were monitored and could be disclosed to courts or regulatory bodies in the course of litigation or regulatory investigations.[4]

Although some legal experts argue that ECPA, which was introduced in 1986, no longer meets America's electronic communications privacy needs, it is still the law. In 2011, Senator Patrick Leahy of Vermont introduced legislation to update ECPA to better reflect twenty-first-century risks, rules, tools, and technologies.[5] Until ECPA is revised, however, employers should continue to exercise their legal right to monitor, and employees should continue to behave accordingly.

---

**BEST PRACTICE ADVICE FOR EMPLOYEES**

Be mindful of what you write, say, or publish online if you hope to land a promotion, keep your current job, or advance your professional standing in the age of social networking.

---

## SOCIAL NETWORKING CAN GET YOU FIRED

While many social networkers, high-profile bloggers, workplace privacy advocates, and employment law experts continue to debate the employer's right to monitor (and fire) employees for inappropriate computer use and online content, one fact remains clear. As of 2011, private employers operating in employment-at-will states do have the legal right to fire at-will employees for just about any reason, including inappropriate or unlawful tweets, Facebook comments, or blog posts.

Many U.S. employers are exercising their right to terminate employees who violate policies governing electronic use and content. As recently as 2009, 5 percent of employers reported that they had fired employees for inappropriate social media use or content, with another 26 terminating workers for Internet violations, and an additional 26 percent dismissing staff for email misuse, according to the *2009 Electronic Business Communication Policies and Procedures Survey* from American Management Association and The ePolicy Institute.[6]

Expect the number of computer-related terminations to increase as social networking use, at work and home, grows. The use of technology definitely is outpacing the law. Until the law catches up with social media use, workers who are concerned about job security are advised to familiarize themselves—and fully comply with—their employers' social media rules, policies, and procedures.

## NLRB TAKES ON SOCIAL MEDIA USE, POLICIES, AND TERMINATIONS

In 2011, the National Labor Relations Board (NLRB) turned its attention to social media use and policies. An independent federal agency, the NLRB is charged with the task of enforcing the National Labor

## REAL-LIFE SOCIAL MEDIA DISASTER STORIES: FIRED FOR FACEBOOK, TERMINATED FOR TWEETING

### Rough Landing on Facebook

Virgin Atlantic fired 13 crew members for participating in a Facebook discussion that was both critical of the airline's safety standards and insulting to passengers. The inappropriate content included "jokes" about faulty engines, cracks about cockroach-infested planes, and insults directed at passengers who were labeled "chavs." Virgin dismissed the workers for using a public forum to damage the company's reputation.[7]

### Gripe Site Grounded

Farm Boy, a Canadian grocery chain, dismissed six employees for creating a Facebook gripe site called "I Got Farm Boy'd." The employees used the site to mock and verbally assault customers and staff. Management fired the workers for displaying their disrespect for customers, the company, and coworkers on the public Internet.[8]

### Bounced for Racist Tweet

A radio host was fired for posting a racist, obscenity-laced tweet following a Dallas Mavericks–San Antonio Spurs basketball game. Venting his frustration over the Mavericks' loss, the announcer tweeted, "Congrats to all the dirty Mexicans in San Antonio." The major league pitcher-turned-radio-personality lost his job and professional reputation over 140 offensive characters.[9]

### CNN Commentator Canned

A senior Middle East editor was fired by CNN after tweeting a controversial comment about Lebanon's deceased Grand Ayatollah Mohammed Hussein Fadlallah. The editor tweeted about her respect for the leader, whom the Associated Press had called "anti-American" and described as linked to bombings that killed hundreds of Americans. The senior editor was dismissed in spite of issuing an apology in which she explained that her comment referred to Fadlallah's position on human rights.[10]

Relations Act. Enacted by Congress in 1935, the National Labor Relations Act is designed to protect the rights of most private-sector employees, unionized or not, to join together in order to improve their wages, working conditions, and other terms of employment.

Section 7 of the National Labor Relations Act gives employees the right to engage in "protected concerted activities," or communications that take place between two or more employees, discussing wages, hours, working conditions, staffing issues, or union organizing. Employers are prohibited from disciplining, terminating, or otherwise retaliating against employees engaged in protected concerted activities or communications. NLRB rules apply equally to traditional, off-line communications, as well as online conversations, including blog posts, tweets, Facebook comments, and other forms of social networking.

When it comes employees' protected concerted activity and employers' NLRB compliance, content counts. It doesn't matter whether an employee is using a company computer or a personal smartphone. It makes no difference whether a post is published on a business blog or a personal Facebook account. The issue is content. If a disgruntled worker uses Twitter to post an individual gripe against the boss, that tweet probably is not protected. On the other hand, if an employees uses YouTube to communicate with at least one coworker about wages, hours, working conditions, or terms of employment, then that communication may be protected by the NLRB.

### Recommendation for employers: Social media rules

On August 18, 2011, the NLRB's acting general counsel released a report detailing the agency's investigation into employees' protected and nonprotected use of social networking sites, as well as employers' lawful and unlawful use of social media rules and policies. That report is available online at https://www.nlrb.gov/news/acting-general-counsel-releases-report-social-media-cases.

Covered employers are advised to have their legal counsel review the NLRB's report on social media. Following that review, conduct a legal analysis of your organization's social media policies (and other electronic business communication policies) to ensure that you have not imposed overbroad rules that are likely to put you at odds with NLRB rules.

## Requirement for employers: Posting notice of employee rights

Effective January 31, 2012, all employers covered by the National Labor Relations Act are required to post a notice of employees' rights under the NLRA. Covered organizations include most private-sector employers, including unions. To determine whether your company is covered, and to receive a copy of the "Employee Rights Under the National Labor Relations Act" poster, visit the agency's website, https://www.nlrb.gov/news/posting-employee-rights-notice-now-required-jan-31-board-postpones-deadline-allow-further-educa.

If your business is covered by the NLRA, then you are obligated to comply with the posting rule, as well as social media requirements, or face potential penalties for noncompliance.

### REAL-LIFE NLRB LAWSUIT: EMPLOYEE'S TERMINATION AND EMPLOYER'S SOCIAL MEDIA POLICY SCUTINIZED

In a widely publicized case that sought to set legal limits on workplace social media and blog policies, the NLRB in 2010 filed suit against a Connecticut ambulance company in response to the firing of a union employee who had posted negative comments about her boss on her personal Facebook page. The employee, emergency medical technician Dawnmarie Souza, called her supervisor a "scumbag" and wrote "Love how the company allows a 17 to be a manager," referring to her employer's numeric code for psychiatric patients.

The NLRB lawsuit argued that the unionized employer, American Medical Response (AMR), had illegally terminated Souza for using her personal Facebook page to criticize her boss, had enforced an overly strict social media and blogging policy, and had denied Souza access to a union representative during the company's investigation into her conduct.

The suit settled in 2011. Financial terms were not disclosed, but AMR did agree to revise its social media and blog policies to ensure that employees are not improperly restricted when discussing wages, hours, or working conditions with coworkers or third parties outside the office. The company also agreed to stop disciplining or dismissing employees for engaging in these discussions. AMR also agreed to fulfill future requests for union representation when employees meet with managers.[11] Because the lawsuit settled, there was no opportunity for a court to issue a ruling or opinion on the case. AMR is the only company affected by the settlement. That said, employers who are covered by the National Labor Relations Act are advised to implement strategic social media policies and procedures, mindful of NLRB compliance obligations.

U.S. employers who are not covered by the NLRA remain free (at least for now) to manage employees' social media use and content through a combination of policy, training, and disciplinary action. Legal experts agree that employees' social media posts, comments, blogs, or tweets that are abusive, defamatory, pornographic, harassing, discriminatory, menacing, or otherwise illegal or inappropriate probably are not protected by the National Labor Relations Act. Employers should continue to adhere to best practices, which call for the implementation of written rules and policies to help manage content and protect company secrets. Just be sure that your policies are as clear and specific as possible.

**BEST PRACTICE RECOMMENDATION**

Have experienced legal counsel review your organization's social media policy, blog policy, and other acceptable use policies governing electronic business communication before distributing them to employees. If your business is covered by the National Labor Relations Act, then use your policies to communicate the fact that your organization is NLRA compliant and supports employees' legal right to engage in protected concerted activity.

For example, you could incorporate a statement like the following into your organization's social media policy: "The Company is covered by and compliant with the National Labor Relations Act (NLRA). The Company supports employees' legal right to engage in protected concerted activity and communication under Section 7 of the NLRA. This Social Media Policy will not be interpreted or applied in a manner that interferes with employees' protected concerted activity or communication. For additional information, see the Company's 'Employee Rights Under the NLRA' poster." (See Chapter 14 for sample policies incorporating NLRA disclaimers.)

The purpose of the legal review is to ensure that your policies are in compliance with federal and state laws, industry and government regulations, union rules, the National Labor Relations Act, and any other laws, regulations, guidelines, or rules that may have an impact on your company or industry.

## SOCIAL MEDIA CAN KEEP YOU FROM BEING HIRED

Job applicants should be mindful of the fact that prospective employers may be viewing the personal content posted by private citizens on public sites. Many organizations review job applicants' social web presence and personal blog posts as a means of uncovering the "real" person hiding behind the formal résumé.

According to American Management Association/ePolicy Institute research, 13 percent of employers in 2009 screened job applicants' social media presence, and another 3 percent rejected job prospects on the basis of the content posted on personal blogs and social networking sites.[12] Expect those numbers to rise steadily, as 70 million Millennials, also known as Generation Y, continue to move into the labor force.

Companies intent on conducting social media background checks can do the work themselves, or they can turn to professional sleuths who specialize in digging into employees' online pasts. Because we live in a web 2.0 world, it should come as no surprise that tech-savvy entrepreneurs are already running companies devoted to researching job candidates' history of Internet activity. For a fee, these organizations will search the social web and compile a dossier of information, positive or negative, about an applicant or employee. The type of information that is commonly sought includes references to drugs, gambling, or other illegal activities; comments that are racist, sexist, anti-Semitic, or otherwise discriminatory or harassing; or other evidence that could cause an employer to rethink or withdraw a job offer.[13]

## U.S. employers beware: Social screenings may trigger discrimination claims

Although using social media to screen potential job candidates is an increasingly common practice, legal experts warn employers to be careful about using the results of social media background checks—unless you want to risk the possibility of a discrimination claim. If an employer passes on a job applicant after viewing comments, photos, videos, or other content on Facebook or a blog, the rejected applicant might be tempted to file a discrimination claim.

United States anti-discrimination law prevents employers from discriminating against persons on the basis of "protected classes" including race, color, religion, national origin, age, sex, familial status, disability, veteran status, genetic information, gender identity (some jurisdictions), or sexual orientation (some jurisdictions). Without access to Facebook or blogs, and short of a face-to-face interview, a hiring manager might never know what a job applicant's race, color, or creed is. Consequently, companies open themselves up to allegations of discrimination when they conduct social media background checks in an effort to uncover information that may not be relevant to job performance.

### *Germany seeks to prohibit social media background checks*

Unlike the United States, where employers are free to conduct social media background checks, some countries, including Germany, take a dim view of using social networks to mine information about current or prospective job candidates. A law proposed in 2010, if passed, would make Germany the first country to restrict companies from snooping for personal information about current or potential workers on Facebook, YouTube, Twitter, or other public social networking sites. The law would, however, allow employers to continue using LinkedIn and other work-related social sites designed specifically to connect would-be employees with prospective bosses.[14]

## PRIVACY LAWS VARY BY JURISDICTION

If you have a social media presence, rest assured that employers, prospective employers, customers, coworkers, teachers, law enforcement personnel, the courts, regulators, malicious intruders, the media, friends, enemies, family members, former spouses, neighbors, and the general public are all likely to view your online content one day—if they haven't done so already.

As of 2011, there is no comprehensive data privacy law in the United States. Each state has its own data privacy laws, so be sure to have your legal counsel or compliance officer thoroughly research—and fully comply with—the privacy laws affecting your industry, company, and employees in every state in which you do business, employ workers, or litigate lawsuits.

We are still waiting for the law to catch up with social media and web 2.0. Consequently, though it may be impossible for an invasion of privacy claim to take root in one state, a terminated employee might succeed in getting a court in another jurisdiction to consider hearing a case involving computer monitoring, policy violations, and privacy expectations. Don't wait for disaster to strike. Plan today for the likelihood of social media-related litigation tomorrow.

### U.S. monitoring laws versus international privacy laws

In the U.S., electronic data is owned and controlled by the data collector, not the data subject. In many countries outside the United States, however, individual privacy is viewed and enforced as a fundamental right. In countries in which individual privacy is a primary concern, electronic data is the property of the subject, not the data collector. In Switzerland, for example, it is illegal to post another person's photo on a social networking site, blog, or website without first securing permission from the photo subject. Violation of this law could result in legal action.[15]

The United Kingdom also places a premium on individual privacy. English law does allow employers to monitor employees' Internet activity and email transmissions; however, the employer must first notify employees that they are being monitored, and the company must use the least intrusive monitoring tools available. Companies operating in the United Kingdom must also adhere to the Data Protection Act, which is in place to protect consumer privacy and private non-business-related information.[16]

---

**BEST PRACTICE RECOMMENDATION**

If you operate in more than one jurisdiction, you must research and comply with the privacy laws and monitoring rules of each state or country in which you have a presence. Do not assume that U.S. monitoring law applies to the European Union, or that New Jersey privacy law applies to Ohio employers. Do your homework first, and then institute formal policies and procedures in compliance with applicable laws.

---

## BEWARE SOCIAL LEAKS AND SPILLED SECRETS

In addition to privacy risks, the use of workplace social media increases the risk of potentially devastating security breaches and data leaks for organizations. Fully 84 percent of chief information officers (CIOs) and chief information security officers (CISOs) surveyed view social networking sites to be serious security threats, according to Symantec's 2011 *State of Enterprise Security Report.*[17]

Computer and security professionals have good reason for alarm, considering that 20 percent of IT decision-makers at large U.S. enterprises investigated the exposure of confidential, sensitive, or private information via social media postings in 2010. That's a 3 percent increase over the previous year, according to the Proofpoint survey, *Outbound Email and Data Loss Prevention in Today's Enterprise, 2010.*[18]

## Putting teeth in security laws: Data breach notification laws

Currently, the United States does not have a nationwide data breach notification law in place to require the reporting of security breaches on the federal level. That may change, however. In 2011, the Obama administration proposed adoption of a federal data breach notification law that would supersede the data breach notification laws that currently exist in more than 40 states, the District of Columbia, Puerto Rico, and the U.S. Virgin Islands. The proposed federal law would require organizations to notify the Federal Trade Commission (FTC), as well as affected parties, in the event of a security breach involving personal identity and financial privacy information.[19]

Until federal legislation is enacted, U.S.-based companies must comply with the data breach notification laws of all states in which you operate or have customers. If your organization touches credit cards, Social Security numbers, customers' private financial data, or other sensitive consumer information, then you must combine policy—including social media, email, computer security, mobile device, and record retention policy—with security and archiving technology solutions to help ensure compliance with data breach notification laws.

## Healing health care breaches: HITECH data security rules

When it comes to the security of electronic health records (EHRs), U.S. health care providers must comply with the data breach notification rules that were instituted in 2009 as part of the federal Health

**REAL-LIFE DATA SECURITY DISASTER STORY: BREACH BLITZES BUCKEYES**

Need convincing of the damage data thieves can do to consumers and companies alike? Consider this real-life cautionary tale. When hackers breached The Ohio State University's computer system in 2010, personal information including the Social Security numbers, birth dates, and addresses of 760,000 current and former students, applicants, faculty, and staff were in danger of identity theft.

The largest security breach of the year, according to the Privacy Rights Clearinghouse, Ohio State's data breach put the university at legal and regulatory risk. In compliance with state data breach notification law, the university mailed notification letters to all 760,000 affected parties, established a dedicated website and toll-free hotline, and offered a free year of credit protection to everyone whose data was on the server. [20]

Information Technology for Economic and Clinical Health (HITECH) Act. When it comes to protecting the privacy and security of EHRs, the Federal Trade Commission has assumed the role of federal health care IT enforcer. In addition to complying with the FTC's federal data breach security laws, health care companies also must adhere to state data breach security laws.[21]

### HITECH enforces encryption on the federal level

The HITECH Act also imposed new, federal encryption rules that are designed to protect individually identifiable health information. When a patient's protected health information (PHI) is transmitted electronically or transported physically outside a health care entity, via smartphone, tablet PC, laptop, or other device, that PHI must be encrypted or otherwise rendered indecipherable to unauthorized parties.

In addition to complying with federal encryption rules, health care companies also must comply with encryption laws on the state level. In 2009, Massachusetts enacted the most comprehensive encryption requirements (201 CMR 17.00) of any state in the nation. The Massachusetts regulations require hospitals, physicians' offices, health care organizations, and all other employers to encrypt all personal information transmitted electronically or wirelessly. Organizations also must encrypt all personal information stored on laptops and other mobile devices including smartphones, cell phones, iPods, and USB drives. In Massachusetts, encryption technology must include anti-spyware, anti-virus, up-to-date patches, virus definitions, and security technology that can receive current updates on a regular basis.[22]

Expect other states to follow Massachusetts' lead, enacting their own state encryption laws to protect patient privacy, consumers' personal financial data, and other confidential company records.

### Mobile devices accelerate health care security risks

The use of smartphones, tablets, and other mobile devices outside the organization's firewall and beyond the reach of content security tools puts confidential patient data at increased risk of interception, theft, or

**REAL-LIFE ENCRYPTION DISASTER STORY: 1.7 MILLION PATIENT RECORDS STOLEN**

Need proof of the damaging impact data theft can have on patient privacy? The security of nearly 2 million New Yorkers was put at risk in 2010, when data thieves stole personal health records from New York City Hospital. While robbing a van, the thieves nabbed backup tapes containing the PHI of over 1.7 million patients, employees, contractors, and vendors. The stolen tapes included patients' full names, addresses, birth dates, telephone numbers, and Social Security numbers. The backup tapes also included 20 years' worth of EPHI including health insurance information, admission and discharge dates, and medical record numbers. Because the backup tapes were not encrypted, a clear violation of federal law, the hospital made it easy for the thieves to take full advantage of the stolen patient data.[23]

loss. By 2012, four in five U.S. physicians are expected to use smartphones for professional communications and consultations, according to a Manhattan Research survey.[24] As of 2010, some 600 U.S. hospitals were using unsecure public social media sites including Facebook, YouTube, Twitter, and blogs, according to FierceHealthIT's Hospital Impact blog.[25] All of that online communication and collaboration can put EPHI at risk, regardless of whether health care professionals are using mobile devices, laptop computers, or desktops.

## Implement confidentiality rules and tools

Regardless of whether your organization is regulated or not, it is essential for all companies operating in the age of social media to put privacy rules and security tools in place to help protect the confidentiality of customer and patient data, as well as the safety of company secrets and intellectual property.

Many of Germany's leading, publicly traded companies are so concerned about industrial espionage and other security risks that they have banned Facebook and Twitter from the workplace. Volkswagen, Porsche, and most of the blue chip firms listed on the DAX 30 financial index have joined forces to prohibit access to social networks. The DAX social media ban is driven by more than concerns over industrial espionage, however. A survey conducted by Clearswift reveals that 30 percent of German companies, including car manufacturer Daimler, fear that unlimited access to social networking sites will decrease employee productivity.[26]

# SOCIAL MEDIA BEST PRACTICES: PRIVACY AND SECURITY

1. Left unmanaged, social media use and content can create potentially costly privacy and security risks for organizations large or small, regulated or unregulated, public or private.
2. Use social media policy and employee training to notify users that the company's computer system is the property of the company.

3. Notify employees that the company has the legal right to monitor computer activity and transmissions—and intends to exercise that legal right.

4. Let employees know that they have no reasonable expectation of privacy when using the company's computer system, sites, accounts, or devices.

5. Conduct formal employee training designed to educate users about privacy and security risks, rules, policies, and procedures.

6. Have experienced legal counsel research—and fully comply with— the privacy and monitoring laws of every jurisdiction in which you operate, have employees, serve customers, or litigate lawsuits.

7. Have your compliance officer research—and fully comply with— relevant industry and government regulatory rules governing privacy and security.

8. Advise employees to safeguard their own privacy, and the privacy of their families and friends, when using public social networking sites.

9. If you touch personal financial data, protected health records, or other sensitive or private consumer information, then you must adopt policies and procedures to ensure compliance with federal and state data breach notification and encryption laws.

10. Take advantage of technology solutions (software, hardware appliances, or cloud technology) designed to monitor social media use, manage content, and minimize threats to customer privacy and data security.

# BLOG RISKS AND COMPLIANCE RULES

No book on workplace social media would be complete without a discussion about blog risks, policies, and compliance management. The blog, after all, is the original social networking platform. The blog has been facilitating interactive two-way communication for business and personal users since the 1999 introduction of Blogger, the first free blog-creation service. Half a decade would pass before the social networking site Facebook (2004) and the microblogging service Twitter (2006) would take the stage and turn social media into a cultural phenomenon.[1]

## BLOGGING IS AT THE HEART OF WEB 2.0

Dubbed a business "prerequisite" by *BusinessWeek* back in 2005,[2] the blog today remains a "go-to" web 2.0 application for organizations large and small, as well as individuals worldwide. What exactly is web 2.0? It's the umbrella term used to describe interactive, Internet-based communication and collaboration tools and technologies. Web 2.0 allows for the creation and exchange of user-generated content. Web 2.0 is all about conversations, collaboration, and customization. Web 2.0 began with blogs and wikis, grew to include social networking, video sharing, and photo sharing—and who knows what the future holds for collaborative cyber-communities.

## BLOG PROGRAM SELF-ASSESSMENT

One fact has remained unchanged since blogs first entered the electronic business communication mix in the 1990s. Unmanaged blog use, inappropriate blog content, and mismanaged blog business records can put your organization's assets, reputation, and future at risk. Without a strategic blog policy and compliance management program in place, employers face the possibility of online disasters that can disrupt business, diminish sales, destroy reputations, and derail relationships.

Where does your organization stand when it comes to strategic blog policy and compliance management? Take a few moments to complete the following self-assessment.

1. Does your company operate a business blog?
   ☐ Yes   ☐ No

2. Are employees allowed to discuss, demonstrate, or otherwise divulge any aspect of the company's business by posting content related to employees, executives, customers, suppliers, products, services, facilities, financials, plans, etc. on their own personal blogs?
   ☐ Yes   ☐ No

3. Are employees allowed to discuss, demonstrate, or otherwise divulge any aspect of the company's business by posting content related to employees, executives, customers, suppliers, products, services, facilities, financials, plans, etc. on external blogs operated by third parties?
   ☐ Yes   ☐ No

4. Does our company currently have a formal, written blog policy in place?
   ☐ Yes      ☐ No

5. If so, how old is your organization's current blog policy? When did you last update it?
   Date: _____

6. Does your blog policy govern employees' personal blog use and content, or does it solely govern employees' use of the organization's business blogs?
   ☐ Personal      ☐ Business      ☐ Personal and Business

7. Does your organization's blog policy address mobile blogging risks and rules?
   ☐ Yes      ☐ No

8. Have you established a mobile device policy governing employee use of smartphones, cell phones, tablet PCs, and other mobile tools?
   ☐ Yes      ☐ No

9. If so, does your mobile device policy address mobile blogging?
   ☐ Yes      ☐ No

10. Have you established formal content rules, spelling out what type of language and content (text, photos, videos, art, etc.) employees may (and may not) post on the organization's business blogs?
    ☐ Yes      ☐ No

11. Have you established formal content rules, spelling out what type of language and content (text, photos, videos, art, and so on) employees may (and may not) post on their own personal blogs or external blogs operated by third parties?
    ☐ Yes      ☐ No

12. Is your company publicly traded?
    ☐ Yes      ☐ No

13. If so, does your blog policy incorporate rules designed to manage and protect financial data in compliance with SOX, SEC, and FINRA guidelines?

☐ Yes   ☐ No

14. Does your company operate within a regulated industry?

☐ Yes   ☐ No

15. If so, does your blog policy incorporate rules designed to manage use, content, and business records in compliance with regulatory guidelines?

☐ Yes   ☐ No

16. Do you allow customers and other third parties to post comments on your business blogs?

☐ Yes   ☐ No

17. If so, do you review all third-party comments before they are published on your organization's business blogs?

☐ Yes   ☐ No

18. Have you established community blogging guidelines for customers and other third parties who wish to post comments on your business blogs?

☐ Yes   ☐ No

19. Does your organization have in place a policy governing the retention of electronic business records, including blog posts and comments?

☐ Yes   ☐ No

20. Do you use technology tools to automatically monitor the content (posts and comments) on company-hosted blogs?

☐ Yes   ☐ No

21. Do you regularly monitor the blogosphere to see what employees are posting on their own personal blogs?

☐ Yes   ☐ No

22. Do you regularly monitor the blogosphere to see what third parties (customers, competitors, and the like) are saying about your company on external blogs?

☐ Yes   ☐ No

Revisit This Self-Assessment Quiz at the Conclusion
of the Chapter
Once you've completed this blog program self-assessment, put
it aside until you have finished reading this entire chapter. By
that point, you should have acquired a comprehensive understanding of current blog risks and recommended best practices.

## BLOG TECHNOLOGY—AND TROUBLES—HAVE EVOLVED; HAS YOUR BLOG POLICY KEPT PACE?

If your organization is still relying on the same blog policy that you established back in 1999 (or even 2009), now is the time for an update. When it comes to blogs, social media, and other web 2.0 applications, best practices call for the creation and implementation of up-to-date acceptable use policies (AUPs) that reflect current risks, current technologies, current laws, current regulations, current user needs, and current compliance requirements. When it comes to mitigating risks and managing use, outdated rules, regulations, policies, and procedures are of no use to employers or employees.

---

**BEST PRACTICE RECOMMENDATION**

Review—and as necessary update—your organization's blog policy, social media policy, and other AUPs annually. See Chapter Nine and Chapter Ten to learn more about the processes of reviewing and writing effective policies governing electronic business communication tools and technologies.

---

### You cannot manage updated tools with outdated rules

In the "old days," bloggers were content to sit at their desks and post content and comments via desktop computers and laptops. That is no longer the case for a quarter of all bloggers. Armed with ever-present smartphones, 25 percent of bloggers now engage in mobile blogging, according to Technorati's 2010 *State of the Blogosphere* report. Of that number, 40 percent say they have adjusted their blogging style and now write shorter, more spontaneous posts to accommodate the space limitations and immediacy of smartphones, tablets, and other mobile devices.[3]

## Mobile blogging accelerates workplace risks

As detailed in Chapter Seven, employees' use of BlackBerries, iPads, cell phones, and other mobile tools ups the ante for employers when it comes to legal, regulatory, security, productivity, and other risks. Consequently, employers are advised to update blog policies to ensure that mobile blogging is addressed, along with other risks and requirements affecting bloggers today.

In addition to addressing the relatively new issue of mobile blogging, AUPs governing workplace blogging should, at a minimum, incorporate rules designed to manage the following seven categories of potentially devastating business risks.

1. **Litigation Risks.** From defamation and copyright infringement to sexual harassment and discrimination, bloggers' posts and readers' comments can expose the organization to a deep pool of legal risks. As discussed in Chapter Eleven, one of the easiest and most effective ways to minimize the possibility of litigation is to manage content. To that end, be sure your organization's blog policy incorporates clear and comprehensive content, language, and netiquette rules. Support policy with employee training. Use policy and training to drive home the point that a policy is a policy. In other words, the company's blog policy and content rules apply to employees who blog at the office during business hours, as well as to those who engage in personal blogging at home at the conclusion of the work day.

2. **Regulatory Risks.** The bad news for regulated businesses and publicly traded companies is that unmanaged blog use, inappropriate blog content, and mismanaged blog business records could land you in hot water for violating the rules set forth by the Securities

and Exchange Commission (SEC), Financial Industry Regulatory Authority (FINRA), Gramm-Leach-Bliley Act (GLBA), Health Insurance Portability and Accountability Act (HIPAA), Federal Trade Commission (FTC), or thousands of other federal, state, and local government and industry regulations.

The good news: regulatory guidelines often spell out the rules governing blog, social media, email, and other online use, content, and records. As a result, compliance should be far less challenging for regulated businesses than it is for unregulated companies, which tend to be on their own when it comes to defining and identifying business records, and establishing and enforcing rules governing electronic use, content, and record retention.

If your blog policy is aging, chances are some of the regulatory rules governing your business or industry have changed since it was first written and introduced to users. If so, you'll want to assign your legal counsel or compliance officer the task of researching the company's current regulatory risks and requirements. First determine which regulatory bodies oversee your business and industry, and then ascertain the rules governing electronic use, content, and business record retention. Armed with that knowledge, you can get to work updating your blog policy.

3. **Security Risks.** Unmanaged blog use opens the organization to a variety of potentially costly security risks, including spam. In the blogosphere, spam takes two shapes: comment spam and splog. Comment spam appears on legitimate blogs in the form of comments from phony readers who have nothing to contribute to the discussion at hand, but simply want to make a sales pitch disguised as a comment. Their goal is to motivate readers to click on a link that will transport them to an unrelated advertiser's site.

A splog, on the other hand, is a fake blog. It may look like a legitimate blog, but it's not. Like comment spammers, sploggers are in business to drive visitors away from legitimate blogs and to secondary sites that are laden with advertising and links to even more advertising.

To help reduce the incidence of comment spam and splog on your system, apply a combination of blog policy, employee training, and security technology. Use policy and training to alert employees to the existence of blog spam, and educate users about how sploggers and comment spammers work. Use policy to prohibit employees from clicking on links embedded within blogs, unless they are 100 percent certain that a blog is, in fact, legitimate. Install an enterprise blogging solution, rather than using a free blog creation and hosting service, to operate and manage your business blog. An enterprise system will give you control over content, posts, and comments—and will help keep your organization safe from security threats that may be levied against public blog hosting services. Finally, assign a trustworthy employee to read third-party comments prior to publication on your business blogs. Delete all obvious comment spam and any other content that violates your organization's blog policy, its community blogging guidelines, or any other workplace policies, laws, or regulations.

4. **Confidentiality Risks.** Employee blogging can create concerns for the safety of confidential company data and the security of private customer information. The law and regulators require all companies to safeguard consumers' private, non-business-related financial information including Social Security numbers, dates of birth, credit card numbers, and debit card numbers. Organizations operating within the health care arena are obligated to protect electronic protected health information (EPHI) related to patients' health status, medical care, treatment plans, and payment issues. All businesses, regardless of industry, must secure their confidential company information including trade secrets, intellectual property, customer lists, marketing plans, company financials, internal email, and the list goes on and on.

Because of their public nature, external blogs give employers ample reason for concern about the safety of sensitive customer and company information. Nearly a third (31 percent) of companies report that they have been affected by the improper exposure or theft of customer information. Another 29 percent of organizations experienced the exposure or theft of intellectual property over a 12-month period, according to Proofpoint's 2010 survey, *Outbound Email and Data Loss Prevention in Today's Enterprise.*[4]

Employers who are eager to safeguard confidential information from improper exposure in the blogosphere are advised to follow these steps: (a) use blog policy to spell out confidentiality risks, rules, and regulations to users; (b) conduct formal employee training to educate users about confidentiality policy; (c) define security-related terms that employees may not be familiar with, including trade secret, intellectual property, data security breach, GLBA, HIPAA, and EPHI, for example; (d) take advantage of technology tools—including URL blocks, monitoring tools, and content filtering solutions—to prevent employees from accessing external blogs and (accidentally or intentionally) posting confidential company information; and (e) make it clear to employees that confidentiality rules apply to business blogging on company-hosted sites, personal blogging via private accounts and devices, and commenting on external third-party blogs. Emphasize the fact that any violation of the organization's confidentiality rules, blog policy, or other employment policies may result in disciplinary action, up to and including termination.

5. **Electronic Discovery Risks.** As Chapter Three makes clear, blog posts and comments create the electronic equivalent of DNA evidence, evidence that may be used to support or sink your company's case in the event of a workplace lawsuit or regulatory investigation.

The courts take e-discovery seriously, and you are obligated to do so as well. To that end, you must make sure employees understand that blog content can rise to the level of a business record; it may be retained and archived by the organization, along with email and other electronically stored information; it could be subpoenaed by courts or regulators in the event of litigation or regulatory investigations; and it must be produced by the organization in compliance with e-discovery rules.

6. **Productivity Risks.** Whether publishing content on business blogs at work, commenting on third-party blogs via smartphones, or posting on private accounts for personal reasons, there's no doubt that employees spend a tremendous amount of time reading, writing, conversing, and commenting on blogs—not to mention all the time spent sending and receiving email, networking via social media, and collaborating on web 2.0 applications.

The best advice: apply personal use rules to block productivity drains. As detailed in Chapter Ten, best practices call for the inclusion of comprehensive and specific personal use rules in all of the organization's acceptable use policies. For example, use blog rules and policy to let employees know just how much personal blogging (if any) is allowed during the work day, when, for how long, and under what circumstances. Similarly, use your mobile device policy to let employees know whether or not they are allowed to engage in mobile blogging on company-provided BlackBerries or personal smartphones. If you choose to outlaw all personal blogging during working hours, clearly state that rule in your blog policy, social media policy, mobile device policy, and any other AUPs or employment policies that employees might turn to for information about personal use of company resources and accounts, as well as their own personal tools and sites.

7. **Public Relations Disasters and Blog Mob Attacks.** The easy, instantaneous, anything-goes culture of the blogosphere is what makes blogging so appealing to some—and so dangerous for others. Anyone armed with a smartphone or tablet PC can create a blog, free of charge, and start posting content in minutes. Unfortunately for business, those posts may include defamatory discussions about customers, critical comments about managers, or negative posts about products and services. With more than half of all bloggers writing about companies, their products, or employees at least once a week, the dangers posed by unmanaged blog content are real.[5]

It's not unheard-of for bloggers to ban together to unleash orchestrated attacks on businesses and individuals. Blogstorms have the potential to destroy reputations, undercut credibility, trigger mainstream media coverage, drive away business, and terrify online victims. Industry analysts believe that at least half of all blog attacks are sponsored by organizations seeking to damage or destroy business rivals by unleashing the fury of the blogosphere on them.[6]

Chapter Eight recommends appointing a social media policy team to help ensure the success of your organization's policy and compliance management program. An important member of your social media policy team is your public relations manager or media relations director. When it comes to blog and social media compliance management, the job of public relations and media relations professionals is twofold: (1) make sure social media and blog policies incorporate rules governing employees' interaction with the media (for example, many organizations prohibit employee-bloggers from responding to press inquiries that may be posted on the comment sections of blogs—if you want employees to direct all media questions, inquiries, and requests to the PR department, use your social media and blog policies to convey that information); and (2) develop a formal reputation management plan to ensure that the company is ready to respond—immediately and effectively—in the event of a blogstorm, cybersmear attack, or other online PR nightmare. See Chapter Thirteen for more information about reputation risks and management in the blogosphere.

## DETERMINE IF BLOGS ARE RIGHT FOR YOUR BUSINESS

In spite of the risks, blogging can deliver valuable benefits to business. Specifically, through a strategic and carefully managed blog program, businesses large and small, public and private, regulated and unregulated can accomplish important marketing, communications, and collaboration tasks:

**Give Your Organization a Personality.** Through tone and content, your organization's business bloggers can help "warm up" the organization, providing readers with a glimpse into the company's culture and a feel for what it's like to work there.

**Position C-Level Executives as "Thought Leaders."** Many organizations use blogs to help position CEOs, CFOs, and CIOs as "thought leaders," expert sources of timely and accurate information about the organization, industry, business world, economy, public policy, trends, and other newsworthy topics. For many organizations, the positioning of senior executives as thought leaders is a strategic public relations initiative. Blogging helps facilitate this task, enabling C-level executives to quickly and easily communicate with—and establish a following among—huge numbers of readers.

**Make the CEO Accessible to Customers, Employees, and the Community.** Use a CEO blog to help put a human face on your most senior executive. A well-written blog can help position the CEO as warm, friendly, and approachable—a "regular" person speaking in a "regular" voice with "regular" people, including customers, investors, employees, and community members. Depending upon the availability and interest of the CEO, it may be a good idea to hire a ghostwriter to write the boss's posts and respond to readers' comments and questions. If so, be sure your ghostwriter captures the CEOs "true" voice and tone, so there is no disconnect between the CEO's written blog posts and the words spoken and messages delivered at shareholder meetings, press conferences, and other public events.

**Facilitate Two-Way Communication.** Created for interactive, two-way communication, the blog is a great way for organizations to initiate and maintain conversations with customers, prospects, job candidates, business partners, and other interested parties. Many organizations use blogs to facilitate technical support or customer service, making it easy for consumers to submit questions and receive answers in the form of public posts or individual email messages. In addition, the blog is an effective tool for companies that want to conduct online polls, solicit consumer feedback, or make customers and other target audiences feel as though their opinions count and their suggestions are heard.

**Pave the Way for Internal Collaboration.** Employees can brainstorm, share knowledge, seek advice, solve problems, and hold confidential password-protected discussions via internal blogs.

**Market, Promote, and Publicize the Company.** Enhance your organization's public relations efforts with an external blog presence. Many consumers turn to blogs for information about companies, brands, products, and services. The mainstream media and online media outlets regularly surf the blogosphere to uncover news stories, locate expert sources, and conduct research. A well-written, regularly updated blog may help create top-of-mind awareness for your company among customers, prospects, reporters, and media decision makers.

**Recruit and Retain Employees.** The operation of a business blog will help position the organization as relevant among current and prospective employees. It's a convenient tool for announcing job openings for current employees who may be eager to make a switch to a different role or division within the company. It's also a good way to educate job candidates about your organization's hiring procedures and job openings.

**Create News and Respond to News.** In the "old days," if the CEO wanted to take a stand on an issue (argue against a proposed regulatory change, for example), respond to a crisis (offer financial support to tornado victims), or make a charitable donation (announce the establishment of a scholarship program), the PR department would issue a news release via fax, email, or the postal service, and then make dozens (possibly hundreds) of follow-up phone calls to ensure that targeted reporters and news producers had received the announcement. Thanks to the blog, the publicist's job has gotten a lot easier. Whether it's making news or responding to breaking news, all you need to do today is post your announcement on your business blog, and then drive the media to it via other social networking tools, including your corporate Twitter, Facebook, and YouTube accounts.

## TIPS FOR MANAGING THIRD-PARTY COMMENTS

"The easiest way to control electronic risk is to control electronic content." That message is repeated throughout this book and is the theme of Chapter Eleven. When it comes to blog content management, employers must be mindful of the risks inherent both in employees' posts and readers' comments, as well.

Remember, accepting and editing comments from customers and other outside readers could make you a publisher in the eyes of the law. As a publisher, you may be held liable, legally and financially, for third parties' inappropriate and potentially illegal content including, for example, defamatory remarks, copyright violations, and comments that may be deemed to be harassing, discriminatory, bullying, or otherwise offensive.

Employers who are eager to manage readers' comments and mitigate potentially costly risks are advised to adhere to these tips for managing third-party blog comments.

### Create community blogging guidelines

If you are going to accept comments from customers and other outside parties on your business blogs, you should create and post a formal policy for visitors, the company's "Community Blogging Guidelines." Your community blogging guidelines are separate from your blog policy for employees. The purpose of your community blogging guidelines is to ensure that all online comments and conversations that take place on the organization's blogs are focused, friendly, civil, productive, and compliant with the law and regulatory guidelines.

Require visitors to your business blogs to register before posting comments. As part of the registration process, inform blog visitors that they must read and agree to the company's community blogging guidelines before posting comments on your site. Use your community blogging guidelines to notify visitors that all comments will be reviewed by the company's chief compliance officer (or another authorized employee) prior to posting. Make clear the fact that comments that are found to be in violation of the company's community blogging guidelines will not be published. See Chapter Fourteen for sample community blogging guidelines.

### Review third-party comments prepublication

Conduct a legal review of all third-party comments prepublication. Yes, it will slow down the blogging process and somewhat diminish the "transparent" nature of blogging, but what's the alternative? You can't afford to take chances with inappropriate comments that could offend readers, trigger lawsuits, violate regulators' rules, ignite public relations firestorms, or crush your company's credibility. Assign a responsible party—a lawyer, compliance officer, or member of the social media policy team (see Chapter Eight)—to review every reader comment before publishing it online—for all the world to read.

### Deactivate the comment function

If you want to minimize comment risks, but don't want to devote resources to reviewing comments prepublication, then you may want to consider deactivating the comment function on your business blogs.

### Address readers' comments

If you do opt to solicit and publish reader comments, then you must adhere to the rules of blog netiquette. When readers take time to post comments on your business blogs, be sure to acknowledge their comments and, when a response is warranted, do so in a polite and professional manner.

### Take advantage of Digital Millennium Copyright Act protections

If you publish a visitor's comments on your business blogs—and that content happens to be protected by another third-party's copyright—your organization could be held vicariously liable for copyright infringement. In other words, regardless of whether the visitor accidentally or intentionally violated copyright law, it's possible that your organization (the blog publisher) could be held legally (and financially) responsible. If deemed to be a third-party copyright infringer, your organization could be subject to treble damages—unless you have followed the procedures necessary to ensure "safe harbor" protection from liability through the Digital Millennium Copyright Act (DMCA).

Under DMCA, your organization is safe from liability even if it has inadvertently fed copyright-protected content into syndication and created a scenario in which the infringed-upon material is available in the blogosphere long after your organization has removed it as required by law.

To qualify for DMCA safe harbor protection from third-party liability for copyright infringement, the organization must follow three steps: (1) designate a DMCA agent with the Library of Congress; (2) list your DMCA agent on your company website. Also on your website, recap the DMCA-mandated protocols that your organization follows when responding to allegations of third-party copyright infringement; and (3) establish a formal plan to handle complaints in compliance with DMCA requirements.[7]

Do ask legal counsel to review all DMCA policies, procedures, and requirements to ensure that your organization has taken all the necessary steps to achieve compliance and safe harbor protection. Do not solicit or post comments by customers or other third parties until your DMCA registration process has been completed and approved by a legal expert.

Along with registering for DMCA protections, be sure to post instructions, notifying visitors how to report claims of copyright infringement. A sample notice follows. Be sure also to spell out exactly how notices should be sent, to whom they should be sent, and how to reach your organization's DMCA agent or other authorized party.

## SAMPLE NOTICE FOR VISITORS

### HOW TO REPORT CLAIMS OF COPYRIGHT INFRINGEMENT

Do you believe your copyright-protected work has been improperly published on a blog, social media site, or website operated by our company? If so, please file a formal notice of copyright infringement with us. Your written notice should contain the following information:

1. Explain that you have identified material on one of our company sites that infringes your copyright (or the copyright of a third party on whose behalf you are authorized to act).
2. Identify the site on which your copyright-protected content is located. Provide the name of the site, the URL, and a screen shot.
3. Describe the copyrighted work that you claim has been infringed (book, article, recorded music, and so on). Provide the title of the work, the full name of the copyright holder, its date of publication, and the country or countries to which the copyright applies.
4. Describe the way(s) in which the copyright-protected material has been infringed. Include a statement that the disputed use of the copyrighted work has not been authorized by the copyright owner (or by a third party who is legally authorized to act on behalf of the copyright owner) and is not otherwise permitted by law.
5. Provide contact information (name, street address, telephone number(s), and email address) for the person who is authorized to discuss or act upon this matter.
6. Include a statement, made under penalty of perjury, that your written notice is truthful and accurate and that you are the copyright owner or an agent who is authorized to act on the copyright owner's behalf.
7. Include the copyright owner's signature (electronic or physical).

## WRITING RULES FOR BUSINESS BLOGGERS

In addition to the personal use rules and content rules spelled out in Chapters Ten and Eleven, employers who want to reduce the likelihood of blogging risks are advised to incorporate the following guidelines for employee-bloggers into the company's formal blog policy.

## Instruct bloggers how to handle media inquiries

A business blog program may lead to an increase in media inquiries from reporters and news producers looking for story ideas and expert sources, conducting research, and covering breaking news. Whether they are writing about the company on business blogs or personal sites, employee-bloggers lend their names and faces the company. Consequently, they are likely to be contacted directly by the media at some point in their blogging careers.

Mindful of that fact, be sure to use blog policy and training to instruct employee-bloggers how to handle media inquiries. If, for example, you want bloggers to route all media calls to the public relations department, then say so—and be sure everyone has the name, phone number, and email address of the company's designated media spokesperson(s). To be safe, you may want to conduct media relations training for all employee-bloggers, so that they are prepared to respond appropriately and effectively to unsolicited media calls.

## Impose financial rules

For publicly traded companies, unmanaged blog content can create devastating regulatory risks. When it comes to the disclosure of financial information, public companies are required to comply with strict regulatory rules. If an unauthorized employee were to jump the gun and prematurely publish information about quarterly revenues and earnings, that public blog post could put the company at risk of an SEC disclosure violation. If employee-bloggers have access to company financials and investor relations information, be sure to educate them—via policy and training—about regulatory risks and requirements, company and regulators' content rules, and the penalties that await organizations (and employees) who violate regulatory and organizational rules and policies. To be safe, you may want to conduct investor relations training for all employee-bloggers to help ensure that financial risks are minimized and compliance is maximized.

## Ban anonymous blogging

For some disgruntled employees, anonymous blogging may provide an easy (and seemingly safe) way to complain about the company, malign management, criticize customers and coworkers, and otherwise gripe about your organization. Be proactive and block employee gripe sites before they get started. Use formal blog policy to notify employees that they are prohibited from blogging anonymously (on their own sites, third-party blogs, or company-hosted sites) about the organization, its activities, financials, plans, people, products, services, customers, suppliers, partners, facilities, resources, or any other business-related matter. Make it clear that if the organization is mentioned in blog posts or comments (in strict accordance with the rules set forth in the company's blog policy), then employees must identify themselves by name, title, and company affiliation.

## Adhere to FTC blogging rules

On December 1, 2009, the United States Federal Trade Commission (FTC) issued revised endorsement guidelines that have an impact on employee blogging (16 CFR 255). Specifically, the FTC requires bloggers to disclose any material connections between themselves and the products or services they discuss in their blog posts. Product, service, or company endorsements must be honest and cannot be deceptive. Failure to comply with FTC endorsement guidelines could create liability concerns for the blogger and advertiser.[8]

What does this mean for your business? Feel free to encourage employee-bloggers to promote the organization's products and services on business blogs, their own personal blogs, and third-party blogs, but require them to disclose their affiliations with the company as part of their blog profiles. Use your organization's written blog policy and blog risks and rules training program to educate employee-bloggers about FTC rules and compliance obligations.

### *Require a legal disclaimer*

Many organizations require employees who operate personal blogs or publish personal posts and comments on business blogs to incorporate a legal disclaimer into their content. A typical disclaimer would state that the blogger's views and opinions belong to the blogger, not the company. For example, you might require employees to post a statement that reads, "The posts and comments on this blog reflect my own personal opinions, views, thoughts, and positions. They do not necessary reflect the opinions, views, thoughts, and positions of my employer, XYZ Company." Although it is unclear how much protection a legal disclaimer would give your organization in the event of a lawsuit, it certainly can't hurt.

### *Review posts prior to publication*

You wouldn't publish an annual report or corporate brochure that hadn't first undergone a thorough review by the communications and legal departments. Why publish blog posts and comments before they have been vetted? As a best practice, screen employee blog posts and reader comments prepublication. The goal is to avoid publishing content that is defamatory or inaccurate, violates copyright law, discloses company financials, reveals confidential customer information, is obscene, offensive, inappropriate, or otherwise violates the law, regulatory guidelines, or company policies. You can automate this all-important compliance task with content management and aggregation technology. Alternatively, you may want to assign an experienced, trusted member of your organization's legal, compliance, or communications department to prescreen content manually.

## SOCIAL MEDIA BEST PRACTICES: BLOGGING

1. The original social networking tool, the blog today remains a "go-to" web 2.0 application for organizations and individuals eager to engage in interactive online conversations and collaboration.

2. Unmanaged blog use, inappropriate blog content, and mismanaged blog business records can put an organization's assets, reputation, and future at risk. Without a strategic blog policy and compliance management program in place, employers face the possibility of online disasters that can disrupt business, diminish sales, destroy reputations, and derail relationships.

3. When it comes to the management of legal, regulatory, security, productivity, and other electronic risks, best practices call for the implementation of blog policies that incorporate clear content rules governing employees' use of business and personal blogs. Use formal content rules to outlaw the writing or posting of any type of content—text, photos, videos, art, or any other form of written, visual, or spoken content—that could trigger legal claims, serve as smoking gun evidence of wrongdoing in litigation, violate regulators' content rules (including the FTC's endorsement guidelines), or otherwise create problems for the organization and its employees.

4. Best practices call for the creation and implementation of up-to-date blog policies that reflect current risks, technologies, laws, regulations, user needs, and compliance requirements. Outdated policies are of no use when it comes to mitigating risks and managing use. Readers who are looking for examples of effective, free-standing blog policies, as well as combination blog and social media policies should turn to Chapter Fourteen.

5. Twenty-five percent of bloggers now engage in mobile blogging via smartphone, tablets, and other mobile devices.[9] Employers should review and as necessary revise blog and mobile device policies to reflect the risks and challenges inherent in mobile blogging.

6. Educate employees. The courts appreciate, and tend to respond favorably to, employment policies and employee training programs that are consistently applied and enforced. Don't leave blog risk management and policy compliance to chance. Support blog policy with formal employee education. Train all employees (authorized employee-bloggers and all other workers, as well) about business

(and personal) blogging risks and rules, policies and procedures, rights and responsibilities.

7. Maintain complete records of your blog policy training program. Keep copies of your blog policy, training sign-in sheets, certification quizzes, signed acknowledgment forms, training manuals, PowerPoint programs and scripts, handout materials, and any other training records and materials. In the event of a lawsuit or regulatory investigation, you may need these records to demonstrate that your organization has done its due diligence and adhered to best practices when it comes to mitigating blog risks, managing bloggers' behavior, and enforcing blog policy compliance. See Chapter Twelve for detailed information about the development and implementation of effective social media and blog policy training programs.

8. Retain and manage blog business records. Just like email messages and attachments, blog posts and comments have the potential to create electronic business records. If your employees or third parties are writing about your company, its people, products, services, suppliers, customers, and competitors, there is a good chance that electronic business records are being created. Compliance requires the preservation, protection, and production of blog posts, reader comments, and other electronically stored information in the event of a workplace lawsuit or regulatory investigation. Manage blog business records effectively through retention policy and archiving technology.

9. Monitor the blogosphere. The easiest and most effective way to stay on top of what employees, ex-employees, competitors, customers, the media, and others are saying about your business online is to monitor the blogosphere. Use an automated monitoring solution (cloud technology, software, or a hardware appliance) to track and manage blog activity on your organization's system and sites. Subscribe to blog search engines to monitor company mentions on external blogs operated by employees and others.

10. Depending upon your geographic location, you may not be legally required to notify employees that management is monitoring the blogosphere. Nonetheless, best practices call for employers to let workers know that the company is keeping an eye on their blog

activity—at work and home. After all, employees who know they are being watched are more likely to comply with policy.

For protection against possible invasion of privacy claims or wrongful termination lawsuits, require employees to sign an acknowledgment form attesting that: (1) they are familiar with and understand your blog policy; (2) they are aware of the fact that the company regularly monitors business, personal, and external blog sites; and (3) they agree to comply with the organization's blog policy or accept the consequences, up to and including termination.

11. Discipline policy violators. If monitoring unearths a violation of blog policy or any employment policy, then you should act immediately to discipline the policy violator. Turn a blind eye to one violation today, and you may find yourself battling a company-wide compliance crisis tomorrow. Use blog policy and training to make clear the penalties, up to and including termination, awaiting policy violators.

12. Institute an anti-blog policy. If you operate within the financial services arena or another heavily regulated industry, you may want to eliminate blogging risks by banning workplace blogging altogether. Operate no business blogs. Institute a policy that prohibits the use of any company or personal resources, including privately owned smartphones or tablets, to operate, access, or view personal or external blogs during the workday. Prohibit employees from writing blog posts, contributing blog comments, or publishing blog content to personal or external blogs during the workday. Support your anti-blog policy with rules governing employees' use of personal and external blogs after working hours. Emphasize the fact that employees must adhere to all employment policies, rules, guidelines, and codes at all times.

Support your anti-blog policy with content security technology, designed to block employees' access to blogs outside the company firewall, so they can't access or post comments on third-party sites. Apply a URL block or content monitoring and filtering solution to automate compliance with regulators' content, use, and retention rules.

# MOBILE DEVICES DRIVE SOCIAL MEDIA RISKS

In the age of social media and web 2.0, the use of mobile devices has shifted into high gear. From smartphones and BlackBerries to iPhones and iPads, employees increasingly are using mobile gadgets to conduct both personal and company business. With employees clamoring to bring their ever-present and increasingly sophisticated smartphones to the office, savvy employers are adapting policy and technology to satisfy workforce demands, while managing workplace risks.

In the not-too-distant past, cell phone policy typically restricted employees to the use of nothing but company-provided BlackBerries to communicate with customers, colleagues, and other business audiences. Citing valid business reasons such as the need to retain business records, safeguard confidential data, and comply with regulatory guidelines, many employers completely banned the use of personal phones for any business-related communication.

That is no longer the case for many organizations. The use of personal smartphones at work is becoming more common. In the United

States alone, 75 million employees are equipped with personal or company-owned mobile phones.[1] A quarter of smartphone owners use their phones as their primary way to access the Internet, and 68 percent report using their devices daily to check email and surf the web.[2] Consequently, many employers are beginning to rethink (and in some cases relax) their old cell phone policies.

## ACCEPTABLE USE POLICIES WILL NEVER GO OUT OF STYLE

While mobile technology continues to evolve—and its authorized (and unauthorized) use in the workplace continues to expand—one fact of strategic compliance management has never changed. Best practices always have—and always will—call for the establishment and enforcement of formal policies designed to maximize compliance with legal, regulatory, and organizational rules, while minimizing business and user risks. Regardless of industry, size, or status as a public or private entity, all organizations must impose acceptable use policies (AUPs) governing mobile devices including cell phones, smartphones, tablet computers, and other portable handheld and hands-free tools.

Regardless of whether your organization provides employees with company-owned BlackBerries, permits the use of personal smartphones, or bans the use of any employee-owned tools for business communication, all employers are advised to review—and as necessary revise—cell phone and smartphone rules and mobile device policies to reflect employee needs and organizational risks as they exist today, not during the last quarter, last year, or last decade.

Even if you don't permit the use of personal smartphones at work, it's likely that your employees are bringing their own phones into the office through the "back door" and are using them to communicate with friends and family, customers and colleagues, and perhaps a competitor or two. Unauthorized and unmanaged use of personal phones is far more dangerous than approved use governed by formal policy.

With no rules in place, employees may use personal phones to transmit confidential customer data in violation of the law or regulatory

guidelines—accidentally or intentionally. They may take embarrassing photos of managers and post them on Facebook. They might shoot
video inside a secret facility and upload it to YouTube. They might jump
the gun and tweet news of quarterly earnings in violation of SEC rules.

Given the potential risks inherent in both authorized and unauthorized use of mobile devices, personal and company-provided, it is
essential for employers to establish and enforce formal mobile device
policy that clearly spells out exactly how, when, why, with whom, and
under what circumstances employees may—and may not—use cell
phones, smartphones, BlackBerries, electronic tablets, and other portable tools that are available today or may be coming on the market
tomorrow.

## HOW MOBILE TOOLS AND RULES AFFECT THE BOTTOM LINE

When managed effectively, employee use of personal smartphones can
help maximize communication and collaboration, internally and externally. Left unmanaged, however, employee use of personal cell phones,
smartphones, and other mobile devices can create a financial burden
for the organization. Take a close look at the pros and cons, costs, and
benefits before establishing formal rules governing employee use of privately owned mobile devices.

### Good news: Personal phones may save employers money

One reason for employers' growing acceptance of employees' personal phones is the fact that their use can deliver financial, productivity, and communications benefits to the organization—provided that
their use is effectively managed with formal rules and written policies.
Spending will decrease and savings will accrue as the need to equip
employees with company-owned BlackBerries declines. Opportunities
for internal collaboration with colleagues and external communication with customers will increase as workers who formerly did not
merit company-owned smartphones now enjoy the freedom of talking,

texting, tweeting, and otherwise conversing and collaborating via personal devices. The ability to conduct confidential, off-the-record conversations rises when executives have access to personal phones that neither record nor retain text and talk—provided those unrecorded conversations do not violate the law or regulatory rules mandating the retention of electronic business records.

## Bad news: Personal phones may cost employers money

Before throwing open the door to unlimited use of personal smartphones and tablets, the flip side of cost must be addressed. Who is going to pay for all of that talking, texting, tweeting, blogging, emailing, and surfing? Is the employee who owns the phone responsible for the monthly bill, or does financial responsibility fall to the company?

There is no one-size-fits-all guideline when it comes to mobile phone reimbursement. Some organizations give each employee a stipend that is equal to the amount the employer used to pay each month to cover company-owned BlackBerries. Some employers split smartphone expenses with employees. One company might cover employees' data packages, while another organization may pick up the cost of voice, but not data. There are companies that cover all employee smartphone costs. And there are companies that reimburse no mobile device costs on the grounds that personal access to corporate data is a voluntary perk for employees.

---

### BEST PRACTICE: ADDRESS REIMBURSEMENT IN YOUR POLICY

State your reimbursement rules clearly within your mobile device policy. Leave no room for misunderstanding or individual interpretation by employees. Spell out exactly how much of their personal smartphone bill employees are required to pay, what portion of the bill the company will cover, how the payment process works, and how penalties for late payments or lack of payments will be handled.

As with all AUPs, require every employee to sign and date a copy of the organization's mobile device policy, attesting to the fact that the user understands the rules, agrees to abide by them, and will accept the consequences—up to and including termination—in the event of a policy violation.

## MOBILE DEVICES MAY INCREASE SECURITY RISKS

Email has long provided a quick and easy way for employees to remove confidential data, trade secrets, and proprietary information from the company system—accidentally or intentionally. Twitter, Facebook, YouTube, blogs, and other social networking platforms have created new opportunities for unauthorized employees to take private information public. Thanks to smartphones, tablets, and other mobile devices, confidential company data and private customer information is at greater risk of exposure—in violation of the law, regulatory rules, and company policy—than ever before.

Increasingly, employees are using personal smartphones to access, transmit, and store company email messages and attachments. Fully 56 percent of U.S. companies surveyed report being "highly concerned" that confidential information will be transmitted out of the system via email sent on mobile devices. Employers have good reason for concern. One in five companies has investigated the exposure of confidential, sensitive, or private information via lost or stolen mobile devices, according to Proofpoint's survey, *Outbound Email and Data Loss Prevention in Today's Enterprise, 2010.*[3]

### BEST PRACTICE: USE MOBILE POLICY TO COMBAT SECURITY RISKS

Use written mobile device policy to help combat security risks associated with lost or misplaced personal gadgets and stolen

*(continued)*

company data. Within your policy, be sure to incorporate rules requiring employees to use the password function and other security features that come standard in their personal smartphones. Make it clear to employees that before using personal devices for business communication, they must set up a secure password that will prevent thieves, coworkers, and outside parties (including family members and friends) from accessing any business data or consumer information that is stored on a personal phone.

Just as the company maintains passwords for employees' desktop and laptop computers, so too should you maintain a list of employees' smartphone passwords. This rule applies regardless of whether phones are company-owned or employee property. Do not be deterred by employee complaints that their personal privacy is being violated. The organization is responsible for protecting and preserving company and customer data. You cannot afford to play fast and loose with business information. Employees either provide the company with their smartphone passwords, or they may not use their personal phones for business communication. It's that simple.

## BEST PRACTICE: ERASE DATA REMOTELY

Support your organization's smartphone password guidelines with a formal rule designed to protect confidential data in the event that an employee's smartphone is lost or stolen, or the employee leaves the company for any reason. Use policy and formal training to notify employees that under those circumstances management will erase all data from devices that are connected to cellular networks. Alert employees that the remote erasure of company data also will result in the loss of all personal information on the phone, including contact numbers, family photos, and personal email. Ideally, the threatened loss of personal data will motivate employees to keep a firm grip on their smartphones.[4]

**BEST PRACTICE: COMPLY WITH INTERNATIONAL PRIVACY LAWS**

Organizations that operate internationally should have legal counsel investigate the security and privacy laws of all of the countries in which they operate or have employees before erasing data remotely. Some countries, including China and South Korea, for example, prohibit employers from erasing data on employees' personal phones.[5] If that's the case, simply prohibit employees in those countries from using personal smartphones for business purposes.

## Regulated firms must comply with security rules

If you operate within the health care arena, financial services profession, or any other heavily regulated industry, you must comply with regulators' security rules (see Chapter Four). The Health Insurance Portability and Accountability Act (HIPAA), for example, requires companies in the medical field to safeguard electronic protected health information (EPHI) related to patients' health status, medical care, treatment plans, and payment issues. Failure to do so may result in regulatory fines, civil litigation, criminal charges, or jail time. If your health care concern is regulated by HIPAA, use policy to prohibit employees from accessing, transmitting, or storing EPHI on personal phones—unless you have in place proven-effective technology designed to keep protected patient data secure.

**BEST PRACTICE: SUPPORT REGULATORY RULES WITH TECHNOLOGY TOOLS**

Some regulated companies have overcome privacy and security challenges with software that isolates part of an employees' personal smartphone for company use. Within the secure, isolated area, the employee can access and view corporate email,

*(continued)*

attachments, and other data. However, that data cannot be downloaded into the device. The isolated area has its own password. Data may be encrypted for further protection. If a smartphone is lost or an employee leaves the company, data within the isolated area is deleted, while personal information remains intact.[6]

If your business (regulated or not) is concerned about the security risks associated with employees' use of personal smartphones, assign IT to research and recommend "the right" technology solutions to help protect your-eyes-only company data and private consumer information.

## MOBILE DEVICES DRIVE LEGAL LIABILITY

In addition to the security risks associated with lost devices and stolen data, organizations' legal risks increase significantly when employees elect to text, talk, blog, post, or surf while driving. Under the legal principle of vicarious liability (see Chapter Two) your organization may be held legally responsible if an employee triggers a traffic accident while communicating via mobile phone. It doesn't matter whether the employee is driving a company-owned vehicle or a personal car at the time of the crash. It makes no difference whether the employee is using a personal smartphone or a company-provided BlackBerry when the accident happens.

Employers have a duty to exercise reasonable care for the safety of the public whenever employees are acting within the scope of their employment. Consequently, your organization could be held legally— and financially—responsible for any accidents, injuries, or deaths caused by distracted employee-drivers who are busy texting, tweeting, talking, blogging, posting, surfing, or are otherwise communicating electronically during business hours. One percent of companies have fought lawsuits triggered by distracted employees texting or talking while driving, according to the *2009 Electronic Business Communication Policies and Procedures Survey* from American Management Association and The ePolicy Institute.[7] Expect that number to rise as workplace use of personal smartphones increases.

## There's a good chance that your employees are driving distracted

Over half (59 percent) of professional and business service workers admit to checking their smartphones while driving, according to a 2010 CareerBuilder survey.[8] Another 47 percent of adults have sent or read text while driving, reports Pew Research.[9] A quarter, 25 percent, of all bloggers report that they engage in mobile blogging, according to Technorati's 2010 *State of the Blogosphere* report.[10] Of Facebook's 800 million active users, 350 million use smartphones and other mobile devices to make and maintain relationships with "friends."[11]

## The high cost of distracted driving

Twenty percent of injury crashes in 2009 involved reports of distracted driving, according to the National Highway Transportation Safety Administration.[12] Employees who text while driving are 23 times more likely to crash than non-distracted drivers.[13] Not surprisingly, distracted driving is a top insurance loss for business, as well as a source of potentially costly legal liability.

---

**REAL-LIFE MOBILE PHONE DISASTER STORIES**

Need convincing of the legal risks associated with distracted employee-drivers? A trucking company paid $18 million to a victim who was left in a permanent vegetative state after being struck by an 18-wheeler driven by an employee who was checking text messages at time of the accident.[14] A lumber company paid $16.2 million to a pedestrian who was struck and disabled by an on-duty salesman who was distracted by his mobile device while driving.[15] Could your organization survive a multimillion-dollar hit to its bottom line and reputation?

---

## Mobile phones make e-discovery easy

Cellular service providers maintain records that make it easy to prove that an employee was texting or talking at or near the time of an accident, and whether or not the conversation was business-related. That's significant because, understandably, juries are unlikely to view texting and talking while behind the wheel as anything other than negligent conduct on the part of a distracted driver.

## The boss may—or may not—be held liable for distracted driving

Based on the legal principle known as vicarious liability, a company may be held liable for the negligence of employees, agents, and independent contractors who are deemed to be acting within the scope of employment or for the benefit of the company. That would include employee-drivers running business-related errands for managers or completing job-related tasks in company cars or private vehicles.

Employers can't escape vicarious liability simply by labeling workers "independent contractors." The courts will look beyond the label to consider the degree of control the employer holds over the worker. In a 2010 case, for example FedEx was held responsible when an allegedly negligent driver, employed by a FedEx contractor, was involved in a multicar accident. A federal appellate court held FedEx liable despite contractual language that disclaimed an employment relationship between FedEx and the contractor's employees. In other words, FedEx may have viewed the driver as an independent contractor, but the court did not.[16]

Employers usually are not held liable for accidents caused by distracted drivers who text with their own phones in their own cars during regular commutes to and from work. However, the company may be held liable if the commuter is transmitting work-related texts on a company-provided phone while driving a company-owned car. For example, an appellate court in 2009 held that an employer could be held liable when an employee was commuting home from a business conference. The worker's commute was considered a "special errand" for the employer since the employer had paid for the employee's accommodations at the conference, and the purpose of the trip was to benefit the employer.[17]

### Road warriors must adhere to talking and texting laws

In June 2011, federal legislation to ban the use of handheld phones and other mobile devices while driving was introduced in the United States House of Representatives.[18] While the debate over that legislation rages, nine states, Washington, D.C., and the U.S. Virgin Islands all enforce bans on handheld cell phones while driving. Thirty-four states, the District of Columbia, and Guam ban text messaging for all drivers. In addition, all U.S. federal employees are prohibited from using any type of cell phone, in any way, for any reason while driving federal vehicles.[19]

Employers must ensure that employee-drivers adhere to the cell phone and texting laws of every state, city, or jurisdiction in which the organization conducts business or has employees. That includes, of course, employees who merely are driving through a jurisdiction while on their way to a business meeting or job-related event. For an up-to-date recap of United States texting and cell phone laws, visit the Governors Highway Safety Association website at http://www.ghsa .org/html/stateinfo/laws/cellphone_laws.html. If you employ workers in other countries or require employees to travel internationally for business, then be sure to research and comply with the laws governing the use of cell phones and other mobile devices in any country in which you or your employees may be driving.

### Conduct "drivers' ed" for employees

Your company may be found negligent if you fail to warn employees about the risks of distracted driving, including the dangers inherent in texting while driving. In addition, your organization could be found liable if employee A were to text employee B during a time when employee A knows that employee B is likely to be driving.[20]

You cannot expect an untrained workforce to be a legally compliant workforce. Best practices call for comprehensive employee training to educate all employees about cell phone and mobile device risks, talking and texting laws, organizational policies, and the penalties (including the possibility of disciplinary action, job termination, civil suits, or criminal charges) awaiting those who violate company policies or laws governing the use, or misuse, of mobile phones while on the road, in the office, or at home.

## Mobile device policy helps combat costly disasters

Could your organization survive a multimillion-dollar legal settlement or jury award triggered by the actions of a distracted employee-driver? Twenty-seven percent of organizations use formal policy to ban cell phone use while driving, and another 26 percent outlaw texting while driving, according to the *2009 Electronic Business Communication Policies and Procedures Survey* from American Management Association and The ePolicy Institute.[21] Follow the lead of these proactive organizations. Establish and enforce a comprehensive, written mobile device policy that clearly spells out organizational, legal, and regulatory rules governing mobile device use, content, records, security, productivity, and other important issues.

To help get your mobile device policy program under way, consider how other employers are using formal guidelines to help manage potential risks. Research conducted by American Management Association and The ePolicy Institute reveals that, as recently as 2009, U.S. employers had in place policies governing the following: personal use of company cell phones (62 percent); use of personal cell phones during work hours (43 percent); personal use of company text messaging (35 percent); use of personal texting tools during work hours (33 percent); cell phone use and language (51 percent); company phones to take/transmit personal video/photos (50 percent); cell phone netiquette (30 percent); and texting use and content (30 percent).[22]

Feel free to use these nationwide findings, coupled with the results of your own social media policy audit, to help formulate your organization's customized and comprehensive mobile device policy and procedures.

# SOCIAL MEDIA BEST PRACTICES: MOBILE DEVICES

1. Establish electronic content rules, language guidelines, and netiquette rules for mobile phone users to help decrease liability, increase productivity, and enhance customer service. Whether texting, tweeting, talking, blogging, posting, or otherwise conversing and communicating, on-the-go employees must employ a professional tone, businesslike language, and appropriate content at all times.

2. Instruct employees to turn off their cell phones or other mobile devices (company-provided or personal, handheld or hands-free) when driving any vehicle (company-owned or personal) during business hours. Insist that they pull off the road to make or take a call; write and send a text; compose and send a tweet; post or comment on blogs; surf the Internet; collaborate on wikis; check text, email, or voice messages; or otherwise engage in any form of mobile communication.

3. Remind employees that a policy is a policy. Mobile device users must comply with the organization's mobile device policy, and all other employment rules and policies, 100 percent of the time—at work, home, or on the road.

4. Inform employees that they must adhere to the organization's personal use rules, regardless of whether they are using a company-provided phone or their own phone. Best practices call for the implementation of mobile device policies that incorporate clear and specific rules governing employees' personal use of company devices, systems, sites, and accounts, as well as the personal use of workers' privately owned phones and accounts.

5. Inform employees that any violation of the company's mobile device policy may result in disciplinary action, up to and including their termination. Also let workers know that they could face civil or criminal charges (carrying possible monetary fines or jail time) if they cause a car crash, hit a pedestrian, or otherwise cause an accident, injury, or death while driving distracted.

6. Make it clear that employees are not to use cell phones or other mobile devices to discuss company business, customer financials,

patients' private medical information, or any other confidential company matter in any public setting in which their conversations could be overheard, text messages could be read, or screens could be seen by unauthorized third parties.

7. Incorporate rules governing the use of smartphone cameras to take, transmit, upload, download, post, publish, or print photos or videos of the company's people, products, services, facilities, customers, and suppliers without formal authorization.

8. Discourage employees from distracting coworkers and customers with unnecessary texting, typing, or talking on their mobile phones in any business setting.

9. Prohibit all employees and executives from driving cars or operating vehicles (company-owned or personal) while texting, talking, tweeting, or otherwise communicating on handheld or hands-free cell phones (company-owned or personal).

10. Review and update mobile device risks, rules, laws, regulations, policies, and procedures annually.

11. Require all employees to sign and date mobile device policy acknowledgment forms, attesting to the fact that they have read the policy, understand the policy, and agree to comply with the policy or accept the consequences, up to and including termination.

12. Distribute your written mobile device policy to employees in the course of formal, mandatory policy training. Do not conclude training until you are certain that all employees fully understand— and agree to comply with—the company's mobile device policy.

13. Collect and file all policy-related and training-related materials, documents, and records to demonstrate your commitment to best practices and compliance, in the event of a regulatory investigation, workplace lawsuit, or criminal complaint.

14. Put some teeth in your mobile device policy. In other words, discipline or dismiss policy violators in accordance with your organization's written rules. Remember, the termination of one policy scofflaw today may prevent the dismissal of an entire department tomorrow.

# SEVEN-STEP ACTION PLAN FOR SUCCESSFUL SOCIAL MEDIA POLICY AND COMPLIANCE MANAGEMENT

8

As detailed throughout this book, business (and personal) social media use is fraught with potentially costly and protracted risks (including lawsuits, regulatory fines, and security breaches, among others) that are best managed through a formal social media policy and compliance management program. To help ensure the success of your organization's social media risk management program, best practices call for adherence to the following seven-step action plan.

### Step One: Form a Social Media Policy Team

Form a social media policy team to oversee the development and implementation of your organization's formal rules, written policies, and ongoing compliance management program. The size and makeup of your team will depend upon the nature of your business, your exposure to online risks, and your available financial and human resources.

### Step Two: Develop a Strategic Social Media Policy and Compliance Management Plan

Develop a strategic plan for the establishment and enforcement of your social media policy and compliance management program. Your plan should spell out specific program-related activities, assignments for policy team members, realistic time lines, and program goals.

### Step Three: Conduct Social Media Policy Audits

Before you start writing social media policy, you'll first want to conduct comprehensive social media policy audits, focusing on management and staff, as detailed in Chapter Nine. Use the audit process to help determine the shape that your workplace social media policy and compliance management program should take, along with the risks and rules that your organization's social media policy, blog policy, mobile device policy, and other acceptable use policies should address.

### Step Four: Write Effective Policies

Once the social media policy audit process is complete, and the results have been analyzed, then it's time to get to work on the creation of well-written, comprehensive policies that clearly communicate legal, regulatory, and organizational rules based on the findings of your social media policy audit. For guidelines on writing the type of effective policies that provide employees with a clear understanding of what constitutes appropriate, acceptable, and lawful social media content and use, see Chapter Ten.

## Step Five: Educate Employees

Once your social media policy has been written (and other acceptable use policies have been created or updated, based on your audit findings), your next step is to introduce your policy and compliance management program to all employees on a company-wide basis. To help maximize policy compliance, manage user behavior, and minimize risks, support your written social media policy with training, training, and more training. See Chapter Twelve for best practices–based training tips, tools, and techniques.

## Step Six: Enforce Policy with Disciplinary Action

You cannot expect an untrained workforce to be a compliant workforce. Nor can you expect to maintain a firm grip on user behavior with relaxed rules. Put some teeth in your social media policy. Let employees know that violations of the company's social media policy (or any AUP or employment policy, for that matter) may result in disciplinary action, up to and including the scofflaw's termination.

## Step Seven: Support Policy with Technology Tools

Support social media policy with technology tools designed to help mitigate legal, regulatory, security, and organizational risks—while helping to manage policy compliance. Just as electronic business communication tools have evolved, so too have the technology solutions that exist to help manage risks, use, content, records, and compliance.

Use your social media policy audit (see Chapter Nine) to help assess the legal, regulatory, and organizational risks facing your company in the age of social media, evaluate the effectiveness of the technology solutions you currently have in place to help manage risks and rules, and make informed decisions about the resources (IT, financial, and human) needed to help maximize compliance and minimize risks.

# FORM A SOCIAL MEDIA POLICY TEAM

Step one of the seven-step social media action plan calls for the formation of a social media policy team. The purpose of the social media policy team is threefold: (1) by marshaling the expertise of executives and managers from various departments, you gain diverse insights into social media-related risks, needs, issues, and challenges; (2) the formation of a policy team helps ensure that the organization's formal social media policy and compliance management program gets under way—and remains active—until the project is completed; (3) the team approach ensures that the demanding, time-consuming jobs of policy research, writing, and implementation will be shared by several trusted managers, rather than thrust on the shoulders of one responsible party.

The makeup of your organization's social media policy and compliance management team will depend upon the size of your organization, the nature of your business, the scope of your social media–related exposures, and the willingness of management to commit financial and human resources to the social media policy and compliance management program. In an ideal world, if resources allow, an effective social media policy and compliance management team would include the following professionals.

## *Senior Executive*

To help convince employees that the company is serious about social media risk management, recruit a senior-level executive (the more senior the better) to serve as the champion, or public face, of the organization's social media policy and compliance management program.

The participation of a top-level executive will signal to employees that the company is fully committed to reducing social media risks, while maximizing compliance with legal, regulatory, and organizational rules. An added bonus: in the event of a lawsuit or regulatory investigation, the fact that your social media policy team is headed by a senior executive may help convince the court and opposing legal counsel that your organization truly is serious about managing social media use, content, records, and compliance.

## Legal Counsel or Compliance Officer

Should your organization become embroiled in social media–related litigation, opposing counsel likely will hire an expert witness (perhaps several expert witnesses) to review and evaluate the effectiveness of your written policies; the training programs you have conducted to educate employees about risks, rules, policies, and procedures; and the technology solutions that you have put in place to help enforce policy.

The presence of an experienced lawyer or compliance officer on your social media policy team will help demonstrate the fact that your organization has done its due diligence when it comes to the development and implementation of a best practices–based policy and compliance management program. Failure to involve legal on your social media policy team, on the other hand, might suggest to opposing legal counsel that your company does not require (or expect) employees to engage in business-appropriate, lawful behavior online.

Be sure to assign your legal expert a lead role in the creation of your social media policy (and all other AUPs and employment policies). No matter how well written or effective you consider your social media policy to be, do not put it into circulation until it has undergone a thorough legal review to ensure that all applicable federal, state, and international laws are addressed, all industry and government regulations are covered, all corporate responsibilities are considered, and all user rights are protected.

## CIO or IT Director

Successful compliance management starts with policy, is supported by training, and is enforced by technology. Your organization's chief information officer (CIO) or IT director can help bridge the gap between people problems (including inappropriate content, excessive personal use, and confidentiality breaches) and technology solutions.

As a member of the social media policy team, your CIO or IT director will play an important role in identifying potential security threats and recommending effective technology solutions to help manage (and in some cases prevent) potentially costly disasters.

## Records Manager

As detailed in Chapter Three, social media content (just like email and other forms of electronically stored information, or ESI) can create written records that must be managed for legal, regulatory, and organizational purposes. Failure to preserve, protect, and produce ESI in response to court subpoenas or citizens' public records requests can land your company in hot water with the law or regulators.

As part of your organization's social media policy and compliance management program, assign a professional records manager (either an in-house professional or an outside consultant) the task of reviewing your current record retention policy, deletion schedule, litigation hold policy, and other rules and procedures related to the management and disposition of electronic business records. Update those policies and procedures, as necessary, in conjunction with the creation of your organization's social media policy program.

## Human Resources Director

Because the human resources (HR) department typically is assigned the task of enforcing employment policies and disciplining policy violators, it is a good idea to include your HR director on the organization's social media policy team. Assign your HR manager a role in every aspect of your compliance management program, from drafting social media policy audit questionnaires, to formulating written policies, to educating employees, to enforcing policies by disciplining rule breakers.

## Training Manager

Policies are only as good as your employees' awareness, understanding, and willingness to comply with them. Formal, ongoing employee education is critical to the success of your organization's social media policy program. Do not expect untrained employees to be aware of or understand social media risks. Do not assume all employees will take the initiative to familiarize themselves with rules, policies, and procedures. Demonstrate your commitment to compliance, communication, and civil online behavior by including your training manager on the social media policy team—and making the ongoing education of employee-networkers a priority.

### Public Relations Manager or Media Relations Director

An important member of your social media policy team should be your public relations (PR) manager or media relations director. One important PR role is to ensure the incorporation of rules governing employees' interaction with the media. For example, many organizations prohibit employees from responding to press inquiries that may be posted on the comment sections of business blogs or personal blogs. If you want employees to direct all media questions and requests to the PR or media relations department, then use your social media and blog policies to convey that information.

Adhere to best practices by having your PR director draft a formal reputation management plan to help ensure that the company is ready to respond—immediately and effectively—in the event of a blogstorm, cybersmear attack, or social networking nightmare. See Chapter Thirteen to learn more about the risks social media and web 2.0 pose to brands and businesses—and why a proactive reputation management plan is essential.

## A WORD FOR SMALL BUSINESS OWNERS

Even if your company is too small to fund, staff, or otherwise support a multimember social media policy team, please note that social media management is an essential task for all businesses, big and small, public and private, regulated and unregulated. Whether you employ one independent contractor, 10 part-time workers, 100 experienced professionals, or 1,000 full-time employees, you must establish formal, written social media rules and policies to help manage user behavior and mitigate legal, regulatory, security, and organizational risks. Small business owners who lack the human or financial resources necessary to form a social media policy team are encouraged to take the time and make the effort to become fully informed about social media risks, policies, and best practices. Start by using this book as your social media policy and compliance management primer. To help meet the compliance needs of your business and industry, feel free to adapt the sample social media policies provided in Chapter Fourteen. Just be sure to run your policies past experienced legal counsel before introducing them to employees.

If you find yourself balking at the cost of a legal review, remember that the up-front investment you make today is nothing compared to the cost of hiring defense counsel, retaining expert witnesses, paying court sanctions, and covering legal settlements or jury awards should your small business one day become embroiled in litigation related to inappropriate social media use or content.

To help round out your social media policy and compliance management education, consider attending online or onsite policy training programs, such as the ones that the author of this book conducts through The ePolicy Institute.

## DEVELOP A SOCIAL MEDIA ACTION PLAN AND TIME LINE

For large and small enterprises alike, the development and implementation of a corporate social media policy and compliance management program can be a daunting and time-consuming task—particularly if your organization (like many companies) is still struggling to manage "good old-fashioned" email and Internet use, records, content, and compliance. Don't let the scope of social media management intimidate you or stop you from moving forward with your policy program.

If human or financial resources are limited, then approach social media policy and compliance management one step at a time. The important

## SAMPLE SOCIAL MEDIA POLICY ACTION PLAN

To help ensure the timely development and implementation of your organization's social media policy and compliance program, be sure to assign roles for policy team members and incorporate specific deadlines for program elements and activities. This sample social media policy action plan allocates two quarters, October 1 to March 31, for an organization to conduct a policy audit, draft and finalize policy, conduct a legal review of policy, review and as necessary update technology solutions in support of policy, and conduct a comprehensive employee education program.

| Action | Responsible Team Member(s) | Date |
| --- | --- | --- |
| Form Team | Senior Executive/ Policy Champion | 10/01 |
| Initial Team Meeting | Entire Policy Team | 10/07 |
| Audit Questionnaires Drafted | IT, HR, Legal | 10/21 |
| Audit Questionnaire Approved | Senior Executive/ Policy Champion | 10/28 |
| Audits Conducted | HR Director | 11/01 – 11/15 |
| Audit Results Tallied | HR Director | 11/15 – 11/30 |
| Audit Findings Summarized | IT, HR, Legal | 12/15 |
| Post-Audit Team Meeting | Entire Policy Team | 12/30 |
| Policy Drafted | HR Director | 1/15 |
| Policy Reviewed | Legal/Compliance | 1/30 |
| Policy Finalized | HR/Legal | 2/15 |
| Technology Solutions Reviewed | IT Director | 2/15 |
| Reputation Management Plan | PR/Media Relations | 2/15 |
| Employee Education | Training Manager | 2/15–3/30 |

As you can see, the first step after forming your policy team is to develop and conduct an organization-wide social media policy audit. Use your initial planning meeting to assign responsibility for drafting audit questionnaires for managers and staff, conducting audits, tallying audit results, and summarizing findings in written form for review by the entire policy team.

Chapter Nine takes you step-by-step through the process of conducting the comprehensive research necessary to develop an effective social media policy program.

thing is that you have taken action and are moving toward your goal of effectively managing social media use and content, records and risks, behavior, and compliance.

## SOCIAL MEDIA BEST PRACTICES: SEVEN-STEP ACTION PLAN FOR POLICY AND COMPLIANCE MANAGEMENT SUCCESS

1. To help ensure the success of your organization's social media policy program, take this seven-step approach: (1) form a social media policy team; (2) develop a strategic plan; (3) conduct a comprehensive social media policy audit; (4) write effective social media policy; (5) educate users; (6) enforce policy with disciplinary action; and (7) support policy with technology tools.

2. If human and financial resources allow, the ideal social media policy team would include these participants: (1) senior executive; (2) legal counsel or compliance officer; (3) CIO or IT; (4) records manager; (5) HR director; (6) training manager; and (7) PR manager.

3. All organizations, regardless of size, are obligated to manage social media risks, use, content, records, and compliance. Small business owners who lack the resources necessary to field a policy team are advised to take advantage of the background information, best practices–based advice, and sample policies offered in this book.

4. Social networking is here, and it is here to stay. Do not wait for a social media disaster to strike your organization. Begin work now on the formation of your social media policy team, development of your strategic policy plan, and the successful management of your organization's social media use, content, records, risks, and legal and regulatory compliance.

# CONDUCT A SOCIAL MEDIA POLICY AUDIT

9

Before committing your organization's formal social media policy and procedures to writing, you'll want to conduct a clear-eyed, comprehensive review of all the social networking–related risks and challenges, laws and regulations, opportunities, and benefits facing your business, employees, customers, prospects, and other audiences with whom you currently communicate—or hope to reach—via external social networking sites, private enterprise-grade networking and collaboration tools, and smartphones and other mobile devices. In other words, conduct a social media policy and procedures audit to determine the shape your workplace social media compliance management program should take, along with the risks and rules your social media policies should address.

## TEN STEPS TO AUDIT SUCCESS

An effective social media policy audit should incorporate the following ten steps:

1. Review all of the social media–related legal risks facing your orga-nization as a whole and its individual users. Assign experienced legal counsel or your company's compliance officer the task of reviewing current laws governing electronic content, use, record retention, e-discovery, monitoring, privacy, security, and other legal issues. Be sure to review the laws of every jurisdiction (fed-eral, state, county, and local) in which you operate, litigate work-place lawsuits, employ workers, serve customers or patients, or otherwise have a business presence.

   If you operate internationally, be sure to retain the services of a legal expert who is familiar with the laws, particularly those related to security, privacy, and monitoring, of every country in which you conduct business, employ workers, or operate facilities.

   Once your comprehensive legal review is complete, the next step is to determine exactly what your organization needs to do—from the standpoint of social media policy, employee training, and technology solutions—to achieve 100 percent legal compliance on the federal, state, county, and local level, as well as internationally, if you operate a multinational business.

   Fail to complete this step, and you may find yourself on the wrong side of a workplace lawsuit triggered by an inappropriate blog post, defamatory tweet, discriminatory video, pornographic photograph, harassing comment, or otherwise illegal, offensive, or inappropriate electronic content.

2. If you operate within the financial services industry, health care arena, or any other regulated industry, then best practices call for a comprehensive review of all of the regulatory risks facing your company and its regulated employees. Assign an experienced legal, compliance, or regulatory expert the task of reviewing

federal, state, industry, and government regulations pertaining to social media content, use, security, privacy, and business records. If you operate internationally, you will need to investigate the regulatory guidelines that govern your business and industry in every country in which you engage in commerce, operate facilities, or employ workers.

Your goal is to determine exactly what your organization needs to do—from the standpoint of social media policy, training, and technology—to adhere to all of the regulatory rules governing your business and industry. Skip this step, and it's possible that careless comments about patients, thoughtless tweets about consumers, or premature posts about company financials could put your organization at risk of regulatory violations and penalties, including potentially steep monetary fines.

3. Review all of the internal, organizational risks facing your company and your employee-networkers. Has excessive personal use of social media led to a slide in workplace productivity? Have you been forced to terminate otherwise valuable employees because of inappropriate tweeting, blogging, commenting, or posting? Do you use social media sites to screen prospective job candidates, opening the organization to possible discrimination claims? Have employee-drivers, distracted by texting, talking, or tweeting, ever caused car crashes, hit pedestrians, or broken federal, state, or local driving laws governing the use of handheld or hands-free cell phones?

When it comes to social media use and electronic business (and personal) communication in general, the list of organizational risks is a long one. Use your social media policy audit to help uncover—and then address through formal rules and written policies—all of the potentially costly exposures facing your organization when employees log onto blogs, social networking sites, or other web 2.0 applications at work, home, or on the road.

4. Review all of the data security risks that social networking and computer use overall poses to your company, customers, and employees.

Are telecommuters, remote workers, and mobile device users accessing the social web outside the security of your corporate network? Do you allow employees to access and download confidential company and customer data via their own personal smartphones? Has your organization's Internet system ever been attacked by hackers or cyber-criminals? Has the electronic protected health information (EPHI) of patients or the private financial data of consumers ever been inappropriately accessed by employees or exposed—accidentally or intentionally—to third parties?

Ever since email and the Internet first entered the workplace, security concerns have kept chief information officers up at night—for good reason. Take advantage of this opportunity to inventory—and address through formal, mandatory, written policies—all of the new and emerging security risks that social media, mobile devices, and other twenty-first-century technology tools have introduced into your place of business.

5. Evaluate the ways in which your organization uses public social networking sites. Do you use Facebook, Twitter, YouTube, Flickr, Digg, Squidoo, LinkedIn, or other external public sites to interact with customers and prospects, vendors and decision makers, shareholders and the media, prospective employees and the general public? Does your company operate an external business blog or maintain a corporate Facebook page? Do your executives use Twitter to connect with the public? Do you produce YouTube videos to educate consumers about products and services? Or, does your company currently lack any form of public social media presence?

6. Assess the ways in which your organization uses enterprise-grade social networking software and internal collaboration tools. Do you operate internal, employee-only blogs or wikis? Do you use private social media sites like Yammer or Socialtext to facilitate secure communication and collaboration, team-building and brainstorming, information-sharing, and relationship-building solely among employees and executives, vendors, and trusted partners?

Increasingly, organizations are discovering that, for business purposes, effective social networking does not necessarily involve participation on free public sites. Many organizations prefer the security of internal social media tools, which offer all of the benefits of in-house social networking—minus many of the risks to confidentiality, privacy, and productivity that are inherent in public social networking.

7. Evaluate employees' personal use of the company's computer system. Do you allow personal use of the company web? Has personal use of business blogs had a negative impact on productivity or job performance? As the popularity of social media grows, are employees spending less time on job-related tasks and more time networking with colleagues and outsiders? Does personal use of social media compromise the company's bandwidth? Do workers use company-provided BlackBerries strictly to conduct business, or are they carrying on personal relationships on your corporate dime? Is your archive a dangerous mix of business-critical email records and insignificant and potentially embarrassing personal posts, messages, and other forms of electronic content?

8. Investigate employees' personal, after-hours use of social media. Are employees using their own personal blogs to whine about their jobs, criticize colleagues, gossip about executives, complain about managers, ridicule customers, or denigrate your products or services? Has a worker ever posted classified business information or confidential consumer data on a private Facebook account, damaging the organization's reputation and triggering a lawsuit or regulatory investigation in the process? Have staff members ever tweeted unauthorized or inappropriate photos of themselves in company uniforms?

Your company's social media policy and training program creates the ideal opportunity to let employees know that all of the organization's employment policies, rules, and guidelines (including social media policy) apply 24 hours a day, seven days a week, 365 days a year, at work and home, on company equipment and private accounts. Don't forfeit the opportunity to deliver that message to employees—loud and clear.

9. Research the level of interest that your customers, prospects, business partners, vendors, job applicants, the media, decision-makers, investors, and other target audiences have in communicating with your company via social media. If you currently have a business blog or company presence on Facebook, Twitter, or YouTube, evaluate the responses (positive or negative) that you have received from your various corporate constituencies. If you have yet to develop a social media presence, this is a good time to consider how your organization's most important audiences—including customers and patients, investors and suppliers, and regulators and decision makers—are likely to react once you dive into the social networking pool (or fail to do so).

   Take advantage of this opportunity to conduct some demographic research related to your customers' and prospects' use of social media. Don't assume, for example, that online networking is strictly a young person's game that holds limited—if any—interest for older customers. Social networking among Americans ages 50 and older nearly doubled in 2010, up to 42 percent from 22 percent the previous year, according to the Pew Internet & American Life Project, 2010.[1] We can safely assume that the adoption of social media by older users will continue to increase, along with overall growth of business and personal use among people of all ages.

   Don't play guessing games with social media. Use your social media policy audit to help determine exactly how to make the most beneficial use of networking tools as a means to promote your brand, position your products and services, and communicate corporate messages to important audiences.

10. Review all of your organization's existing policies governing social media, blogs, mobile devices, email, the Internet, instant messenger, text messaging, and all other electronic business

communication tools. Do you have in place free-standing policies governing all of the electronic tools and technologies that employees currently are using at work, home, and on the road? You should.

When was the last time your formal rules and written policies were updated? If it's been more than a year, that's too long.

Are your acceptable use policies (AUPs) well written, easy to read, understand, and adhere to? Are your policies well designed and visually appealing?

How do you distribute policies to employees? Best practices call for formal, onsite employee training, yet most employers rely solely on the employee handbook or Intranet to introduce AUPs to users. Where do you stand?

In addition to auditing social media and other electronic policies, now is the time to review all of your organization's business rules and employment policies. Use the social media policy audit process as an opportunity to take a strategic look at, for example, your current harassment and discrimination policy, employee code of conduct, confidentiality policy, writing style guidelines, ethics rules, mobile device policy, dress code, and all other workplace policies. Ideally, you have the human and financial resources necessary to update all of your organization's employment policies simultaneous to the development and implementation of your social media policy program.

Also, take advantage of opportunities to "cross promote" policies. Use blog policy, for example, to inform employees that they must adhere to the company's ethics guidelines when blogging. Use harassment and discrimination policy to remind workers that the rules apply, regardless of whether they are communicating internally or externally, for business or personal reasons, in-person or online via social media or any other electronic communication tool. Finally, use your policy program to remind the workforce that a policy is a policy, and all employees must adhere to all employment policies at all times.

# STRUCTURING AN EFFECTIVE SOCIAL MEDIA AUDIT

As a first step toward social media audit success, you'll want to develop questionnaires that are designed to elicit "the right" information from executives and employees.

## Create two separate audit questionnaires: One for management, the other for staff

Use the social media policy audit process to gauge policy awareness, understanding, and compliance from the standpoint of both management and staff. To that end, your social media policy team will need to draft and distribute two separate audit questionnaires: one for managers, supervisors, and executives; the other for employees.

The management questionnaire should be designed to yield information about the legal, regulatory, organizational, security, and other risks facing your business. It also should reveal information about the company's policy needs and challenges, as perceived by the people who supervise computer users, discipline policy violators, and otherwise encounter and handle policy-related issues, needs, and challenges on a daily basis. By comparing management's audit responses with those of employees, you'll learn whether executives and supervisors really have an accurate read on employees' online behavior, content, and compliance.

Ideally, your employee questionnaire and audit will generate honest responses about workers' computer use, awareness of risks, understanding of policies, adherence to company rules, compliance with laws and regulatory guidelines, and attitudes toward the organization's employment policies in general and social media policy in particular.

## Motivating employee participation in the audit process

Consider kicking off your social media policy audit with a company-wide informational meeting. If a company-wide gathering is not viable, then consider hosting a series of onsite informational sessions, live webcasts, or video conferences. Use your mandatory company-wide rally to announce your planned social media policy program, introduce your social media policy team, and explain the fact that, as a first step, you will be gathering information about employees' current (and past) use of the company's computer system, social media sites (business and personal), and other electronic communication sites, accounts, tools, and devices (company owned and private).

In order to generate honest responses and open participation by employees, it is essential that the audit be conducted anonymously and "safely." Among the assurances to give employees: (1) the audit will be conducted in a confidential manner; (2) employees will not be required to sign completed questionnaires or otherwise identify themselves as respondents; (3) management will make no effort to identify respondents via numbered questionnaires or any other method; and (4) the company will not discipline employees who admit to violating any computer policies or other employment rules or misusing electronic resources in the past—accidentally or intentionally. Make it clear to employees that they are free to answer all questions truthfully and without fear of reprisal from management. Finally, let employees know that management will share the final results of the audit with employees in the course of a formal social media policy training program.

**SAMPLE SOCIAL MEDIA POLICY AUDIT QUESTIONNAIRE FOR MANAGERS, SUPERVISORS, AND EXECUTIVES**

**Legal Risks and Compliance**
1. Have you reviewed current federal and state laws governing electronic content, usage, monitoring, privacy, e-discovery, data encryption, business records, and other legal issues in all jurisdictions in which you operate, have employees, serve customers, or litigate lawsuits?
   ☐  Yes     ☐  No     ☐  Don't Know

2. Has employee email ever triggered a workplace lawsuit?
   ☐ Yes   ☐ No   ☐ Don't Know

3. Has offensive or inappropriate social media content (blog posts, tweets, Facebook profiles, third-party blog comments, YouTube videos, and so on) ever triggered a workplace lawsuit?
   ☐ Yes   ☐ No   ☐ Don't Know

4. Has employee Internet use (surfing, viewing, downloading, uploading, and so on) ever triggered a workplace lawsuit?
   ☐ Yes   ☐ No   ☐ Don't Know

5. Have employee-written business blog posts or third-party comments ever triggered a workplace lawsuit?
   ☐ Yes   ☐ No   ☐ Don't Know

**E-Discovery Risks and Compliance**

6. Has employee email ever been subpoenaed by a court or regulatory body?
   ☐ Yes   ☐ No   ☐ Don't Know

7. Have business-related tweets, Facebook posts, YouTube videos, or other social networking content ever been subpoenaed by a court or regulator?
   ☐ Yes   ☐ No   ☐ Don't Know

8. Have business blog posts ever been subpoenaed by a court or regulator?
   ☐ Yes   ☐ No   ☐ Don't Know

9. Has email or other electronically stored information (ESI) ever been used as evidence—for or against your company—in litigation?
   ☐ Yes   ☐ No   ☐ Don't Know

10. Have you provided employees with a formal definition of "electronic business record"?
    ☐ Yes   ☐ No   ☐ Don't Know

11. Do your employees know the difference between business-critical email that must be retained for legal and regulatory purposes versus personal email and otherwise insignificant messages that may be purged?

   ☐ Yes     ☐ No     ☐ Don't Know

12. Do you rely on an archiving solution to automatically preserve, protect, and produce legally compliant email and other ESI?

   ☐ Yes     ☐ No     ☐ Don't Know

13. Could you locate and produce legally compliant business blog posts, email messages, text messages, and other ESI in 99 days if ordered by a court to do so?

   ☐ Yes     ☐ No     ☐ Don't Know

14. Are you familiar and compliant with the amended Federal Rules of Civil Procedure (FRCP)?

   ☐ Yes     ☐ No     ☐ Don't Know

15. Are you familiar and compliant with the state rules of civil procedure in every state in which you operate, have employees, or litigate lawsuits?

   ☐ Yes     ☐ No     ☐ Don't Know

**Records Management**

16. Do you have a formal electronic business record retention policy in place, governing the retention of all electronically stored information?

   ☐ Yes     ☐ No     ☐ Don't Know

17. Have you established a record lifecycle schedule and formal deletion schedule for your organization's electronic business records?

   ☐ Yes     ☐ No     ☐ Don't Know

18. Do you have a formal litigation hold policy and related procedures in place?

   ☐ Yes     ☐ No     ☐ Don't Know

19. If your organization is a public entity, are you confident of your ability to respond in a timely and complete manner to a public records request?
    ☐ Yes        ☐ No        ☐ Don't Know

20. If your organization is a public entity, have you ever responded to a federal Freedom of Information Act (FOIA) request or a state public records request?
    ☐ Yes        ☐ No        ☐ Don't Know

## Regulatory Risks and Compliance

21. Do you know and understand all of the industry and government regulations that govern your organization's electronic use, content, records, data security, customer data, consumer privacy, or e-discovery obligations?
    ☐ Yes        ☐ No        ☐ Don't Know

22. Have you educated your regulated employees about electronic risks and compliance vis-à-vis regulators' rules and guidelines?
    ☐ Yes        ☐ No        ☐ Don't Know

23. Has content posted on your organization's business blog ever triggered a regulatory investigation?
    ☐ Yes        ☐ No        ☐ Don't Know

24. Has content posted on your organization's public Facebook page or other external public social media site (Twitter, YouTube, and so on) ever triggered a regulatory investigation?
    ☐ Yes        ☐ No        ☐ Don't Know

25. Has content posted on your organization's private, enterprise-grade social media sites, internal blogs, or in-house wikis ever triggered a regulatory investigation?
    ☐ Yes        ☐ No        ☐ Don't Know

26. Has content posted on an employee's personal blog ever triggered a regulatory investigation against your company?
    ☐ Yes        ☐ No        ☐ Don't Know

27. Has content posted by an employee on a personal Facebook, Twitter, YouTube, or other social networking account ever triggered a regulatory investigation against your organization?

    ☐ Yes        ☐ No        ☐ Don't Know

28. If your organization is in the health care industry, have you ever terminated an employee for improperly accessing, reviewing, or exposing a patient's electronic protected health information (EPHI) in violation of HIPAA?

    ☐ Yes        ☐ No        ☐ Don't Know

29. If your organization is in the health care industry, have you ever terminated an employee for posting a patient's EPHI on a public social media site in violation of HIPAA?

    ☐ Yes        ☐ No        ☐ Don't Know

30. If your organization is in the financial services industry, have you ever terminated an employee for posting private consumer financial data on a public social networking site (Facebook, Twitter, YouTube, and so on) in violation of the Gramm-Leach-Bliley Act (GLBA)?

    ☐ Yes        ☐ No        ☐ Don't Know

31. If your organization is in the financial services industry, have you ever terminated an employee for posting confidential company financial data on a public social media site in violation of SEC, FINRA, or other regulatory bodies?

    ☐ Yes        ☐ No        ☐ Don't Know

## Organizational and Productivity Risks and Compliance

32. Has excessive personal use of email led to a slide in workplace productivity?

    ☐ Yes        ☐ No        ☐ Don't Know

33. Has excessive personal use of the Internet led to a slide in workplace productivity?

    ☐ Yes        ☐ No        ☐ Don't Know

34. Has excessive personal use of public social networking sites led to a slide in workplace productivity?

☐ Yes ☐ No ☐ Don't Know

35. Has excessive personal use of the organization's private, enterprise-grade social networking sites led to a slide in workplace productivity?

☐ Yes ☑ No ☐ Don't Know

36. Do you review job applicants' personal blogs, Facebook pages, and other personal social media presence as part of the interview process?

☐ Yes ☐ No ☐ Don't Know

37. Has your review of job applicants' personal blogs, Facebook profiles, and other social networking sites ever triggered a discrimination claim against your company?

☐ Yes ☐ No ☐ Don't Know

38. Do you allow employees to engage in video snacking via personal or company-owned systems and accounts?

☐ Yes ☐ No ☐ Don't Know

39. Have you ever terminated an employee for violating email policy?

☐ Yes ☐ No ☐ Don't Know

40. Have you ever terminated an employee for violating Internet policy?

☐ Yes ☐ No ☐ Don't Know

41. Have you ever terminated an employee for violating Intranet policy?

☐ Yes ☐ No ☐ Don't Know

42. Have you ever terminated an employee for violating blog policy?

☐ Yes ☐ No ☐ Don't Know

43. Have you ever terminated an employee for violating social media policy?

☐ Yes   ☐ No   ☐ Don't Know

44. What does your company consider to be a termination-worthy social media violation? (Check all that apply.)

☐ Violation of social media policy

☐ Violation of any company employment policy

☐ Inappropriate or offensive language or content

☐ Excessive personal use

☐ Breach of confidentiality rules

☐ Violation of regulatory guidelines

☐ Other

45. What does your company consider to be a termination-worthy blog violation? (Check all that apply.)

☐ Violation of blog policy

☐ Violation of any company employment policy

☐ Inappropriate or offensive language or content

☐ Excessive personal use

☐ Breach of confidentiality rules

☐ Violation of regulatory guidelines

☐ Other

46. What does your company consider to be a termination-worthy email violation? (Check all that apply.)

☐ Violation of email policy

☐ Violation of any company employment policy

☐ Inappropriate or offensive language or content

☐ Excessive personal use

☐ Breach of confidentiality rules

☐ Violation of regulatory guidelines

☐ Other

47. What does your company consider to be a termination-worthy Internet violation? (Check all that apply.)

☐ Violation of Internet policy

☐ Violation of any company employment policy

☐ Inappropriate or offensive language or content

☐ Excessive personal use

☐ Breach of confidentiality rules

☐ Violation of regulatory guidelines

☐ Other

48. On average, how much personal use of the organization's computer systems (social media, blogs, Internet, email, texting, and so forth) do you engage in daily?

☐ 0 to 30 minutes

☐ 30 minutes to 2 hours

☐ 2 hours to 4 hours

☐ 4-plus hours

## Security Risks and Compliance

49. Are telecommuters, remote workers, and mobile device users accessing the web, public social networking sites, and external blogs outside the security of your corporate network?

☐ Yes  ☒ No  ☐ Don't Know

50. Has your organization ever been attacked by malicious intruders, hackers, or cybercriminals?

☐ Yes  ☐ No  ☐ Don't Know

51. Have leaked internal email messages ever triggered negative media coverage, a drop in stock valuation, a regulatory audit, or other negative consequences?

☒ Yes  ☐ No  ☐ Don't Know

52. Have employees ever posted confidential information about the company or its customers on social networking sites or blogs, triggering negative media coverage, a drop in stock valuation, a regulatory audit, or other negative consequences?

    ☐ Yes     ☐ No     ☐ Don't Know

53. Has compromised customer financial data (Social Security numbers, credit card numbers, debit card numbers, financial account numbers) ever put your organization at risk of Gramm-Leach-Bliley (GLBA) violations?

    ☐ Yes     ☐ No     ☐ Don't Know

54. Has HIPAA-protected electronic protected health information (related to patients' health status, medical care, treatment plans, and payment issues) ever been exposed—accidentally or intentionally—to unauthorized third parties?

    ☐ Yes     ☐ No     ☐ Don't Know

55. Have cybercriminals ever launched phishing attacks against your organization's IT system?

    ☐ Yes     ☐ No     ☐ Don't Know

56. Are you familiar and compliant with the data security breach notification laws of every state in which you operate facilities, have customers, or do business?

    ☐ Yes     ☐ No     ☐ Don't Know

57. Are you familiar with the state encryption laws of every state in which you operate facilities, have customers, or do business?

    ☐ Yes     ☐ No     ☐ Don't Know

58. Does your technology support roaming and remote workers, safeguarding your systems, sites, and secrets regardless of an employee's geographic location?

    ☐ Yes     ☐ No     ☐ Don't Know

## Mobile Device Risks and Compliance

59. Does your organization provide employees with mobile devices of any kind (smartphones, BlackBerries, iPhones, cell phones, tablets, iPads)?

    ☐ Yes   ☐ No   ☐ Don't Know

60. Are employees permitted to use company-provided smartphones or other company-owned mobile devices for personal reasons?

    ☐ Yes   ☐ No   ☐ Don't Know

61. Are employees allowed to use personal smartphones or other privately owned mobile devices to create, post, access, transmit, or download company or customer data?

    ☐ Yes   ☐ No   ☐ Don't Know

62. Are employees allowed to access the corporate email system via personal smartphones or privately owned mobile devices?

    ☐ Yes   ☐ No   ☐ Don't Know

63. Do employees use text messaging for internal communication with coworkers or for external business communication with customers, prospects, suppliers, and other business audiences?

    ☐ Yes   ☐ No   ☐ Don't Know

64. Has an employee-driver ever caused a traffic accident or hit a pedestrian while texting, talking, blogging, posting, social networking, surfing, emailing, or otherwise engaged in distracting behavior while driving?

    ☐ Yes   ☐ No   ☐ Don't Know

65. Has the organization ever battled a lawsuit triggered by a distracted employee-driver?

    ☐ Yes   ☐ No   ☐ Don't Know

66. Does the company remotely delete business data from employees' personal smartphones in the event that phones are lost or stolen, or when employees leave the company for any reason?

    ☐ Yes   ☐ No   ☐ Don't Know

67. Does the company prohibit employees from talking, texting, blogging, posting, social networking, web surfing, emailing, or otherwise using mobile phones to communicate, converse, or collaborate while driving?

☐ Yes    ☐ No    ☐ Don't Know

68. Do your employees engage in mobile blogging for business or personal reasons?

☐ Yes    ☐ No    ☐ Don't Know

**Personal Use**

69. Do employees ever use their own personal social networking accounts, public sites, or external blogs to comment on your business, employees, executives, customers, products, services, or other company matters?

☐ Yes    ☐ No    ☐ Don't Know

70. Have employees ever used their own personal social networking accounts, public sites, or external blogs to gossip, whine, or complain about your business, employees, executives, customers, products, services, or other company matters?

☐ Yes    ☐ No    ☐ Don't Know

71. On their own time and using their own computer resources, have employees ever—accidentally or intentionally—leaked confidential company data or private consumer information that has triggered a regulatory investigation, sparked a lawsuit, damaged the organization's reputation, or otherwise harmed the company?

☐ Yes    ☐ No    ☐ Don't Know

72. Do you monitor employees' personal blogs?

☐ Yes    ☐ No    ☐ Don't Know

73. Do you monitor employees' personal social networking presence and activity?

☐ Yes    ☐ No    ☐ Don't Know

**Business Use**

74. Does your organization use public social media sites (Facebook, Twitter, YouTube, LinkedIn, and so on) to communicate, collaborate, and converse with customers, prospects, vendors, decision makers, shareholders, the media, business partners, and other important audiences?

    ☐ Yes    ☐ No    ☐ Don't Know

75. Does your organization use enterprise-grade social media software, in-house wikis, and internal blogs for knowledge sharing, brainstorming, communication, and collaboration among employees, executives, suppliers, business partners, or other authorized parties?

    ☐ Yes    ☐ No    ☐ Don't Know

76. Do you maintain a business blog(s)?

    ☐ Yes    ☐ No    ☐ Don't Know

77. Do you provide employees access to instant messaging (IM) for internal chat with colleagues?

    ☐ Yes    ☐ No    ☐ Don't Know

78. Do you provide employees access to public instant messaging (IM) for external chat with customers, prospects, and other outsiders?

    ☐ Yes    ☐ No    ☐ Don't Know

79. What type of IM tool(s) do your employees use during the workday? (Check all that apply.)

    ☐ Company-owned enterprise IM system

    ☐ Free IM accessed via the public web

80. Does your organization use technology (URL blocks) to prevent employees from accessing off-limits websites?

    ☐ Yes    ☐ No    ☐ Don't Know

81. If yes, what type of sites does your organization block? (Check all that apply.)

    ☐ Social networking sites

    ☐ External blogs

- ☐ "Adult" sites (sexual, pornographic, or romantic content)
- ☐ Game sites
- ☐ News sites
- ☐ Shopping or auction sites
- ☐ Entertainment sites
- ☐ Sports sites
- ☐ Gambling sites
- ☐ Illegal or otherwise inappropriate or offensive sites

### Acceptable Use Policies (AUPs)

82. What type of acceptable use policies (AUPs) does your organization currently have in place? (Check all that apply.)

- ☐ Social media policy (governing business use and content)
- ☐ Social media policy (governing personal use and content)
- ☐ Blog policy (governing business use and content)
- ☐ Blog policy (governing personal use and content)
- ☐ Business record retention policy
- ☐ Email policy (governing business use and content)
- ☐ Email policy (governing personal use and content)
- ☐ Internet policy (governing business use and content)
- ☐ Internet policy (governing personal use and content)
- ☐ Instant messenger (IM) policy (governing business use and content)
- ☐ Instant messenger (IM) policy (governing personal use and content)
- ☐ Text messaging policy (governing business use and content)
- ☐ Text messaging policy (governing personal use and content)
- ☐ Smartphone/cell phone policy (governing business use and content)

☐ Smartphone/cell phone policy (governing personal use and content)

☐ Mobile device policy (governing business use and content)

☐ Mobile device policy (governing personal use and content)

83. Have all of your AUPs been reviewed and updated as necessary within the past 12 months?
☐ Yes      ☐ No      ☐ Don't Know

84. Are your AUPs easy to ready, understand, and adhere to?
☐ Yes      ☐ No      ☐ Don't Know

85. How do you distribute AUPs to employees? (Check all that apply.)
☐ Formal employee training programs
☐ Employee handbook
☐ Company Intranet
☐ Email
☐ Online policy portal

86. Do you conduct mandatory employee training related to each AUP your company has developed and distributed to employees?
☐ Yes      ☐ No      ☐ Don't Know

87. Do you clearly date each new or revised AUP?
☐ Yes      ☐ No      ☐ Don't Know

88. Do you take old AUPs out of circulation when new AUPs are introduced?
☐ Yes      ☐ No      ☐ Don't Know

89. In the event of a lawsuit, are you confident that your organization could demonstrate to the court that it has established a best-practices-based AUP program that combines effective policies, supported by comprehensive employee education, and enforced by best-in-class technology tools?
☐ Yes      ☐ No      ☐ Don't Know

**SAMPLE SOCIAL MEDIA POLICY AUDIT QUESTIONNAIRE FOR EMPLOYEES**

1. How familiar are you with your employer's acceptable use policies (AUPs)? Please identify all of the policies that you are familiar with. (Check all that apply.)

   ☐ Social media policy (governing business use and content)

   ☐ Social media policy (governing personal use and content)

   ☐ Blog policy (governing business use and content)

   ☐ Blog policy (governing personal use and content)

   ☐ Business record retention policy

   ☐ Email policy (governing business use and content)

   ☐ Email policy (governing personal use and content)

   ☐ Internet policy (governing business use and content)

   ☐ Internet policy (governing personal use and content)

   ☐ Instant messenger (IM) policy (governing business use and content)

   ☐ Instant messenger (IM) policy (governing personal use and content)

   ☐ Text messaging policy (governing business use and content)

   ☐ Text messaging policy (governing personal use and content)

   ☐ Smartphone/cell phone policy (governing business use and content)

   ☐ Smartphone/cell phone policy (governing personal use and content)

   ☐ Mobile device policy (governing business use and content)

   ☐ Mobile device policy (governing personal use and content)

2. On average, how much personal use of the corporate email system do you engage in during the workday (emailing for personal, nonbusiness reasons)?

☐ 0 to 30 minutes

☐ 30 minutes to 2 hours

☐ 2 hours to 4 hours

☐ 4-plus hours

3. On average, how much personal use of the corporate Internet system do you engage in daily (web surfing, social networking, or blogging for personal, nonbusiness reasons)?

☐ 0 to 30 minutes

☐ 30 minutes to 2 hours

☐ 2 hours to 4 hours

☐ 4-plus hours

4. On average, how much personal use of company-provided mobile devices (smartphones, cell phones, tablets) do you engage in daily (talking, texting, web surfing, social networking, blogging, or emailing for personal, nonbusiness reasons)?

☐ 0 to 30 minutes

☐ 30 minutes to 2 hours

☐ 2 hours to 4 hours

☐ 4-plus hours

5. Do you ever use your own personal mobile devices (smartphone, cell phone, tablet) to engage in personal, nonbusiness-related talking, texting, web surfing, social networking, blogging, or emailing during the workday?

☐ Yes     ☐ No     ☐ Don't Know

6. Do you know what an "electronic business record" is?

☐ Yes     ☐ No     ☐ Don't Know

7. Do you know the difference between business-critical email that must be retained for legal and regulatory purposes (business record email) versus personal or otherwise insignificant messages that may be deleted and purged from the system?
   ☐ Yes        ☐ No        ☐ Don't Know

8. Have you ever used the company computer system to create, access, post, forward, view, download, upload, transmit, copy, or print pornographic, obscene, sexually oriented, or otherwise offensive content?
   ☐ Yes        ☐ No        ☐ Don't Know

9. Have you ever used the company computer system to access, view, transmit, or post confidential customer data (credit card numbers, debit card account numbers, Social Security numbers, bank account numbers, and so forth)?
   ☐ Yes        ☐ No        ☐ Don't Know

10. Have you ever used the company computer system to access, view, transmit, post, copy, print, or save electronic protected health information related to patients' health status, medical care, treatment plans, and payment issues, in violation of HIPAA regulations?
    ☐ Yes        ☐ No        ☐ Don't Know

11. Have you ever intentionally or accidentally violated the organization's email policy?
    ☐ Yes        ☐ No        ☐ Don't Know

12. Have you ever intentionally or accidentally violated the organization's Internet policy?
    ☐ Yes        ☐ No        ☐ Don't Know

13. Have you ever intentionally or accidentally violated the organization's social media policy?
    ☐ Yes        ☐ No        ☐ Don't Know

14. Have you ever intentionally or accidentally violated the organization's cell phone/smartphone/mobile device policy?
    ☐ Yes        ☐ No        ☐ Don't Know

15. Have you ever received formal training that focused on any of the company's acceptable use policies?

☐ Yes   ☐ No   ☐ Don't Know

16. If yes, please identify the acceptable use policies for which you have received formal training. (Check all that apply.)

☐ Social media policy (governing business use and content)

☐ Social media policy (governing personal use and content)

☐ Blog policy (governing business use and content)

☐ Blog policy (governing personal use and content)

☐ Business record retention policy

☐ Email policy (governing business use and content)

☐ Email policy (governing personal use and content)

☐ Internet policy (governing business use and content)

☐ Internet policy (governing personal use and content)

☐ Instant messenger (IM) policy (governing business use and content)

☐ Instant messenger (IM) policy (governing personal use and content)

☐ Text messaging policy (governing business use and content)

☐ Text messaging policy (governing personal use and content)

☐ Smartphone/cell phone policy (governing business use and content)

☐ Smartphone/cell phone policy (governing personal use and content)

☐ Mobile device policy (governing business use and content)

☐ Mobile device policy (governing personal use and content)

17. Have you ever received a warning from management or been disciplined for violating any of the company's acceptable use policies?

    ☐  Yes      ☐  No      ☐  Don't Know

18. If yes, please identify the acceptable use policy you violated. (Check all that apply.)

    ☐  Social media policy (governing business use and content)

    ☐  Social media policy (governing personal use and content)

    ☐  Blog policy (governing business use and content)

    ☐  Blog policy (governing personal use and content)

    ☐  Business record retention policy

    ☐  Email policy (governing business use and content)

    ☐  Email policy (governing personal use and content)

    ☐  Internet policy (governing business use and content)

    ☐  Internet policy (governing personal use and content)

    ☐  Instant messenger (IM) policy (governing business use and content)

    ☐  Instant messenger (IM) policy (governing personal use and content)

    ☐  Text messaging policy (governing business use and content)

    ☐  Text messaging policy (governing personal use and content)

    ☐  Smartphone/cell phone policy (governing business use and content)

    ☐  Smartphone/cell phone policy (governing personal use and content)

    ☐  Mobile device policy (governing business use and content)

    ☐  Mobile device policy (governing personal use and content)

19. Have you been notified of the company's computer monitoring policy and procedures?

☐ Yes    ☐ No    ☐ Don't Know

20. Does the company have the right to terminate employees for personal blog posts, personal Facebook content, personal tweets, personal YouTube videos, or any other personal content that is created and posted on the employee's own personal time, in the employee's own home, using the employee's private accounts and personal tools?

☐ Yes    ☐ No    ☐ Don't Know

## PUTTING YOUR SOCIAL MEDIA AUDIT RESULTS TO WORK

Based on the findings of your comprehensive social media policy audit, you now are ready to update old rules and policies and, as necessary, create new AUPs. In order to maximize users' understanding of the rules and compliance with your policies, you should establish one free-standing policy per technology tool. That means one policy for social media, a separate policy for mobile devices, another policy for email, and the list goes on and on.

Once new policies are written (or old AUPs are updated), it's time for a formal policy review by your legal counsel. No matter how well written or effective you consider your social media policy and other AUPs to be, do not put them into circulation until they have undergone a thorough legal review to ensure that all applicable federal, state, local, and international laws are addressed, all industry and government regulations are covered, all corporate responsibilities are met, and all individual rights are protected.

Following your legal review of policies, be sure to date each new or revised policy. Collect and destroy all but one file copy of all old and out-of-date acceptable use policies. Distribute one copy of the new social media policy and other revised or new AUPs to every employee at the conclusion of mandatory policy training. See Chapter Twelve for best practices–based advice on using comprehensive and continuing employee education to help enforce social media policy and other company rules.

Because technology in general and social media in particular continue to evolve, you should repeat your comprehensive social media policy audit and other acceptable use policy audits annually, updating and creating new policies as necessary based on the results of your annual reviews of risks, rules, laws, regulations, use, content, policies, and procedures.

## SOCIAL MEDIA BEST PRACTICES: POLICY AUDITS

1. Before committing your organization's formal social media policy to writing, conduct a comprehensive review all of the social networking–related risks and challenges, laws and regulations, opportunities, and benefits facing your business and employees, customers, prospects, and other audiences with whom you currently communicate—or hope to reach—via public social networking sites, enterprise-grade social networking solutions, mobile devices, and other related tools and technologies.

2. Create two separate social media policy audit questionnaires: one for managers, supervisors, and executives; the other for staff.

3. To help generate honest responses and ensure full participation by users, conduct your employee audit anonymously. Make it clear to employees that they are free to answer all questions truthfully and without fear of reprisal from management.

4. Use the results of your social media policy audit to update old policies and, as necessary, create new AUPs.

5. Best practices call for the creation of one freestanding policy for each electronic business communication tool. In other words, draft one social media policy, a separate email policy, another policy for the Internet, and so on.

6. Assign an experienced legal expert the task of reviewing your social media policy and all other AUPs before distributing them to employees.

7. Collect and destroy all but one file copy of any old, outdated policy that you are replacing with a new, updated version. Be sure to date each version of every AUP that you put into circulation.

8. Audit and, as necessary, revise social media policy and other AUPs annually.

# WRITING EFFECTIVE SOCIAL MEDIA POLICIES

## 10

Although online tools and technologies will continue to evolve, one fact of strategic electronic compliance management will never change. Best practices always have—and always will—call for the establishment and enforcement of well-written acceptable use policies (AUPs) designed to maximize compliance with legal, regulatory, security, and organizational rules—while minimizing risks to business and individual users.

Regardless of your organization's industry, size, or status as a public or private, regulated or unregulated entity, you must impose AUPs governing all forms of electronic business communication, including social networking and web surfing, blogging and mobile blogging, photo sharing and video sharing, email messaging and instant messaging, and texting and talking via smartphones, tablet computers, and other mobile devices.

# TWENTY-FIRST-CENTURY TOOLS REQUIRE TWENTY-FIRST-CENTURY RULES

In general, effective AUPs should incorporate formal rules governing business and personal use, language and content, and the retention and management of business records. More specifically, use the results of your social media policy audit (see Chapter Nine) to create customized social media policies, designed to help manage the unique risks and requirements of your particular organization and its employees.

## *Our relationships with technology are evolving*

As technology has evolved, so too has the business community's relationship with it. Not long ago, for example, it was common for organizations to impose across-the-board bans on personal, nonbusiness-related web surfing, as well as the use of private email accounts, employee-owned cell phones, and other personal technology tools and accounts in the workplace.

Using policy and technology to ban and block personal accounts, private use, and employee-owned mobile devices is no longer the most appropriate course of action for many organizations. With the exception of the financial services industry and other heavily regulated businesses that must strictly control online access and use, content and records for legal, regulatory, and security reasons, it simply is not realistic in the twenty-first century to prohibit all access to all private accounts and all personal technology tools during the workday.

Employees—particularly younger employees who have more or less grown up online—expect ready access to all forms of electronic communication, including social media, blogs, and other web 2.0 applications dedicated to the creation, communication, and exchange of user-generated content. Impose a strict ban on personal tweeting and texting, blogging and posting, video sharing and photo sharing, and you're likely to find some of your most valuable workers seeking employment elsewhere. The cost of replacing experienced staff with untrained employees can be staggering, even in a tight economy with high unemployment.

When it comes to the development and implementation of social media policies and other web 2.0 AUPs, the goal is to marry your employees' desire to converse and collaborate with your organization's need to comply with legal, regulatory, and business guidelines. In other words, establish and enforce twenty-first-century rules to govern employees' use of twenty-first-century tools.

## PERSONAL USE DEMANDS CLEAR AND SPECIFIC RULES

Though you may not want to outlaw all personal access, use, and content, best practices nonetheless call for the adoption of formal rules governing the exact amount and specific type of personal use employees may engage in during working hours. When it comes to personal use of the organization's social networking sites, business blogs, Internet system, email system, and other company-owned systems and sites, accounts, and devices, you must draft clear and specific rules that are not open to interpretation by individual employees.

It is not enough, in other words, to say that employees are allowed a "limited amount of appropriate personal use of social media during working hours." To some employees, on the one hand, "appropriate personal use" may mean eight hours a day spent conversing with "friends" on Facebook, updating followers on Twitter, uploading (potentially embarrassing) family photos to Flickr, or viewing entertaining (and possibly inappropriate) YouTube videos.

To the company's CEO, on the other hand, "appropriate personal use" may mean 15 minutes of "essential" personal communication with family members, child care providers, physicians, or other approved parties before and after regular business hours, during the lunch hour, and in the course of established work breaks.

**RECOMMENDED BEST PRACTICE**

Use your organization's social media policy (and other AUPs) to spell out exactly how much personal social networking, posting, tweeting, blogging, surfing, communicating, conversing, and collaborating employees may engage in, with whom, under what circumstances, for how long, and during what periods of the workday.

Also, be sure to remind employees that although the organization's social media policy does allow for some personal networking, all use of the organization's computer system is monitored in the ordinary course of business. Consequently, employees' personal Facebook posts, private tweets, non-business-related blog comments, and other online content will be monitored, may be retained, and might be archived alongside the organization's legitimate, business-related electronic business records. In the event of a lawsuit, all electronically stored information, including personal posts and private photos, is likely to be subpoenaed as evidence, which the company is obligated to turn over to the court. The knowledge that lawyers, judges, juries, expert witnesses, forensic experts, and the media could potentially read their personal social networking conversations and view their private photo files is likely to motivate many employees to toe the line when online.

## What constitutes effective personal use rules?

Best practices call for the creation of social media policies that provide employees with clear and specific rules governing their online behavior, content, and use. In order to create truly effective social media policies, you must focus on—and address—every potential risk facing the organization.

Consider, for example, the following personal use policy and rules. These detailed and specific rules, which are part of an even more comprehensive social media policy, leave employees with absolutely no question about or confusion over the company's stance on personal social networking. These guidelines make clear what type of personal social media use is permitted—and what sort of online behavior, content, and activity is prohibited.

## SAMPLE PERSONAL USE POLICY AND RULES

During the workday, and strictly in accordance with the rules detailed below, the company allows employees to access both external, public social media sites (including Facebook, Twitter, YouTube, and blogs), as well as our own internal, private social networking sites (including Yammer and Socialtext). The company makes private (internal) and public (external) social media access available in order to facilitate business-specific conversations and business-related collaboration with business audiences for business reasons.

Compliance with the company's social media policy and personal use rules is mandatory, not an option. When engaged in social networking (at the office, in your home, on the road for business, or at a third-party location, such as a vendor's office), employees are required to adhere to the following social media–related personal use rules:

1. During working hours, employees are prohibited from using any company-owned computer resources—including company systems, accounts, sites, or devices (desktops, laptops, smartphones, or mobile devices)—to engage in any form of personal, non-business-related social networking.

2. Using your own personal smartphones or other mobile devices and your own private accounts, employees may use the company's Internet system to access public, external social media sites and engage in strictly personal, non-business-related communication during the workday.

3. Whether using company computer resources or your own personal accounts, sites, and devices, personal social networking is limited to a maximum of 15 minutes a day

during regular, otherwise productive business hours. In addition to those 15 minutes, employees also may engage in personal social networking (in accordance with the rules set forth in this document) during lunch breaks and other authorized break times.

4.  All business-related social media and blog content must be created, transmitted, posted, published, acquired, accessed, uploaded, downloaded, copied, printed, or stored via the company's computer system, using company accounts and company-provided devices including but not limited to desktops, laptops, tablets, and other mobile devices.

5.  In other words, employees are prohibited from using personal accounts, personal sites, or private devices to create, transmit, post, publish, acquire, access, upload, download, copy, print, or store business-related content of any kind including but not limited to customers' personal, non-business-related data; confidential company information; company financials; internal email and other in-house documents; or any other electronic content that concerns the organization or rises to the level of a business record.

6.  Whether using company resources or your own personal accounts, sites, and devices to engage in social networking or blogging for business or personal reasons, employees must adhere fully to the company's content and language rules, ethics guidelines, code of conduct, harassment and discrimination policy, social media policy, mobile device policy, confidentiality rules, and all other employment policies, codes, rules, and guidelines.

7.  Employees' personal (and business) social media use, content, and behavior must at all times be compliant with all applicable laws and regulatory rules governing our company and industry.

8.  Failure to comply with the company's personal use policy and rules (or any other company rules or policies) may result in disciplinary action, up to and including termination.

## Personal use rules apply to personal tools, too

To increase employee compliance (and reduce the likelihood of content-related risks), use your organization's social media policy and training program to make clear the fact that employees must adhere to personal use rules, social media policy, and all other AUPs and employment rules, guidelines, and codes 24 hours a day, seven days a week, 365 days a year.

Explain that a policy is a policy, and rules are rules. Emphasize the fact that compliance with rules and policies is mandatory, regardless of whether employees are at work using corporate resources, at home using their own personal accounts and devices, or on the road using resources provided by hotels, airports, suppliers, customers, or any other entity.

## Banning and blocking sites is a growing challenge

In addition to spelling out how much personal social networking employees may engage in, also use your social media policy to clarify what type of personal, non-business-related social networking sites, blogs, or other external websites employees may—and may not—visit during the workday, via the company system and resources as well as their own devices and accounts.

You might, for example, allow employees to read and comment on authorized external blogs, follow friends on Facebook, view industry-related YouTube videos, conduct online banking, or visit Internet news sites. On the other hand, you may want to ban visits to and participation on "controversial" websites that are related to politics or religion, for example. And you definitely want to prohibit workday access to sites that are in any way inappropriate (pornography), illegal (gambling), or otherwise offensive (sites that promote violence, hatred, discrimination, harassment, or bullying, for example).

If your organization is regulated, you may want to ban access to public social networking sites in order to decrease the likelihood of confidential company, customer, or patient information being posted in violation of SEC, FINRA, HIPAA, or other regulatory guidelines.

If it's been a while since your organization established a list of sites that are "banned and blocked" based on general content or specific URL, now is the time to revisit the issue. Banning and blocking websites today can be a complex and time-consuming task. The web is more crowded than ever, thanks to blogs, social networking sites, web 2.0, the shift toward online news, the introduction of e-books, the acceptance of online banking and commerce, and the seemingly non-stop growth of electronic content.

## Beware video snacking

Web content providers who track and cater to audience interests and needs add to the challenge for employers. Mindful that workers' Internet usage increases during the lunch hour, many content producers create short online programs, known as "video snacks," that employees can tune into via their own smartphones and tablets, or the organization's desktops and laptops, at midday. ComedyCentral .com and PoliticalLunch.com are two examples of high-profile sites that cater to workers' desire for lunchtime entertainment and information by programming abbreviated shows and short webcasts at noon. In addition, video snackers can turn to YouTube and video blogs, or vlogs, to access free video content. Proof of the popularity of video snacking—online advertisers charge higher rates for the ads that accompany video snacks.[1]

Not surprisingly, video snacking opens the organization to possible risks, including lost productivity (when video snackers stretch noon lunch breaks into mid-afternoon), bandwidth waste (as employees download large videos that are unrelated to business), and security breaches (thanks to viruses, spyware, and malicious intruders who enter your system through infected content).

As part of your organization's social media policy audit (see Chapter Nine), be sure to investigate video snacking. Determine whether or not employees are using company (or personal) resources to video snack. Ascertain what sites they are snacking on, how often, and for how long. Armed with that information, you can use policy to spell out video snacking guidelines. Or, you may decide to ban video snacking altogether.

Once you have researched and established your company's list of outlawed sites (specific URLs and specific site categories), you'll want to use policy, supported by training and technology, including URL blocks, to help enforce employee compliance with the rules.

## WHAT CONSTITUTES EFFECTIVE WRITTEN POLICY?

Before you start writing social media policy, take a close look at your audience and goals. You also may want to consider how other employers are using policy to help manage social media risks and compliance.

### Consider your audience

Before you start writing social media policy, spend some time thinking about your audience and goals. Traditionally, effective AUPs communicate organizational, legal, and regulatory rules to full-time and part-time employees, executives and board members, independent contractors and consultants, and other internal and external parties working on behalf of your organization.

### Create community guidelines for social media and blogs

In the case of social media, however, you'll need to expand that list to include outside parties who may not be working on behalf of the organization, but who nonetheless are commenting publicly on your business blogs, Facebook page, Twitter account, and other company-hosted public social networking sites.

To that end, employers are advised to create and put into circulation two separate policy documents: (1) social media policy for employees and others working on the company's behalf; and (2) community social networking and blogging guidelines, governing the content posted by third parties on the organization's sites. For more about community guidelines, see Chapters Six and Fourteen.

## Focus on your policy goals

What do you hope to accomplish through your organization's social media policy program? Effective social media policy should provide employees with a clear understanding of what constitutes appropriate, acceptable, and lawful business behavior. Well-written community guidelines should give customers and other outsiders a solid understanding of what type of content, language, and behavior is considered appropriate and welcome, versus that which is deemed offensive and therefore banned.

In addition, clear, comprehensive, strategically written policies and community guidelines will help your organization demonstrate to courts, regulators, employees, applicants, customers, investors, the media, decision makers, and other important audiences that the organization is committed to operating an online business environment that is civil, compliant, and correct. The mere existence of a current, comprehensive, formal policy may provide you with some defense from liability, should you one day find yourself battling a hostile work environment claim, allegations of sexual harassment, or another workplace lawsuit.

## Where do other employers stand?

Increasingly, employers are using formal policies to help control a broad range of potentially costly social media risks. According to the *Electronic Business Communication Policies and Procedures Survey* from American Management Association and The ePolicy Institute, employers in 2009 were using social media policies as follows:

Policy governing the exposure of company secrets, financial data, rumors, or gossip on business-related or personal social media sites: 61 percent.

Policy governing the viewing, downloading, or uploading of videos to video-sharing sites during working hours: 54 percent.

Policy governing the use of personal social media during working hours: 46 percent.

Policy governing the use of words, photos, signage, uniforms, logos, or any other means to identify yourself as a company employee on personal social media sites: 43 percent.

Policy governing discussions about the company on business-related social networking sites: 41 percent.

Policy governing the uploading of business-related photos or videos to personal social media sites: 40 percent.

Policy governing the use of business-related social networking sites during working hours: 32 percent.[2]

## TIPS FOR WRITING EFFECTIVE POLICIES

Your goal as a policy writer is to communicate rules, not to confuse readers. To that end, here are a few proven-effective tips for writing effective social media and acceptable use policies.

### Use clear and specific language

As discussed in depth in Chapter Eleven, effective written policies should incorporate clear and specific language that is not open to interpretation by individual employees. The same rule holds true for written community guidelines for social networking and blogging.

### Include content rules in social media polices and community guidelines

Included among the content rules that you'll want to incorporate into social media policies, community guidelines, and all other AUPs governing any form of electronic business communication are the following:

No violations of regulators' content rules.

No illegal content.

No harassment or discrimination based on race, color, religion, sex, sexual orientation, national origin, age, disability, or any other status protected by law.

No disclosure of confidential company, executive, or employee data.

No exposure of customers' personal financial data to outside parties.

No disclosure of patients' electronic protected health information to third parties.

No rumors, gossip, or defamatory comments—about anyone.

No whining or complaining about the company, customers, or business.

No external distribution of internal email messages or other eyes-only data.

No disclosure of company financials to outside parties.

No "funny" jokes, cartoons, videos, photos, files, or art.

No obscene, off-color, pornographic, sexually charged, or otherwise inappropriate and offensive language, art, or other content.

No netiquette (electronic etiquette) breaches.

### Define key concepts and terms

Don't assume that all of your employees and external community members are familiar with or understand all of the key concepts and terms included in the company's social media policy or community guidelines for blogging and social networking. If you use potentially confusing words or terms in written policies or guidelines, be sure to provide a definition, either within the text itself or as part of a glossary of terms at the end of the document. To help ensure comprehension and compliance, consider defining important terms including "social networking," "web 2.0," "blogging," "mobile blogging," "photo sharing," "video sharing," "mobile device," "confidential data," "intellectual property," "trade secret," "electronic protected health information," "electronic business record," "private consumer data," "record retention," and the list goes on and on.

Remember, just because you, the policy writer, are familiar with legal, regulatory, and technology terms, that does not mean all of your employees or community members are equally well informed. Increase comprehension and compliance by giving internal users and external parties the tools they need in order to understand—and act upon—written rules.

## Write policies and guidelines in plain English

To help mitigate organizational risks, maximize employee compliance with rules, and minimize the likelihood of third parties posting objectionable comments, be sure to write social media policies and community guidelines in plain English. No legal gobbledygook. No confusing technology terms. No acronyms or abbreviations that may not be understood by all employees or third-party commenters.

As a policy writer, you must focus on your reader, not yourself. Remember, the purpose of social media policy is to establish rules and enforce compliance. The goal of community guidelines is to encourage civility. To those ends, policies and guidelines must communicate with users—not confuse them.

## Adhere to the ABCs of effective policy writing

### A is for accuracy

As the writer of employment policies and community guidelines, your organization relies on you to do your legal and regulatory homework, get your facts straight, and present accurate, reliable, trustworthy information and rules. Accuracy also requires you to adhere to the rules of grammar, punctuation, and style. Compliance management rides on the information you present in written policies and guidelines, so be sure you always get everything right.

### B is for brevity

Unless you want employees' eyes to glaze over, do not produce one massive policy document that covers, for example, the use of all electronic business communication tools and technologies, including social media, blogs, wikis, web 2.0, email, instant messenger, text messaging, software, smartphones, BlackBerries, cell phones, tablets, and so forth.

Instead, you will increase the odds of having employees read, remember, and adhere to your written rules and policies by writing and distributing separate, brief policy documents covering the use of each individual business communication tool (or closely related technologies). For example, you might produce one policy for social networking and blogging, a separate policy for mobile devices, and another freestanding policy for email use and content. Keep each policy short, simple, and straight to the point. Period.

### C is for clarity

Clarity is essential to communication and compliance success. Your job as a policy writer is to present employee rules and community guidelines in a clear and compelling manner. You must make it easy for employee-posters and reader-commenters to read through policies from beginning to end, and then take appropriate action: comply with the rules.

You simply cannot expect employees or visitors to your social networking sites or blogs to take time to decipher illogical sentences and paragraphs, struggle through policies or guidelines that are riddled with grammar goofs and spelling errors, or adhere to policies and procedures that put them to sleep.

## *Use effective design to enhance readability*

As stated earlier, policies and guidelines must communicate with users, not confuse them. To that end, policy writers should consider incorporating a few design tricks that are guaranteed to enhance the readability of social media policies, community guidelines, and all other employment rules and codes of conduct.

1. Use white space or blank space to enhance policy readability and add visual impact.
2. Keep policies brief. A four-page, double-spaced policy that is accessible and easy to read is considerably less intimidating than

a two-page, single-spaced policy that is crammed full of dense information written in a tiny typeface.

3. Rely on boldface headlines and subheads to emphasize important copy points.

4. Communicate rules and other important policy information in small, bite-size chunks.

5. Use bulleted or numbered lists to enhance readability.

6. If, for some reason, you must write a lengthy policy document, then be sure to include a table of contents to help users locate information quickly when questions or concerns arise.

7. Include a glossary of social media, legal, regulatory, technology, business, or other terms to help eliminate confusion, enhance awareness, and support compliance.

8. Include contact information for policy team members. Let employees know who to contact when questions related to social media use, content, and policy arise.

## SUPPORT WRITTEN POLICY WITH EMPLOYEE— AND COMMUNITY—EDUCATION

No matter how well written your social media policy may be, it serves no purpose unless your users fully understand and comply with it. To that end, best practices call for a comprehensive, company-wide training program to help introduce social media risks, rules, policies, and procedures to employees.

### Support policy with employee education

Now that you have completed your policy audit (see Chapter Nine) and written or revised your organization's social media policy, it's time to get to work educating users about social media risks, policy, and compliance. Here are a few tips for effective policy training. For a detailed discussion about best practices–based training programs and procedures, see Chapter Twelve.

1. Before distributing social media policy to employees in the course of formal training, be sure to have the organization's legal counsel review and sign off on your policy document. The purpose of a legal review is to ensure that your social media policy addresses and supports compliance with the laws of every jurisdiction in which you operate or litigate lawsuits, as well as all industry and government regulations impacting your business.

   Policy that has been reviewed and approved by legal counsel will help put your organization on firmer legal ground, should you one day find yourself battling a workplace lawsuit or facing a regulatory investigation.

2. You cannot expect an untrained workforce to be a compliant workforce. Educate all employees, from entry-level staff to C-level executives, about the organization's social media policy and compliance management program. Cover social media risks, rules, records, regulations, policy, and procedures.

3. In the eyes of the law, you may be held liable for the actions of any individual who works on behalf of your company. In addition to training full-time and part-time employees, managers, and executives about your social media policy and compliance management program, be sure to educate your board of directors, business consultants, freelancers, independent contractors, interns, and anyone else who provides time and talent, information and energy, or products and services to benefit your organization.

4. In the course of training, make clear the fact that policy compliance is mandatory, not an option.

5. Approach policy training as an ongoing, continuing education program, not a one-time event.

6. Best practices call for live, onsite training, giving users the opportunity to ask questions and discuss issues and challenges with an experienced professional trainer. Alternatively, you may conduct social media policy training via live webcasts or interactive online training modules.

7. Use training to review all policy-related risks (legal, regulatory, security, productivity, public relations, career, and so on) facing individual users and the organization as a whole.

8. Remind users that the easiest way to control social media risks is to control content. In other words, be mindful of what you say, write, or capture on film.

9. Stress the fact that a policy is a policy. Make sure users understand that the organization's social media policy and all other employment policies, guidelines, rules, and codes apply 24 hours a day, seven days a week, 365 days a year—at work, home, or elsewhere.

10. Educate employees about trade secrets and confidential data. Explain the legal and regulatory risks facing the company if customers' financial data or patients' electronic protected health information is breached, or company secrets are revealed.

11. Review monitoring policies and procedures. Discuss privacy expectations and realities.

12. Define "electronic business record" and share the organization's record retention policy and procedures.

13. Define "personal use" and review the organization's personal use rules.

14. Provide every employee with a hard copy of the social media policy.

15. Train until you are certain that every employee understands the company's social media policy and is clear on what constitutes appropriate (and inappropriate) use, content, and behavior.

16. Require all employees to sign and date acknowledgment forms attesting that they understand your social media policy and will adhere to it or face the consequences, up to and including their termination.

### Support community guidelines with visitor education

In addition to educating employees about your social media policy, you'll also want to inform visitors to your social media sites and business blogs about your community guidelines for social networking and blogging.

Consider producing and posting a brief informational video on each of your social media and blog sites. Enlist the organization's CEO, CIO, chief compliance officer, or public relations director to serve as the on-camera spokesperson. Use the 30-second video to explain why you have created community guidelines, how comments are reviewed, and on what basis comments may be rejected. The goal is to produce an appealing video that helps motivate visitors to be responsible and respectful members of your online community.

Here's a sample script: "We value the comments of our online community, and we hope you decide to join us. To help ensure a polite and productive exchange of opinions and information, we have developed community guidelines for social media and blogs. Please click on the community guidelines link at the bottom of your screen to review our guidelines and register as a member of our online community. Once registered, you are welcome to post comments on this site, in accordance with our published guidelines. Thank you for taking time to join our online community. We look forward to reading your opinions and comments."

## SOCIAL MEDIA BEST PRACTICES: WRITING EFFECTIVE POLICY

1. The ever-expanding universe of technology tools facilitates users' ability to quickly and conveniently transmit business-critical data and stay connected with colleagues and customers around the globe. That's the good news. The bad news: new and emerging technologies dramatically increase employers' exposure to potentially costly and protracted risks, including workplace lawsuits, regulatory fines, security breaches, and productivity drains, among others.

2. Fortunately, for savvy employers determined to manage technology use and minimize risks, there is a solution. Through the strategic implementation of a comprehensive social media policy, supported

by employee education and technology tools, organizations can successfully manage (and in some cases prevent) legal, regulatory, security, productivity, and public relations risks, while maximizing compliance.

3. In general, social media policies should incorporate formal rules governing business and personal use, language and content, and business record retention. More specifically, use the results of your social media policy audit to create customized social media policies designed to help manage the unique risks and requirements of your particular organization and employees.

4. Using policy and technology to ban and block all personal accounts, sites, and devices is no longer the most appropriate course of action for many organizations. When it comes to social media policies, the goal is to marry employees' desire to converse and collaborate with the organization's need to comply with legal, regulatory, and organizational rules. In other words, establish twenty-first-century rules to govern use of twenty-first-century technologies and tools.

5. In addition to establishing social media policies for employees, employers are advised to publish community guidelines for social media and blogs, governing the content posted by third parties on company-hosted sites.

6. Social media policies should be well written and adhere to the ABCs (accuracy, brevity, clarity) of effective business writing.

7. Support social media policy with formal employee education.

8. Support community blogging and social networking guidelines with a visitor education program that combines an informational video, written rules, and a registration process for third parties seeking to comment on your business sites.

9. Put some teeth in your social media policy. Let users know that policy compliance is mandatory, not an option. Failure to comply with the organization's social media policy could result in the dismissal of employees or the termination of consultants' contracts.

# CONTENT RULES ARE CRITICAL TO COMPLIANCE

11

The rapid-fire adoption of social networking and an overall increase in online activity (business and personal) have ushered in a "new era" of web-related risks, including litigation, regulatory violations, security breaches, and public relations nightmares, among others. In the age of social media, blogs, and other web 2.0 applications, millions of workers worldwide are busy conversing and collaborating with online contacts, followers, and "friends" anytime, anywhere, and about anything.

Consequently, workplace lawsuits, regulatory audits, and bruised brands are no longer restricted to inappropriate email use and unmanaged Internet surfing. Employees today are using smartphones to transmit "sext" messages, including obscene photos and off-color text, to coworkers. Angry workers are using Twitter and blogs to defame customers and malign managers. Resentful ex-employees and poorly trained staff are using YouTube and Facebook to reveal company secrets, gossip about patients, and expose consumer data. Still others are using tablet computers and other mobile devices to transmit and post inappropriate, unlawful, impolite, or otherwise objectionable content on social networking sites—accidentally or intentionally.

## USE CONTENT RULES TO HELP MANAGE COMPLIANCE

As a result of the growing electronic conversation, employers face increased exposure to lawsuits, including hostile work environment claims, sexual harassment and discrimination suits, and defamation claims, among others. In fact, 15 percent of companies surveyed in 2010 named "legal risks" as their primary concern about web 2.0, according to the McAfee report, *Web 2.0: A Complex Balancing Act.*[1]

When employees transmit, post, and publish unlawful, offensive, or otherwise inappropriate content to social media sites—regardless of whether they use apps, the web, corporate email systems, or personal text messaging accounts for their posts—the results can be disastrous for business. Twenty percent of IT decision makers at large U.S. enterprises report that adult, obscene, or potentially offensive content is "common" or "very common" in social media communications and outbound instant messaging from their organizations, according to *Outbound Email and Data Loss Prevention in Today's Enterprise, 2010* from Proofpoint.[2]

Thanks to inappropriate online content, employers also face the increased likelihood of lengthy regulatory investigations and monetary fines stemming from violations of the Gramm-Leach-Bliley Act (GLBA), Health Insurance Portability and Accountability Act (HIPAA), Securities and Exchange Commission (SEC) regulations, Federal Trade Commission (FTC) blogging rules, or other regulatory guidelines designed to protect consumer and business data. See Chapter Four for more information about content risks and compliance requirements facing regulated businesses and industries that are engaged in social networking, blogging, and web 2.0.

When it comes to the management of legal, regulatory, and other electronic risks, best practices call for the implementation of social media policies that incorporate clear content rules governing employees' business and personal use of corporate and private social networking sites and accounts. Use formal content rules to outlaw the creation, posting, transmission, acquisition, accessing, or publishing of any type of content—text, photos, videos, art, or any other written, visual, or spoken content—that could trigger legal claims, serve as smoking-gun evidence of wrongdoing in litigation, violate regulators' content rules, or otherwise create problems for the organization and its employees.

## CONTENT CAN DESTROY CAREERS, COMPANIES, AND CREDIBILITY

When it comes to social networking and blogging, just how important are content rules? Consider these real-life examples of what can go wrong when electronic content and online behavior are left unmanaged.

### *Tweets trip up congressman*

Six-term United States Congressman Anthony Weiner made headlines worldwide in June, 2011, when it was revealed that the married representative from New York's Ninth Congressional District had been using Twitter to send risqué tweets and racy photos of himself—at times posed in nothing more than his underwear, a towel, or his birthday suit—to several women over a period of years.

Relentless news coverage, possible violations of congressional rules and ethics guidelines, and the revelation that Representative Weiner had shot some of the offending photos in the locker room of the congressional gym prompted the Democratic congressional caucus to call for Weiner's resignation, spurred President Barack Obama to say that stepping down might be the right course of action, and finally drove the embattled congressman to resign from office two weeks after his twisted tweets first came to light.

A modern-day cautionary tale, the Twittering congressman literally tweeted away his credibility and congressional career, thanks to inappropriate content and unmanaged online behavior.

## Sexual harassment isn't about being chased around the desk anymore

Social media, mobile devices, and the ability to transmit just about any type of electronic content—anytime, to anyone—have ushered in a "new era" of sexual harassment. In the "old days," sexual harassment claims and hostile work environment allegations often were "he said/she said" events, in which one party accused another of some sort of wrongdoing, which most likely occurred face-to-face and without witnesses.

Thanks to the social web, that no longer is the case. As detailed in Chapter Three, tweets, posts, text messages, email, photo-sharing applications, and YouTube videos all create the electronic equivalent of DNA evidence, which can (and will) be subpoenaed and used to support (or sink) claims of workplace sexual harassment and other forms of bad behavior and unlawful conduct.

Unmanaged electronic content and inappropriate online behavior have contributed to an ever-growing number of sexual harassment suits, hostile work environment claims, and the related fallout including ruined reputations, shattered careers, and negative publicity. Consider, for example, the Florida-based Hooters waitress who filed a sexual harassment claim against the restaurant in 2009, alleging that a manager had used a cell phone to send her explicit "sext" messages and offensive photos.[3] The same year, the director of a county jail in Ohio resigned after he was caught using his personal cell phone to take and transmit inappropriate photos to a female employee, while on duty and in uniform.[4]

The bad news for employers: mobile devices and social media make it easier than ever for rogue employees to engage in offensive or otherwise inappropriate behavior, for which the boss typically is held legally responsible.

The good news for victims of uncivil online behavior: U.S. courts recognize electronically stored information—including text messages, photos, videos, email, blog posts, tweets, profiles, and other content—as discoverable evidence that can be used to help prove allegations of sexual harassment, discrimination, or other types of wrongdoing in the workplace.

## Tweets trigger terminations

Thanks to social media, content-related terminations are becoming increasingly common. In Beverly Hills, California, a waiter found himself out of a job after tweeting unflattering comments about a television actress who first skipped out on her bill, then failed to include a tip when she sent her agent in to pay the tab the next day. When she discovered the waiter's tweets the following month, the actress stopped by the restaurant to settle the $3 tip and complain to management about the waiter's online comments. The waiter was fired, thanks to spiteful 140-character tweets.[5]

With Twitter users sending over 50 million tweets a day, the potential for career-shattering gaffes is unlimited.[6]

## Boundaries broken—and bosses bothered—by bloggers

When bloggers behave badly, business and personal reputations may be ruined, and jobs may be lost. Take the case of the twenty-something staff assistant to a United States senator. The staffer lost her job—and gained international notoriety—when she opted to blog about her active Capitol Hill sex life. The blogger's anonymous posts, which were written to entertain a few close friends and amuse the blogger herself, included detailed information about the blogger's sexual partners, the spanking games they sometimes engaged in, and the cash gifts she sometimes received in exchange for services rendered. When one of her "close friends" shared the X-rated posts with an online gossip site, the blogger's identity was revealed, and she was dismissed from the senator's staff.[7]

When bloggers are terminated (or "dooced" in blog parlance) for inappropriate content, their violations often revolve around inappropriate comments and complaints about colleagues and customers. In Southern California, for example, 27 auto club employees were dismissed after they wrote offensive and harassing blog posts in which club members were criticized and the weight and sexual orientation of coworkers were commented upon.[8] For these bloggers and others like them, there can be no doubt that the long-term pain of unemployment outweighs whatever momentary "pleasure" they may have derived from taking online jabs at colleagues and customers.

### YouTube video vexes city leaders

A citywide uproar was triggered in Columbus, Ohio, when a police officer and her sister produced and posted offensive YouTube videos in which they disparaged Jews, blacks, Cubans, and illegal immigrants. The discovery of the videos prompted a departmental investigation into the officer's conduct. The Anti-Defamation League denounced the videos as anti-Semitic, racist, and hateful. The mayor and city leaders fretted over the negative impact the videos had on the city's reputation. A city of more than 1 million people suffered a potentially significant public relations blow, courtesy of two women armed only with a video camera and a free public forum to share their hateful opinions with anyone willing to listen.[9]

## THINK BEFORE YOU POST OR PUBLISH

The easiest way to control social networking risks is to control content, regardless of whether that content is in written, spoken, photographic, or video form. Before you post or publish your next tweet, blog, comment, photo, or video, consider the potential consequences—to yourself, your employer, your reputation, your family, and your friends. When in doubt about the appropriateness of content, ask yourself the following questions:

1. Would I be embarrassed if I were identified as the blogger behind this anonymous post?
   ☐ Yes   ☐ No

2. Do my online comments have the potential to offend, frighten, embarrass, menace, defame, or otherwise harm another person?
   ☐ Yes   ☐ No

3. Does this post reflect the "real" me? Is this actually how I think and talk? Would I ever say this out loud in a formal business meeting, casual gathering of coworkers, or luncheon with customers?
   ☐ Yes   ☐ No

4. Would I be embarrassed if my parents, children, spouse, friends, neighbors, or boss watched this YouTube video that I produced and star in?
   ☐ Yes   ☐ No

5. Should I take time to cool off before I transmit this intentionally negative and nasty tweet?
   ☐ Yes   ☐ No

6. Is it possible that I have misinterpreted or misunderstood another blogger's post? Is my anger toward this blogger misplaced?
   ☐ Yes   ☐ No

7. Do the comments I have written and published online violate any of my company's employment policies, guidelines, rules, or codes? Am I in violation of the organization's social media policy, smartphone policy, netiquette guidelines, content rules, code of conduct, ethics policy, harassment and discrimination policy, or any other formal guideline?
   ☐ Yes   ☐ No

8. Do the photos I have posted and filed online violate any of my company's employment policies, guidelines, rules, or codes? Am I in violation of the organization's social media policy, smartphone policy, netiquette guidelines, content rules, code of conduct, ethics policy, harassment and discrimination policy, or any other formal guidelines?
   ☐ Yes   ☐ No

9.  Do the videos I have produced and uploaded to YouTube violate any of my company's employment policies, guidelines, rules, or codes? Am I in violation of the organization's social media policy, smartphone policy, netiquette guidelines, content rules, code of conduct, ethics policy, harassment and discrimination policy, or any other formal guideline?
☐ Yes    ☐ No

10. Does my social media or blog content violate any laws? Could my comments be construed by readers, my employer, or the court as hostile, harassing, discriminatory, defamatory, menacing, threatening, bullying, obscene, pornographic, or otherwise unlawful or objectionable?
☐ Yes    ☐ No

11. Would I be upset if my spouse, children, parents, or friends were on the receiving end of a comment like this?
☐ Yes    ☐ No

12. Would I be hurt if a stranger made a statement like this about me?
☐ Yes    ☐ No

13. Could the content posted on my personal blog possibly create problems for me during a future job interview?
☐ Yes    ☐ No

14. Does my online writing, content, language, and style accurately reflect my education, professionalism, and career ambitions?
☐ Yes    ☐ No

15. Will my blogs and comments, tweets and posts help me achieve my career goals?
☐ Yes    ☐ No

16. Could any of the photos I have posted, uploaded, or filed online be viewed as obscene, pornographic, sexually charged, or otherwise offensive or inappropriate?
☐ Yes    ☐ No

17. Could the jokes I have posted online be taken the wrong way by readers? Is there any level on which my "funny" comments might be deemed offensive?
☐ Yes   ☐ No

18. Does my blog content violate copyright law? Do I have the copyright holder's written permission to publish this material online?
☐ Yes   ☐ No

19. Does this post make me look foolish, petty, or unprofessional?
☐ Yes   ☐ No

20. Do I really want my employer to retain and archive this particular post alongside legitimate business records? Would I be humiliated if this content were produced in the course of e-discovery, for lawyers, the court, and the media to read?
☐ Yes   ☐ No

21. Do my online comments diminish the online conversation?
☐ Yes   ☐ No

22. Am I willing to risk my job over this comment?
☐ Yes   ☐ No

If you answered yes to any of these questions, then you would benefit from adhering to the following list of dos, don'ts, and best practices–based social media content rules.

## DOS AND DON'TS TO HELP MANAGE SOCIAL MEDIA CONTENT, BEHAVIOR, AND RISKS

Employers who are eager to manage online behavior and risks should consider incorporating the following list of content-related dos and don'ts into the organization's social media policy (and all other acceptable use policies governing electronic business communication tools and technologies).

## Don'ts

1. Don't violate regulators' content rules.

2. Don't write, post, transmit, access, acquire, file, publish, or otherwise communicate content that could be deemed unlawful. Illegal content includes but is not limited to that which is fraudulent, obscene, harassing, discriminatory, bullying, defamatory, or otherwise prohibited by law or company policy.

3. Don't harass or discriminate against others based on race, color, religion, sex, sexual orientation, national origin, age, disability, or other status protected by U.S. law.

4. Don't disclose confidential company, executive, director, or employee data.

5. Don't expose customers' personal financial data or other private, non-business-related information to outside parties.

6. Don't access patients' electronic protected health information (EPHI) without authorization, and don't expose EPHI to third parties.

7. Don't spread rumors, gossip, or defamatory comments about anyone, within the organization or without.

8. Don't whine or complain about the company, its customers, employees, or business.

9. Don't share internal business information, including company email or other "eyes-only" data intended solely for in-house readers, with external parties.

10. Don't disclose company financials to outside parties. Company financials include but are not limited to information about revenues, earnings, sales, projections, marketing plans, inventories, strategies, share price, stock valuation, quarterly reports, annual reports, mergers, acquisitions, executive salaries, performance bonuses, and severance packages.

11. Don't post, create, transmit, access, acquire, file, upload, download, publish, or otherwise communicate "funny" jokes, cartoons, videos, photos, files, or art. Remember, the joke that strikes you as hilarious may be offensive to someone else.

12. Don't post, create, transmit, access, acquire, file, upload, download, publish, or otherwise communicate obscene, off-color, pornographic, sexually oriented, or otherwise inappropriate and offensive text, language, photographs, illustrations, videos, art, or other content.

13. Don't violate netiquette, or electronic etiquette, guidelines. Social media content should be civil, polite, and business-appropriate.

14. Don't comment on any lawsuits in which the company currently is embroiled, previously has been engaged in, or may become involved in at some future time. Employees are prohibited from discussing, commenting on, or answering questions about legal claims, financial settlements, jury awards, legal strategies, or any other aspects of litigation involving the company. Refer all litigation-related questions or comments that may be posted by third parties on your business or personal blogs or social networking sites to the company's legal department.

15. Don't plagiarize. Create your own original content. Express your own opinions. Share your own expertise. Whenever you use or refer to outside content, be sure to cite the original source and, whenever possible, provide a link to your source.

16. Don't post, copy, transfer, rename, or edit copyright-protected material without written permission from the copyright owner. Employees may not link to copyright-protected content without first receiving permission from the copyright holder. Copyright infringement may result in disciplinary action, up to and including termination, as well as legal action by the copyright holder.

17. Don't expect or assume privacy when using the company's public (external) or private (internal) blogs, social networking sites, web 2.0 applications, or Internet system. The company reserves the right to access and monitor all blog posts, social media content, Internet activity, email transmissions, and other electronic content and records transmitted, posted, or stored on the company's system, as deemed necessary and appropriate.

The company also reserves the right to monitor the public blogosphere and the Internet as a whole, including employees' personal blogs, tweets, YouTube videos, Facebook posts, photos, and other online content that employees may create, post, transmit, or publish on their own time, using their own personal accounts, via their own electronic devices, in their own homes.

18. Remember that any content that is posted on the public web (via Facebook, Twitter, LinkedIn, YouTube, third-party blogs, and so on) is public, not private, communication. Violation of the company's content rules, social media policy, blog policy, mobile device policy, or any other company policy, rule, guideline, or code may result in disciplinary action, up to and including termination, regardless of whether the violation occurs at work using company-owned resources or at home using personal accounts and devices.

## Dos

1. Do adhere to all of the company's employment policies at all times. Whether using company accounts, systems, and devices, or your own personal accounts and tools, bloggers and social networkers are obligated to adhere to all company policies, codes, and guidelines including but not limited to social media policy, mobile device policy, privacy policy, confidentiality policy, computer security policy, media relations policy, investor relations policy, ethics guidelines, corporate code of conduct, content and language rules, and netiquette guidelines.

2. Do focus on your expertise and interests as an online writer. The social web offers employees the chance to share their unique perspectives on what's happening within our organization, around the globe, and within your own lives. This is your opportunity to share your know-how with the world. Do so in a polished and professional manner.

3. Do add value to the online conversation. If you are writing on behalf of the company, please be sure that your content provides value to our customers, prospects, employees, executives, suppliers,

business partners, the general public, and other readers. Try to post content that answers a question, solves a problem, helps people do their jobs, or creates greater awareness and understanding of our company's mission.

4. Do keep confidential company business and proprietary information under wraps. Never reveal company secrets including but not limited to confidential data, company financials, internal email and other in-house documents, intellectual property, customer lists, marketing plans, salary and benefits packages, or company secrets of any kind.

5. Do keep your personal business private. Never share private information that could potentially harm or embarrass your family, friends, or yourself. You never know who may be reading your blog, following your tweets, or viewing your YouTube videos. Be discreet.

6. Do be completely honest. The blogosphere and social media world are attuned to honesty—and dishonesty. If you have a vested interested in a topic, be sure to mention it. If you are writing about our company, identify yourself by name, title, and role within the company.

7. Do bear in mind the fact that employees are responsible for their own business and personal blog and social media content including text, audio, photos, videos, and other images. Fraudulent, obscene, vulgar, abusive, harassing, profane, discriminatory, sexually suggestive, intimidating, misleading, defamatory, bullying, or otherwise offensive, objectionable, inappropriate, or illegal content is prohibited. Jokes, disparaging remarks, and inappropriate comments related to ethnicity, race, color, religion, sex, age, disabilities, physique, sexual orientation, and sexual preference are prohibited by law and company policy.

8. Do adhere to the financial industry's regulatory rules, if applicable. That means no exposure of customers' personal financial data to unauthorized employees or outside parties. Private financial data includes, but is not limited to, credit card numbers, debit card numbers, Social Security numbers, dates of birth, mailing addresses, and so on.

9. Do comply with the health care industry's regulatory rules, if applicable. That means no exposure of patients' electronic protected health information (EPHI) to unauthorized employees or outside parties. EPHI includes patients' health status, medical care, treatment plans, and payment issues. Failure to do so can result in regulatory fines, civil litigation, criminal charges, and jail time.

10. Do adhere to Federal Trade Commission (FTC) "blogging rules," requiring bloggers, tweeters, and other online posters to disclose any material connections between themselves and the products or services they endorse in their posts. You may promote the organization's products and services on your own (or third-party) personal blogs and social sites, but you must disclose your affiliation with the company as part of your online profiles. Failure to comply with FTC endorsement guidelines would violate company policy and could result in regulatory fines of up to $11,000, imposed against you, the individual blogger.

11. Do write as you speak. Be conversational, yet professional. Put a human face on your posts and our company. Your written posts should reflect your normal speaking style and the tone you would use in any business situation—chatting with coworkers or explaining concepts to customers, for example. Short, simple sentences are best. Make an effort to engage your readers by asking questions and initiating thought-provoking, ongoing discussions.

12. Do forward all business-related media inquiries to the company's media relations director. Many reporters turn to blogs and social media for story ideas and news sources. If you are contacted directly by a reporter or news producer, you must first seek permission from the company's media relations director before responding to media inquiries, conducting interviews, providing background material, or otherwise engaging in business-related media relations activities.

13. Do forward all company-related financial inquiries to the investor relations director. That would include questions or requests for information about sales and earnings, mergers and acquisitions,

salaries and benefits, marketing plans and financial projections, or other issues related to the company's financials. If you are contacted directly by a reporter, industry analyst, or investor, you must first seek permission from the company's investor relations director before responding to inquiries, conducting interviews, providing background material, or otherwise engaging in conversations related to company financials.

14. Do bear in mind the fact that all blog posts and social media content written, transmitted, accessed, acquired, published, or stored on the company's system are the property of the organization, and should be considered public information. The company reserves the right to access and monitor all blog and social networking posts, comments, and archives on the company's system as deemed necessary and appropriate. Blog and social media content is public, not private, communication. All posts and comments, including text and images, can be disclosed by the company to law enforcement agencies, courts, regulatory bodies, and other third parties without the prior consent of the employee who created, transmitted, acquired, or posted the information.

   The company also reserves the right to monitor the blogosphere and the Internet as a whole, including personal blogs, tweets, YouTube videos, Facebook pages, and other online content that employees may create and post on their own time, using their own personal accounts, via their own electronic devices.

   Violation of the company's content rules and social media policy may result in disciplinary action, up to and including termination, regardless of whether the violation occurs on a company-hosted account, site, or device, or the employee's own personal blog or social media site.

15. Do adhere to the rules of netiquette, or electronic etiquette, when communicating online. In other words, be polite, polished, and professional. Write, post, and publish content that is 100 percent appropriate, civil, and compliant with all company policies, regulatory rules, and laws.

16. Do post this legal disclaimer on both your business and personal blog profiles: "The opinions and content expressed on this site are my own. They do not necessarily reflect the views of my employer, the company."

## SOCIAL MEDIA BEST PRACTICES: CONTENT MANAGEMENT

1. Remind employees that the easiest way to control social networking risks is to control published content including written text, spoken comments, photos, videos, art, and any other form of online content.

2. Use social media rules and policy to spell out clear and specific content, language, and netiquette rules that are not open to interpretation by individual users. Follow the lead of proactive companies that have already implemented content rules and policies governing the exposure of business secrets, financial data, and rumors on business or personal social media sites (61 percent); the use of YouTube during working hours (54 percent); and the uploading of business-related photos or videos to personal social media sites (40 percent), according to the *2009 Electronic Business Communication Policies and Procedures Survey* from American Management Association and The ePolicy Institute.[10]

3. Do not allow employees to dismiss netiquette, or electronic etiquette, guidelines as frivolous or insignificant. As an employer, part of your job is to ensure that the online business environment is civil, appropriate, and free from harassment or hostility of any kind. Netiquette rules will help you achieve that important goal.

4. Through a combination of policy and training, notify employees that the organization's content rules (and social media policy as a whole) apply 24 hours a day, seven days a week, 365 days a year. Regardless of whether employees are using business resources at the office or personal accounts and devices at home, compliance with all employment rules and policies is mandatory at all times.

5. Social media content, just like email messages and other forms of electronic communication, can trigger workplace lawsuits or serve as smoking-gun evidence in litigation, including but not limited to defamation, sexual harassment, hostile work environment, and copyright infringement claims. Use social media policy and employee training to educate employees about organizational legal risks and individual compliance obligations. See Chapter Two for more information about lawful social media content, use, and behavior.

6. Employees' posts, tweets, photos, videos, and other forms of social networking and electronic content can put employers at risk of regulatory violations. If your organization is regulated, be sure to provide employees with the content guidelines of the regulatory bodies that oversee your industry, as well as their usage and records rules. See Chapter Four for an overview of regulatory risks, requirements, and best practices in the age of social media.

7. In addition to alerting employees to legal and regulatory risks and rules, best practices call for the implementation of a comprehensive employee education program to help ensure that employees recognize the risks social networking poses to the company and individual users, understand the organization's employment rules and social media policies, and agree to comply with policies or accept the consequences. See Chapter Twelve for a detailed discussion about social media policy training.

8. Put some teeth in your content rules and social media policies. Make clear the fact that policy violators are subject to disciplinary action, up to and including termination.

9. Support content rules, social media policy, and all of the organization's electronic policies and general business policies with technology tools designed to enforce compliance by monitoring, filtering, blocking, and otherwise managing content.

# ENFORCE POLICY COMPLIANCE WITH EDUCATION 12

Once you have completed your social media policy audit (see Chapter Nine) and have written or updated your social media policy (see Chapter Ten), it's now time to get to work educating your employees about workplace social media, its risks, rules, policies, and procedures. Here are a few best practices–based tips to help your organization develop and implement a successful social media policy training program, designed to help minimize legal and regulatory risks and maximize individual and organizational compliance.

## TIPS FOR EFFECTIVE SOCIAL MEDIA POLICY TRAINING

### Educate everyone

You cannot expect an untrained workforce to be a compliant workforce, so educate everyone, from your summer interns to your C-level executives, about your organizational, legal, and regulatory risks and rules, policies and procedures. You may one day need to prove to a court or regulatory body that your organization is wholly committed to managing social media behavior and use, content, and compliance. A mandatory, company-wide social media policy training program will help convince the courts that you are serious about policy enforcement and compliance management.

As detailed in Chapter Two, employers cannot escape vicarious liability simply by labeling workers as "independent contractors." In the event of a workplace lawsuit, the court will look beyond the "independent contractor" or "freelancer" label and consider just how much control the employer holds over the worker. Consequently, employers who are eager to manage social media risks and reduce the likelihood of lawsuits should make social media policy training mandatory for everyone over whom the company exerts control. That includes full-time and part-time employees, managers and supervisors, executives and board members, independent contractors and consultants, and all other internal and external parties working on behalf of your organization.

## Take advantage of onsite, online, and interactive training options

To maximize the effectiveness of social media policy training, employers are advised to conduct policy-related educational programs live and onsite, giving participants the opportunity to interact with an experienced training professional who has proven expertise in workplace social media. Onsite training makes it easy for employees to ask questions, discuss challenges, brainstorm solutions, and gain a thorough understanding of the organization's social media–related risks, policies, and procedures.

If you employ a geographically disperse workforce for whom onsite training is not an option, you may want to conduct training via live webcast or interactive online training modules. A live webcast (or possibly a series of live webinars) will give your employees one-on-one access to a professional trainer. A benefit to live webcasts: you can record and archive the training program for replay in the future by new hires or employees who were unable to attend training on the day of the live webcast.

Alternatively, you may want to consider the production of customized interactive online training modules, complete with recorded voiceovers. Some organizations prefer the convenience and flexibility of interactive online training modules, which can be archived and accessed on-demand by employees at their convenience.

## Incorporate certification quizzes

Whether you conduct training onsite, via live webcasts, or in the form of customized interactive online training modules, be sure to incorporate a certification quiz, or a series of certification quizzes, into your training program.

The purpose of certification quizzes is twofold. First, a certification quiz will give users the opportunity to demonstrate to management their understanding of social media risks, their awareness of company rules, and their commitment to policy compliance.

In addition, should the organization one day become embroiled in litigation or a regulatory review, you can use completed certification quizzes to prove to courts or regulators that the company is committed to educating its users and maintaining a civil and lawful online business environment.

## Help shield your organization from liability

Unfortunately, there is no such thing as a 100 percent risk-free social media environment. Resentful ex-employees may intentionally use Twitter, Facebook, YouTube, or blogs to gossip about management, complain about customers, or bad-mouth your brand. Employees may accidentally post content that triggers litigation or serves as smoking-gun evidence in the event of a workplace lawsuit.

Fortunately, the strategic adoption of social media policy coupled with employee training may provide your organization with some defense from liability, should you one day find yourself battling a hostile work environment claim, allegations of sexual harassment, a copyright infringement suit, or any other type of workplace lawsuit stemming from employees' use of social media, blogs, web 2.0, or other electronic business communication tools or technologies.

As discussed previously, based on the legal principle known as "vicarious liability," an employer may be held liable for the wrong acts (intentional or accidental) of employees, including full-time professionals, part-time workers, independent contractors, or other parties who are deemed to be working on behalf of the organization. That's the bad news.

The good news is that, in the United States, the courts tend to appreciate and react positively to policy management programs that combine clearly written rules with formal employee education. An added benefit: A formal compliance management program that combines social media policy with user education will demonstrate to important audiences, including employees, job applicants, customers, prospects, investors, the media, decision makers, and the public, that the organization truly is committed to operating an electronic business environment that is civil, compliant, and correct.

## Address privacy expectations and monitoring realities

If you are a U.S.-based employer, be sure to use policy and training to make clear the fact that employees have no reasonable expectation of privacy when using the company's computer system, sites, devices, or accounts, including but not limited to external and internal social networking sites and blogs.

Use your formal employee training program to notify users that the organization's computer resources—systems, accounts, sites, and devices—are the property of the company. Also inform employees that all of the content that is written, created, posted, transmitted, acquired, accessed, uploaded, downloaded, printed, copied, or stored on your company's system belongs to the organization. Stress the fact that employees should never post any written comments, photos, videos, or other content that could potentially haunt them, harm the company, or embarrass their family and friends were it to be retained and read by management, the courts, regulators, law enforcement agencies, the media, the public, or any other parties.

Research—and take time to explain to employees—the monitoring rights, policies, and procedures that apply to every country and jurisdiction in which you operate facilities, employ workers, or litigate lawsuits. In the United States, for example, the federal Electronic Communications Privacy Act (ECPA) makes it clear that the computer system is the property of the employer, who has the legal right to monitor all activity, transmissions, use, and content. Though only two states, Delaware and Connecticut, require employers to notify employees that they are being monitored, best practices call for all employers to let workers know if you are watching their online activity, why you are monitoring them, how monitoring technology works, and what you are (and are not) looking for.

Also notify employees that, in the United States, private employers operating in employment-at-will states have the legal right to dismiss employees for just about any reason, as long as federal discrimination guidelines, whistle-blower laws, or National Labor Relations Board (NLRB) rules aren't violated. This also is a good opportunity to discuss issues including online privacy, the freedom of speech, the First Amendment, and the National Labor Relations Act.

Emphasize the fact that employees have absolutely no reasonable expectation of privacy when using your company computer systems, accounts, sites, or devices. Explain that the First Amendment only restricts government control of speech. It says nothing about the private employer's right to control what employees write, say, transmit, post, upload, download, or otherwise communicate online. Remind your staff that violations of the organization's social media policy, blog policy, or any other employment policy could result in disciplinary action, up to and including their termination.

## *Training should be ongoing, not a one-time event*

Social media, blog, and web 2.0 tools and technologies are constantly evolving, along with related risks, laws, regulations, and user needs.

Best practices call for social media policies (and all acceptable use policies) to be reviewed and updated, as necessary, every 12 months. Similarly, your organization should conduct formal, policy-related training on an annual basis.

Use your yearly policy review and training program as the opportunity to provide each employee with a copy of every new or revised policy—and to remove copies of old policies from circulation. This is your chance to inform users about any changes to the law that may have been implemented over the past year, any new or revised regulatory requirements that may have taken effect, and any new tools or technologies that the organization may have added to the electronic business communication mix during the year.

In addition to revisiting company-wide policy training each year, you should work throughout the year to reinforce users' understanding of social media risks, awareness of policies, and commitment to compliance. To that end, consider holding periodic policy-related webcasts to reinforce rules or address problems that may pop up during the year. Use the organization's Intranet site and internal blogs, wikis, email, and text messaging system to post policy updates, alert employees to compliance requirements, and reinforce the message that management is serious about social media policy and compliance management.

### Review content rules

Use formal training to remind users that the easiest way to control social media, blog, and other online risks is to control content—written, spoken, and visual content. Review the organization's formal language, content, and netiquette guidelines. If you operate within a regulated industry, be sure to alert employees to regulatory guidelines governing electronic content, records, and use. Discuss language and the law. Make sure employees understand what they legally may—and may not—write, say, post, publish, transmit, download, upload, view, or otherwise communicate online. To that end, you'll want to define legal terms including, for example, "copyright law," "protected classes," and "concerted activities."

## Compliance is mandatory, not an option

Stress the fact that a policy is a policy. Make sure employees understand that social media policy, blog policy, mobile device policy, and all other acceptable use policies and employment rules, guidelines, and codes apply 24 hours a day, seven days a week, 365 days a year, at work, home, and on the road.

Let employees know, for example, that social networkers and bloggers must comply with harassment and discrimination policy, confidentiality rules, and ethics guidelines, as well as social media policy and blog policy. Explain that any violation of any company policy is likely to result in disciplinary action, possibly even termination.

## Keep secrets safe

Educate employees about trade secrets, confidential data, intellectual property, and proprietary information. Explain the legal and regulatory risks facing the company if consumers' personal financial data is breached, patients' electronic protected health information is exposed, company secrets are revealed, or business partners' intellectual property is shared with unauthorized third parties.

Instruct employees to keep their own personal information under wraps, too. This may be a good time to revisit the issues of monitoring, record retention, and personal use. Remind employees that if they use company resources or systems for personal reasons, their private (potentially embarrassing or harmful) conversations may be monitored, could be retained, and might be turned over to courts, regulators, or other third parties in the course of a workplace lawsuit or regulatory audit.

## Discuss business record retention and disposition

The term "electronic business record" tends to confuse employees and executives alike. Even records managers and IT professionals sometimes find themselves challenged by the task of defining and managing electronic business records. Users who traditionally have struggled to distinguish business-critical email, which must be retained, from insignificant messages, which may be deleted, now face the added burden of determining what constitutes a business record tweet, post, or comment in the world of social networking.

Use your social media training program to educate employees about electronic record management and e-discovery (see Chapter Three). Start by defining key terms including "business record," "electronically stored information," "e-discovery," "retention," "litigation hold," "deletion," and "archiving" among others. Review the organization's record retention policy and deletion schedule with users. Explain what data the company retains and archives, why, for how long, and how. Let employees know what roles they play, if any, when it comes to the retention and deletion of the organization's electronic business records.

### Review regulatory rules and requirements

If you operate within the health care arena, financial services world, or any other heavily regulated industry, you should address regulatory risks and rules as part of your social media policy training program. Regulators including the Securities and Exchange Commission (SEC) and Financial Industry Regulatory Authority (FINRA) take electronic content and records management seriously—and expect your organization to do so, too. Best practices call for the application of policy, training, and technology to help ensure regulatory compliance.

### Require users to sign acknowledgment forms

Do not conclude training until you are certain that every employee understands every rule and each guideline contained in your social media policy. At the conclusion of training, require all attendees to sign and date acknowledgment forms, attesting to the fact that they have read the policy, understand the policy, and agree to comply with the policy—or accept the consequences, up to and including termination.

Securing signed acknowledgment forms may help stave off potential lawsuits alleging invasion of privacy (in response to monitoring) or wrongful termination (when policy violations lead to employee dismissals).

Signed acknowledgment forms also can help demonstrate to courts and regulators that the organization takes seriously the tasks of managing online content and behavior, minimizing electronic risks, and maximizing compliance with laws and regulatory guidelines.

## Maintain complete records of your policy training program

Should you one day become embroiled in a workplace lawsuit, you may need to prove to the court that your organization is indeed committed to social media compliance management. To that end, you should maintain and manage comprehensive records related to your organization's social media policy and training program.

Keep copies of written policies (retain one copy of each new or revised policy, and be sure to date every new policy that goes into circulation). Maintain copies of training sign-in sheets or attendance records. Collect and retain employees' policy acknowledgment forms, signed and dated by users and attesting to the fact that they have read the policy, understand it, and agree to adhere to it.

Keep one copy of all policy-related training materials including instructor training manuals, participant workbooks, PowerPoint slides, presentation scripts, and participant handouts. Hold onto participants' completed, graded, signed, and dated certification quizzes. You'll also want to record and maintain an archive of your organization's live training webcasts. If education is conducted via videotape or audiotape, maintain copies of those recorded materials. Written announcements of training or invitations to seminars should be retained, along with any other records related to the organization's social media policy training program.

## Provide every employee with a copy of policy

In the course of training, provide every user (employees, executives, board members, independent contractors, and all other internal and external parties working on behalf of your organization) with the most current version of your social media policy, along with any other policy (blog policy, web 2.0 policy, mobile device policy, and harassment and discrimination policy, for example) that you may address in the course of social media policy training. In addition to distributing hard copies, you also may want to make policies available in the employee handbook, new hire orientation packets, on the company Intranet, or via an online policy portal solution.

By putting hard copies of policy into employees' hands during training, you reduce the likelihood of employees one day claiming that they have never seen your social media policy, or were never notified of the company's monitoring policy, or were unaware that policy violations could result in disciplinary action, up to and including termination of employment.

### Enforce policy and training with disciplinary action

Speaking of employment termination, to help ensure compliance with social networking rules and other employment policies, you'll want to put some teeth in your social media policy. Let employees know that compliance with policy is mandatory, and violations of policy may result in disciplinary action, up to and including termination.

Reprimanding one policy violator today may motivate other users to comply with the rules, and could save you from disciplining an entire department of scofflaws tomorrow. An added bonus: If you can walk into court and demonstrate a consistent pattern of policy enforcement, that may help support your case should you one day find yourself battling a social media–related lawsuit.

What type of disciplinary action is recommended? Some organizations suspend policy violators' Internet access or other computer privileges. Other companies impose monetary fines, with the monies collected earmarked for charity or another worthy cause.

More than half of all employers surveyed have dismissed employees for policy violations, including violations of the rules governing the Internet (26 percent), email (26 percent), social networking

(2 percent), video-sharing sites (1 percent), corporate blogs (1 percent), and personal blogs (1 percent), according to the *2009 Electronic Business Communication Policies and Procedures Survey* from American Management Association and The ePolicy Institute.[1]

## EDUCATE YOUR EXTERNAL ONLINE COMMUNITY, TOO

In the case of social networking, employers are advised to create and put into circulation two separate policy documents: (1) a social media policy for employees and other users working on the company's behalf; and (2) a comment policy, or community guidelines, for social media and blogs, governing the comments posted by customers and other third parties on the organization's sites.

In addition to conducting social media policy training for employees, you'll also want to educate visitors to your social networking sites and business blogs about your community guidelines for social media and blogs. To that end, consider producing and posting a brief informational video on each of your external social networking and blog sites. Enlist the organization's CEO, CIO, chief compliance officer, or public relations director to serve as on-camera spokesperson. Use the 30-second video to explain why you have created community guidelines, how comments are reviewed, and on what basis comments may be rejected. The goal is to produce an appealing video that helps motivate visitors to be part of your community and behave compliantly.

Here's a sample video script: "We value the comments of our online community, and we hope you decide to join us. To help ensure a polite and productive exchange of opinions and information, we have developed community guidelines for blogging and social networking. Please click on the community guidelines link at the bottom of your screen to review our guidelines and register as a member of our online community. Once registered, you are welcome to post comments on this site, in accordance with our published guidelines. Thank you for taking time to join our online community. We look forward to reading your opinions and comments."

# SOCIAL MEDIA BEST PRACTICES: POLICY TRAINING

1. You cannot expect an untrained workforce to be a compliant workforce, so support social media policy with formal employee education.

2. Under the legal principle known as vicarious liability, employers may be held legally responsible for the wrong acts, accidental and intentional, of employees. To help protect your organization from social media–related liability, educate everyone: full-time employees and executives, part-time workers, board members, independent contractors, consultants, freelancers, and anyone else who works for the benefit of your organization.

3. The courts and regulators have consistently demonstrated their appreciation for acceptable use policies that are clearly written and supported by comprehensive employee education.

4. Conduct formal, company-wide social media policy training annually, in conjunction with your organization's yearly policy audit and policy updates.

5. Communicate the fact that social media policy (and all of the organization's acceptable use policies and employment rules) apply at all times, regardless of whether employees are using company resources to network and blog at the office or are at home using their own devices, accounts, and sites.

6. Remind employees that the easiest way to control social media risks is to control online content. Spell out content rules, language guidelines, and netiquette policy. Review personal-use dos and don'ts. Discuss lawful content versus illegal content.

7. Help protect the company's confidential information and consumer's private financial data by educating users about the organization's confidentiality rules, computer security policy, and other applicable guidelines. Review key terms including, for example, "confidential," "trade secret," "data security breach," "Gramm-Leach-Bliley Act," and "HIPAA."

8. If you operate within a regulated industry, be sure to address regulators' electronic content, use, and record retention rules as part of your employee education program.

9. Conclude training with a certification quiz, or series of quizzes, designed to demonstrate users' understanding of the rules, as well as the organization's commitment to operating a compliant and business-appropriate electronic environment.

10. Require all employees to sign and date a copy of the organization's social media policy, attesting to the fact that they understand and agree to adhere to the rules.

11. Put some teeth in your social media policy. In the United States, private employers operating in employment-at-will states have the legal right to fire employees for just about any reason, including violations of social media policy, as long as federal discrimination guidelines or NLRB rules are not violated. Let employees know that when it comes to social media policy and other acceptable use policies, rule-breakers are subject to disciplinary action, up to and including termination.

12. Maintain complete records related to your organization's social media policy, training, and compliance management program. In the event of a lawsuit or regulatory audit, you may need those records to demonstrate that you have done your due diligence and adhered to best practices related to managing online behavior, mitigating social media risks, and maximizing compliance with legal, regulatory, and organizational rules.

# REPUTATION MANAGEMENT 13

## RESPONDING TO AND RECOVERING FROM A SOCIAL NETWORKING NIGHTMARE

The upside of social networking is that it can quickly, conveniently, and cost-effectively facilitate online conversations, communication, and collaboration among customers, colleagues, and communities. The downside of social networking is that all that tweeting, texting, blogging, and posting can savage corporate reputations and short-circuit otherwise promising careers.

Thanks to social media, blogs, and web 2.0, the rules of engagement between business and the public have changed. The social web has leveled the playing field between deep-pocketed corporations (that historically have controlled their own positioning and messages through mainstream media channels) and deeply committed individuals (who are intent on maligning managers, embarrassing executives, and criticizing companies on Facebook, Twitter, YouTube, the blogosphere, and other social networking sites). No wonder 9 percent of organizations surveyed about social media risks claim "reputation" as their primary concern, according to McAfee's *Web 2.0: A Complex Balancing Act.*[1]

Back in the pre-Internet days, it took the substantial financial and human resources of major corporations with multimillion-dollar marketing and advertising budgets to capture media attention and sway public opinion regarding any given issue, cause, or crisis. No longer is that the case. Today, thanks largely to the power of free and publicly accessible social media sites, any individual who is armed with a smartphone and data package can launch a successful assault on any organization, at any time, for any reason, potentially capturing the attention of thousands (perhaps even millions) of worldwide followers in the process.

### Ten reasons why twenty-first-century critics rely on social media to bring down businesses

There is no denying that social media have increased the number and effectiveness of public attacks against businesses, government entities, school systems, the media, and organizations of all types. What makes social networking such an effective tool for ruining reputations and busting brands? Here are the ten top reasons why twenty-first-century critics rely on the social web to help bring down businesses, large and small.

1. Online attacks are quick, easy, and inexpensive. Anyone equipped with a smartphone or digital camera and Internet access can post and publish damaging text, photos, or videos in a matter of seconds.

2. Online attackers can hide behind anonymous posts. There is no law requiring people to blog, post, tweet, or network under their real names. Consequently, it can be difficult (at times impossible) for business executives to identify and battle their detractors.

3. Social media use is pervasive and global. As of 2011, Facebook boasted 800 million active users; Twitter was acquiring 300,000 new users a day; and YouTube fans were uploading 35 hours of video every minute.[2] It is impossible to control what millions of people—strangers, competitors, corporate friends and enemies, customers, job applicants, employees and ex-employees, decision

makers, and the public—will say about your organization on blogs, Facebook, Twitter, YouTube, or any other social networking site.

4. According to Forbes, more than half of all orchestrated blog attacks are sponsored by business rivals who are willing to underwrite online smear campaigns in order to damage their competitors' reputations and revenues.[3] Corporate rivalries have always existed. Thanks to the social web, however, business battles can now be played out publicly and may attract the attention of tens of thousands of observers to root against (or for) your organization.

5. Under section 230 of the United States Communications Decency Act, no party is responsible for the speech of a third party. Because blog hosts are considered "neutral carriers" of Internet content, they are protected from liability for anything posted on the sites they host. Consequently, the host of a wildly popular blog catering to millions of readers has little incentive to ensure that the posts bloggers publish about a company's people or products, services or systems are honest, fair, or factual. On the contrary, bloggers posting on public sites are free to say whatever they like about whomever or whatever they choose.[4]

6. Unlike the mainstream media (print newspapers and magazines, network and cable television, local and nationally syndicated radio), the hosts of new-media sites (blogs, Twitter, YouTube, Facebook, and so on) do not rely on professional fact-checkers to ensure that published comments are factually accurate, appropriate for publication, and otherwise correct. If a blogger makes an inaccurate comment—intentionally or accidentally—readers may point out the error, but the blogger alone decides whether to acknowledge and correct the mistake, or simply let it ride.

7. Thanks to social bookmarking sites like Digg, news aggregation sites like Techmeme, content syndication tools, links, and permalinks, damaging social networking content and defamatory blog posts can remain online and accessible to new readers forever. Even if your organization convinces a blogger to remove an unflattering post about your people, products, or services, you will never succeed in locating (let alone removing) every link to and every copy

of the offending post. Once published, blog posts and other forms of social networking content are no longer under the control of the writer or the writer's subject. They "belong" to the social web, where they will live (in one form or another) forever.

8. Facebook is used by 69 percent of Fortune Global 100 companies in the United States; 52 percent in Europe; and 40 percent in Asia. When it comes to corporate blog use, 50 percent Asia's Fortune 100 blog for business reasons, trailed by 34 percent in the United States, and 25 percent in Europe, according to Burson-Marsteller's *The Global Social Media Check-Up.*[5]

   That data, collected between November 2009 and January 2010, indicates that a substantial number of major multinational corporations have yet to engage in social media use. An organization that has not yet adopted a social media presence cannot be expected to monitor cyber-attacks or manage its online reputation. That lack of participation and oversight makes these companies relatively easy targets for blog mobs and Twitter troops.

   Organizations that are accustomed to communicating solely through traditional, well-funded media channels cannot afford to ignore social media. Do continue to use established marketing communications methods and tools, but don't overlook the power of social networking as a proven-effective weapon in the battle for position, persuasion, and reputation.

9. A tech-savvy individual who is intent on ruining a corporate reputation or defaming an individual manager would find it relatively easy to doctor and post images that falsely depict an unsuspecting victim engaging in inappropriate, embarrassing, or even criminal activity. Were an employee to use a company blog, social networking site, photo-sharing site, or video-sharing site to post a doctored image that falsely depicts a third-party engaged in a crime, then both the employee and employer could be slapped with a "false light" defamation claim. However, if an anonymous blogger posts a phony photo on a private site, then the unfortunate victim likely would face a steep uphill battle against an unknown assailant hiding

behind the safety of anonymity and the U.S. Communications Decency Act, as detailed in point 5.[6]

10. As of 2011, some 350 million active users were accessing Facebook through mobile devices. In addition, 25 percent of bloggers were engaged in mobile blogging, according to Technorati's *State of the Blogosphere* report.[7] Unfortunately for business, smartphones and other mobile devices make it easy for disgruntled, disturbed, or demanding people to post just about any thoughts that pop into their minds at just about any given moment, without taking time to cool off and think before publishing. From restaurateurs and realtors to retailers and riggers, businesses suffer when angry consumers and corporate enemies log on to vent about disappointing customer service, poorly performing products, or other issues—real or imagined.

## REAL-LIFE CAUTIONARY TALE: SOCIAL WEB ATTACKS OFTEN COME FROM WITHOUT

Although many corporations have been slow to add social media to the electronic business communication mix, individual users (including plenty of people with axes to grind) have been quick to identify—and take full advantage of—the communications power inherent in Twitter, Facebook, YouTube, blogs, and other social networking sites.

In 2010, for example, one angry man successfully used Twitter to stir up ongoing public resentment for BP, following the Deepwater Horizon oil spill (also known as the BP oil spill). Writing under the alias Leroy Stick, this frustrated and fed-up citizen posed as a representative of a bogus BP public relations division and tweeted about silly, made-up PR missteps related to the oil spill and other frivolous matters, including, for example, the lunch menu at the bogus PR division.

Blogging on "The Huffington Post" on June 3, 2010, the tweeter explained that he had chosen Leroy Stick as his pen name because, "social media, and in this particular case

Twitter, has given average people like me the ability to use and invent all sorts of brand new sticks" to beat bad corporate citizens like BP, which was offering "no solutions, no urgency, no sincerity, no nothing" in response to the largest accidental marine oil spill in the history of the petroleum industry.

The oil spill raged for three months, destroying the environment and economy of the Gulf of Mexico. During that time, Stick attracted more than 100,000 followers to his @BPGlobalPR Twitter account. His anti-BP/pro-environment message was so popular that, in one week's time, he generated $10,000 by selling "bp cares" tee shirts, the proceeds of which he donated to the environmental group healthygulf.org.[8]

By co-opting BP's Twitter presence and ridiculing what he deemed to be an ineffective PR response by the oil industry giant, Stick fed the rage of the American public—and stymied BP's efforts to restore its reputation and salvage the public's belief in its brand. That's the power of the individual activist in the age of social media.

## REAL-LIFE CAUTIONARY TALE: ASSAULTS ON REPUTATION MAY COME FROM WITHIN, TOO

In addition to battling external attacks, employers also face the possibility of social media nightmares that are dreamt up by employees. Consider the case of pizza giant Domino's, which was publicly humiliated in 2009 after two employees produced a "prank" video and posted it to YouTube. The "funny" video captured one of the employees handling food inappropriately (stuffing it up his nose) while preparing it for delivery. The "wacky" YouTube video became an online—and mainstream media—sensation. Massive news coverage forced Domino's to spend time and money addressing negative food-prep allegations, via YouTube and mainstream media, in order to salvage its corporate reputation, respond to customer concerns, and keep its business on track.[9]

### *Brand warfare: The best defense is a good offense*

Is your organization capable of responding quickly and effectively when social networkers post inaccurate, embarrassing, or potentially harmful information about your company, its people, products, or services? When it comes to cybersmears, blogstorms, and other types of social media attacks, the best defense is a good offense. In other words, be proactive.

A strategic social media reputation management plan can help you respond to PR nightmares immediately, minimizing damage to your organization's brand and business, reputation and revenues, financials and future, should you come under fire in the blogosphere or on Facebook, Twitter, YouTube, or any other social networking site. To that end, following are fifteen best practices designed to help your organization manage its social media risks, maintain its reputation, and build its brand online.

## SOCIAL MEDIA BEST PRACTICES: REPUTATION MANAGEMENT

1. **Establish and enforce written social media policy and related acceptable use policies (AUPs).** You cannot control what outside parties say about your organization, but you can use written policy to help manage employees' content, comments, and conversations about the company's people, products, services, sales, financials, future, customers, and confidential data. Use social media policy and other AUPs to help govern the online behavior, use, and content of all employees—full-time professionals, part-time staff, student interns, managers and executives, board members, independent contractors, consultants, and anyone else who works on behalf of or for the benefit of your organization. Make it clear to employees that the organization's social media policy, AUPs, and all other employment policies apply, regardless of whether employees are using the company's computer resources, their own personal accounts and devices, or third-party blogs and

social networking sites. Let users know exactly what you expect of them, and they will be more likely to comply with rules and policies, laws, and regulations.

2. **Support social media policy with employee education.** Inform employees about the reputation risks facing the organization (as well as individual workers, managers, and executives) in the age of social media. Notify employees that, if the company sustains significant brand damage online, the resulting loss of reputation and customers, sales, and revenues could lead to a reduction in working hours or a loss of jobs.

   Recruit employees to act as the organization's first line of defense, watching for online attacks against the company and promptly reporting blistering blog posts, defamatory tweets, organized Facebook protests, and critical YouTube videos to designated managers. Let employees know how reputation risks and brand management affects them personally, and they will be more likely to help defend the corporate ship from online pirates.

3. **Monitor blogs and social media sites.** As a best practice, all employers operating in the United States should take advantage of their legal right to monitor all employee computer activity and transmissions. As detailed in Chapter Five, the federal Electronic Communications Privacy Act (ECPA) makes it clear that the computer system is the property of the employer, and employees have no reasonable expectation of privacy when using company systems, accounts, sites, or devices. Keep an eye on Internet use, including visits to external blogs and social networking sites; external and internal email and attachments; instant messenger chat; text messaging; and all other forms of electronic business communication. International companies are advised to monitor employees' online use, content, and behavior in compliance with the laws set forth in the countries in which you operate or have employees.

   In addition to monitoring your organization's own computer systems and accounts, be sure to track external blogs and public social media sites to learn what competitors, customers, employees, ex-employees, corporate friends, business enemies, community activists, the media, the investment community, decision makers, and other important audiences are saying about your organization. Take advantage of Google, Technorati, and other technology tools to conduct automatic online searches and effective social media surveillance. Consider assigning a responsible employee the task of manually inspecting the Internet on a regular basis to help uncover company-related posts, favorable and unfavorable alike. A search (automatic or manual) of your company name, brands, products, executives, trademarks, competitors, and other key terms is likely to unearth a lot of content, good and bad. Remember, when it comes to brand management on the social web, knowledge definitely is power.

4. **Ban anonymous blogging and commenting, tweeting and posting.** For some disgruntled employees, anonymous blogging or social networking may provide an easy (and seemingly safe) way to complain about the company, malign management, criticize customers, carp about coworkers, or otherwise gripe about the organization. Be proactive. Block employee gripe sites before they get started. Use written social media policy, formal blog policy, and other relevant AUPs to notify employees that they are prohibited from anonymously blogging, posting, commenting, or otherwise communicating—on their own sites, third-party blogs, or company-hosted sites—about the organization, its activities, financials, plans, people, products, services, customers, suppliers, partners, facilities, resources, or any other business-related matter.

Make it clear that, if the organization is mentioned by employees on blogs or social networking sites, the posters must identify themselves by name, title, and company affiliation, in strict accordance with the rules set forth in the company's social media policy and blog policy, as well as the Federal Trade Commission's blogging rules (see point 9). Let employees know, through policy and training, that they are expected to take ownership of their online comments, opinions, and actions. Anonymous posting will not be tolerated during the workday or after hours.

5. **Be social media savvy.** If your organization has not yet adopted a social media strategy, now is the time to get educated and become engaged. Your social media presence will help give your organization a personality and "warm up" the organization, providing readers with a glimpse into the company's culture and a feel for what it's like to work there. Let the online community know what your organization is all about, and they may be less likely to criticize you online.

   Created for interactive, two-way communication, blogs, Twitter, Facebook, and other social networking sites provide a great way for organizations to initiate and maintain conversations with customers, prospects, job candidates, business partners, community activists, and other interested parties. Many organizations use blogs, Twitter, Facebook, and YouTube to facilitate technical support or customer service, making it easy for customers to submit questions and receive answers in the form of public posts or individual email messages. In addition, blogs and social networking sites are effective tools for companies that want to conduct online polls, solicit consumer feedback, or make customers and other target audiences feel as though their opinions count and their suggestions are heard. Let people know that you are listening, and they may be less inclined to lash out against your organization on the social web.

6. **Use business blogs and social networking sites to help position the organization as relevant to younger employees and prospective employees.** Social media provide convenient tools for announcing job openings and educating job candidates about your organization's hiring procedures and corporate culture. Let job seekers know you are looking for qualified workers, and they may become online cheerleaders for your organization.

7. **Create news and respond to news.** In the pre–social networking era, if the CEO wanted to take a stand on an issue (argue against a proposed law or regulatory change, for example), respond to a crisis (offer financial support to tornado victims), or make a charitable donation (announce the establishment of a scholarship program), the company's media relations department would issue a

news release via fax, email, and the postal service, and then make follow-up phone calls to ensure that targeted reporters and news producers had received the announcement. Thanks to social media, the corporate publicist's job has gotten a lot easier. Whether it's making news or responding to breaking news, all you need to do today is post a tweet or blog, then drive the media and public to your corporate website, business blogs, and company Facebook page to learn more. Let the public know about your support of worthwhile causes, and then watch your ranking as a "good corporate citizen" rise.

8. **Operate C-level executive blogs.** As part of your strategic reputation management initiative, you'll want to use blogs to help position the company's chief executive officer (CEO), chief financial officer (CFO), and chief information officer (CIO) as "thought leaders," expert sources of timely and accurate information about the organization, industry, business world, the economy, public policy, trends, and newsworthy topics.

Blogging enables C-level executives to quickly and easily communicate with—and establish a following among—huge numbers of readers. Use blogs to help put human faces on your most senior executives, positioning them as warm, friendly, and approachable. In other words, let the blogosphere know that your CEO, CFO, and CIO are just "regular" folks who speak in "regular" voices and are eager to interact with customers, investors, employees, or anyone else who would like to engage in a civil and mutually productive online conversation.

9. **Put executives and employees to work posting, publishing, and promoting on behalf of the company after business hours.** If you are a U.S.-based employer, however, please note that the Federal Trade Commission (FTC) in 2009 issued revised "endorsement guidelines" that impact employee blogging. Specifically, the FTC requires bloggers to disclose any material connections between themselves and the products or services they discuss in their blog posts. Product, service, or company endorsements must be honest and cannot be deceptive. Failure to comply

with FTC endorsement guidelines could create liability concerns for the blogger and advertiser.

What does this mean for your business? Feel free to encourage employee-bloggers to promote the organization's products and services on your business blogs, their own personal blogs, and external blogs operated by third parties, but require them to disclose their affiliations with the company as part of their blog profiles. Use your organization's written blog policy and blog risks and rules training program to educate employee-bloggers about FTC rules and compliance obligations. Let employee-bloggers know exactly what it takes to maintain regulatory and organizational compliance.

10. **Establish and grow relationships with influential bloggers, tweeters, and social networkers.** The social web is an active and involved community made up of bloggers, tweeters, and other social networkers. Your business cannot afford to sit passively on the social media sidelines. Once you establish a business blog and corporate presence on Twitter, Facebook, YouTube, LinkedIn, and other networking sites, it's time to get busy introducing yourself to the most influential, high-profile bloggers and networkers in your industry. Invite those online influencers to follow, friend, and favorite you. Ask them to contribute to the electronic conversation. As appropriate, send the industry's most influential bloggers product samples for review on their sites. The influential friends you make online today can help defend your organization tomorrow, in the event of a blogstorm or cybersmear campaign.

11. **Encourage and engage brand bloggers and customer evangelists.** Customer evangelists are dedicated buyers and fans who would be delighted to blog, tweet, post, and otherwise talk up your company, products, and services. Brand bloggers take customer evangelism one step further. On their own time and using their own resources, brand bloggers create and operate blogs devoted to their favorite (or least favorite) brands.

If your monitoring of the blogosphere and social media sites reveals the existence of customer evangelists or brand bloggers who feel passionately and positively about your organization or products, you're in luck. Reach out to these online cheerleaders. Send them free samples, tchotchkes featuring the company logo, or other business-related goodies. Invite influential brand bloggers to attend the company's annual meeting, tour the factory, or stop by your booth at trade shows. Assign a member of the PR team to stay in touch regularly via email, text, and tweets with your customer evangelists and brand bloggers. Send thank-you notes in response to particularly positive posts.

In the event that an online attack or protest is launched against the company, your army of loyal customer evangelists and brand bloggers can provide a valuable communications channel and help you counter any negative claims that are circulating.

12. **Respond swiftly when attacked.** The beauty of social networking is that it facilitates speedy communication. If your organization is under assault online, then take advantage of the rapid-fire nature of Twitter, Facebook, YouTube, and blogs to get your response out—immediately. Social media have changed the public relations game—permanently. If your business is being attacked on the social web, you must respond nimbly. You cannot afford to spend days brainstorming the "right" response, hammering out a press release, or fine-tuning the "perfect" 140-character tweet. A delayed response simply gives the opposition more time to beat up your brand.

13. **Draft a strategic media relations plan that addresses social media disasters.** As part of your strategic communications plan, instruct employee-bloggers and social networkers how to handle media inquiries. Your organization's business blog and social networking programs may lead to an increase in media inquiries from reporters and news producers looking for story ideas and expert sources, conducting research, and covering breaking news. Whether they are writing about the company on business blogs or personal social networking sites, employees lend their names and faces to the company every time they post content. Consequently, they are likely to be contacted directly by the media at some point in their online publishing careers.

Mindful of that fact, be sure to use social media policy, blog policy, and formal training to instruct employee-bloggers and social networkers how to handle media inquiries. If, for example, you want bloggers to route all media calls to the public relations department, then say so—and make sure everyone has the name, phone number, and email address of the company's designated media spokesperson(s).

To be safe, you may want to conduct media relations training for all employees who engage in business-related or personal blogging and social networking, so they are prepared to respond appropriately and effectively to unsolicited media calls.

14. **Draft a strategic financial relations plan that addresses blog and social media crises.** For publicly traded companies, unmanaged blog content can create devastating regulatory risks. When it comes to the disclosure of financial information, public companies are required to comply with strict regulatory rules. If an unauthorized employee were to jump the gun and prematurely publish information about quarterly revenues and earnings, that public blog post could put the company at risk of a Securities and Exchange Commission (SEC) disclosure violation.

    If employee-bloggers or social networkers have access to company financials and investor relations information, be sure to educate them—via policy and training—about regulatory risks and requirements, company and regulators' content rules, and the penalties that await organizations (and employees) who violate regulatory and organizational rules and policies. To help ensure that financial risks are minimized and compliance is maximized, consider conducting mandatory investor relations training for all employee-bloggers and all employees who are engaged in social networking at work or after business hours.

15. **If all else fails, file a cybersmear lawsuit.** If you feel you have been defamed online, you may want to contact an experienced legal professional and explore your legal options. Growing numbers of businesses and individuals are taking to the courts in an

effort to battle bloggers, tweeters, and other social networkers who have posted false, damaging, critical, or otherwise defamatory content on the web. However, because many bloggers and social networkers opt to hide behind a nom de plume, it can be difficult to mount a successful legal challenge against an individual who is attacking your reputation online. You can ask the court to force Internet service providers to provide the names of anonymous posters, but you may not succeed in your mission. To date, the U.S. courts have been inconsistent in their rulings in these types of cases. Until the courts arrive at a consensus on this issue, you will have to weigh the pros and cons of litigation.[10]

It's important to note that a lawsuit filed by a multinational corporation against an individual blogger could be viewed as overkill, a grossly inappropriate show of force. If the online media, mainstream media, blogosphere, and social networking community decide that your company, the big guy, is beating up a little guy unfairly, then your lawsuit may turn into an additional public relations nightmare, further eroding your corporation's good name.

# SAMPLE POLICIES

## SOCIAL MEDIA, BLOGS, AND RELATED AUPS

Need help developing effective, well-written social media policies? This chapter contains sample policies to help employers write and implement their own formal policies. Sample policies are offered in several categories: (1) social media policy; (2) social media and blog policy; (3) blog policy; (4) community guidelines for blogs and social media; (5) social networking and video-sharing policy; (6) cell phone and text messaging policy; (7) smartphone and mobile device policy; (8) email policy in the age of social media; (9) Internet policy in the age of social media; (10) sexual harassment policy in the age of social media; and (11) electronic business communication code of conduct.

## BEST PRACTICES CALL FOR A COMPREHENSIVE LEGAL REVIEW OF POLICY

These sample policies are intended as guidelines only. Any employer using these sample policies should feel free to adjust them as necessary and adapt them as appropriate for your particular business and industry needs, corporate culture, and legal and regulatory compliance requirements.

Best practices call for social media policies—and other employment policies—to be developed and implemented with assistance from competent legal counsel. Whether using one of the following samples as your policy template or writing policy from scratch, be sure to have your legal counsel review and sign-off on policy before introducing it to employees. The purpose of a legal review is to ensure that your policy addresses and supports compliance with laws (federal, state, and international) and regulations (government and industry) affecting your business. Policy that has been reviewed by legal counsel will help put your organization on firmer legal ground should you one day find yourself battling a workplace lawsuit or facing a regulatory investigation.

## SAMPLE SOCIAL MEDIA POLICY, 1

The organization has created this eleven-point Social Media Policy, which applies to all employees who contribute to social networks, blogs, wikis, or any other form of social media including but not limited to Facebook, Twitter, YouTube, and LinkedIn. These guidelines apply to organization-hosted blogs and social media sites and users' own personal accounts and sites.

1. Be honest and transparent about your identity and purpose. Always use your real name; never write anonymously. If you are writing about the organization or any business-related matter, you must identify yourself as an employee of the organization. If you have a vested interest in the topic at hand, Federal Trade Commission compliance requires you to say so. Honesty is valued in the blogosphere and social media world.

2. When writing about the organization's competitors, be polite and diplomatic. Make sure your comments are appropriate, your facts are correct, and your details are accurate. Do not post comments that are defamatory, disparaging, untruthful, unlawful, or otherwise offensive and inappropriate.

3. Never write about, comment on, or answer questions regarding any legal matter, litigation, or party to a lawsuit involving the organization. Refer all legal inquiries to the organization's law director.

4. In the event of a business-related crisis (for example, a warehouse fire or data security breach) employees are prohibited from participating in crisis-related discussions online. Do not answer questions, rush to the company's defense, respond to rumors, or spread gossip. Even anonymous comments could be traced back to your IP address or the organization's system. Refer any comments, questions, or interview requests that come to your blogs or social networking sites to the media relations director.

5. Protect your privacy and the privacy of the organization. Think carefully before posting comments that could come back to haunt you or harm the company. Privacy settings on social media sites are constantly in flux, so you cannot assume personal information is protected. The web has a long memory, and secrets never die online.

6. Keep an eye on spelling, grammar, and punctuation. You wouldn't walk into a business meeting and start speaking gibberish. Why post online content that is anything less than 100 percent accurate and correct? A goal of business blogging and social networking is to attract and grow an audience of loyal readers who will follow you for expert advice and information. It's impossible to establish that sort of influence if your writing is riddled with grammatical goofs and mechanical missteps.

7. Be gracious to readers and commenters. If a reader takes time to respond to your posts, then you should acknowledge his or her comment quickly and graciously. That said, don't feel obligated to post or reply to any comments that are offensive or otherwise inappropriate. The organization reviews all posts, comments, and queries prepublication. We reject any content that is unlawful or contrary to our code of conduct. We advise you to do the same. Keep your blogs and social media sites clean, civil, and compliant.

8. Mistakes happen. If you make an online misstep, quickly acknowledge it, correct it, and then move on.

9. You are required to comply with all of the organization's employment policies at all times, whether using the organization's blogs, sites, systems, and devices, or your own personal accounts, sites, and devices. Among the policies with which bloggers and social networkers must comply are the organization's Social Media Policy, Record Retention Policy, Harassment & Discrimination Policy, Ethics Policy, Confidentiality Policy, Mobile Device Policy, Investor Relations Policy, Media Relations Policy, Email Policy,

Internet Policy, Computer Security Policy, and Netiquette Policy.

10. The Company is covered by and compliant with the National Labor Relations Act (NLRA). The Company supports employees' legal right to engage in protected concerted activity and communication under Section 7 of the NLRA. This Social Media Policy will not be interpreted or applied in a manner that interferes with employees' protected concerted activity or communication. For additional information, see the Company's "Employee Rights Under the NLRA" poster.

11. When using the organization's blogs, social media sites, or Internet system, employees have no reasonable expectation of privacy. The federal Electronic Communications Privacy Act (ECPA) gives management the legal right to access and monitor all blog posts, social media content, business records, personal data, and archives on the organization's system as deemed necessary and appropriate.

The organization also reserves the right to monitor the blogosphere and the Internet as a whole, including personal blogs, tweets, YouTube videos, Facebook profiles, and other online content that employees may create and post on their own time, using their own personal accounts, via their own electronic devices. Remember, blog and social media content is public, not private, communication.

Violation of the organization's Social Media Policy—or any other company policy, rule, guideline, or code—may result in disciplinary action, up to and including your employment or contract termination.

## Acknowledgment and Signature

If you have any questions about this Social Media Policy, please address them to the Human Resources Director before signing the following agreement.

I have read the organization's Social Media Policy, and I agree to abide by it. I understand that a violation of any of the above rules, policies, or procedures may result in disciplinary action, up to and including my termination.

Employee Name (Printed): _____

Employee Signature: _____

Date: _____

*Source:* ©2012, The ePolicy Institute, www.epolicyinstitute.com, Executive Director Nancy Flynn. For informational purposes only. Individual policies should be developed with assistance from competent legal counsel.

## SAMPLE SOCIAL MEDIA POLICY, 2

### I. Overview

Social media provide a new and valuable means for employees and executives of the Company to communicate with customers, collaborate with colleagues, and connect with the community. We also recognize the fact that social media play an important role in the personal lives of many Company employees. The personal use of social media can have an impact—positive or negative—on employees' job performance, as well as the public positioning of our organization. Consequently, this Social Media Policy applies not only to employees' use of Company-hosted business-related social networking sites, but also employees' own personal social networking accounts and sites.

### II. Definitions of Key Terms

To help ensure understanding of and compliance with the Company's Social Media Policy, we offer the following definitions of several relatively new and potentially confusing social networking, legal, and technology terms contained in this policy.

**Blog.** Short for weblog. A blog is a self-published online journal that contains written content, links, and photos, which are regularly updated. Blogs enable anyone with a computer and Internet access to publish their thoughts, ideas, and opinions for anyone else to read and comment upon.

**Blogosphere.** The universe of blogs, or the community of bloggers.

**Breach Notification Laws.** The law takes data theft—and corporate compliance with security laws and procedures—seriously. All of the states in which the Company operates have enacted breach notification laws, requiring the Company to notify customers and other affected parties in the event of a data security breach, such as the electronic theft of customers' Social Security numbers, credit card numbers, or other personal information.

**Business Record.** Social media posts and other electronic content may create evidence of business-related activities, events, and transactions. This type of content is defined as a business record. For legal and regulatory reasons, the Company is required to retain business record posts, tweets, email, text messages, videos, and other electronic information that is created, transmitted, acquired, posted, or stored on the Company's computer system.

**Comments.** Blogs and other social networking sites often include comment features that allow readers to participate in the electronic conversation by asking questions, injecting opinions, and otherwise commenting.

**Copyright.** The exclusive right granted to authors under the U.S. Copyright Act to copy, adapt, distribute, rent, publicly perform, and publicly display their works of authorship, such as literary works, databases, musical works, sound recordings, photographs and other still images, and motion pictures and other audiovisual works.

**Electronic Communications Privacy Act (ECPA).** The federal law that gives U.S. employers the legal right to monitor all employee computer activity and transmissions. The ECPA makes clear the fact that the Company's computer system is the property of the employer, and employees have no reasonable expectation of privacy when using Company computer systems, accounts, sites, or devices.

**Entry.** Commentary, also called a post, written on a social networking site or blog. Some users write multiple entries every day. Most entries are relatively short and may include links to external sites.

**Facebook.** The world's largest social networking site, Facebook announced in 2011 that it had 800 million active users worldwide. Facebook encourages people to introduce themselves to the online community, make "friends," share information, participate in the electronic conversation, and build business-related and personal relationships.

**Links.** Social networkers and bloggers strive to increase traffic and readership by incorporating incoming and outgoing links into their sites. Users can enhance the relevance of their sites, and provide readers with a service, by including outgoing links to sites that contain relevant content or otherwise are likely to appeal to readers. High-quality content (a timely topic, compelling writing, and high search engine rankings) helps motivate other social networkers and bloggers to create links into a site.

**LinkedIn.** LinkedIn is an invitation-only business networking site that relies heavily on the power of personal referrals. Unlike Facebook and other social networking sites that create opportunities for strangers to meet and become "friends," LinkedIn is designed for professional networking with people, or "connections," you already know.

**Netiquette.** Etiquette rules governing online use, language, and behavior.

**Page.** The specific portion of a social media site on which content is displayed and managed by an individual or, in the case of Company sites, employees with administrative rights.

**Post.** Commentary, also called an entry, written on a social networking site or blog. Some users write multiple entries every day. Most entries are relatively short and may include links to external sites.

**Profile.** Biographical (or "about me" information) that users post about themselves on social media sites and blogs.

**Social Media.** A category of Internet-based resources that facilitate user participation and user-generated content. Social media include but are not limited to social networking sites (Facebook, MySpace), microblogging sites (Twitter), photo- and video-sharing sites (Flickr, YouTube), wikis (Wikipedia), blogs (The Huffington Post), and news aggregation sites (Digg, Reddit).

**Social Networks.** Social networks are online platforms where users create profiles, post content, share information, and socialize with others.

**Tweets.** The 140-character messages that are posted on Twitter.

**Twitter.** A microblogging site that limits messages, or tweets, to 140 characters. Readers who follow a writer's tweets are called "followers."

**Video-Sharing Site.** Thanks to YouTube and other video sites, anyone whose smartphone, cell phone, or mobile device is equipped with a video recorder can capture and upload potentially embarrassing or otherwise damaging videos of company executives and employees, facilities, and secrets. Like social networking sites, video sites increase the risk of confidentiality breaches and information leaks when employees and ex-employees take and post unauthorized videos of a company's people, products, and proprietary information.

**Wiki.** Reported to be an acronym for "what I know is," a wiki is a website with pages that any reader can contribute content to or edit. Readers are encouraged to add pages, edit content, or comment on other writers' remarks. The term "wiki" is adapted from the Hawaiian phrase "wiki wiki," which means quick. Wikis primarily are used in the business arena as an internal collaboration platform for employees.

**YouTube.** The "granddaddy" of video-sharing sites. YouTube offers users the ability to upload, tag, describe, share, find, watch, and comment on videos. YouTube has embraced, and been embraced by, the business community. Many organizations use YouTube to educate consumers about services, deliver how-to advice, build brand awareness, communicate a position, deliver a message, or promote people, products, and businesses. It's not unusual for popular YouTube videos to "go viral," attracting millions of viewers in the process.

## III. Business-Related Use of Social Media

Employees are encouraged to engage in social networking as a means to communicate with external audiences (customers, prospects, prospective employees, and the public) and internal audiences (coworkers, managers, and executives). When using the Company's social media sites, accounts, and tools, employees must adhere to the following rules:

a. Clearly state the purpose of each business-related site you operate. For example, "This ePolicy Institute blog is designed to help employers minimize social media risks and maximize compliance with legal and regulatory rules."

b. As appropriate, link from your business-related site to the Company's official website and relevant Company-hosted social networking sites and blogs.

c. Social media content must by lawful and in compliance with all federal and state laws including but not limited to copyright, harassment, and discrimination laws.

d. Social media use and content must comply with all of the Company's employment policies including but not limited to Social Media Policy, Blog Policy, Mobile Device Policy, Internet Policy, Email Policy, Computer Security Policy, Harassment and Discrimination Policy, Media Relations Policy, Privacy Policy, Investor Relations Policy, and Confidentiality Policy.

e. Prior to publication on Company-hosted sites, all social media content (employees' posts and readers' comments) must be reviewed by the Chief Compliance Officer.

f. Provide a link from every Company-hosted site to the Company's Community Guidelines for Social Media. Inform visitors that they must read and agree to the Company's Community Guidelines for Social Media before posting questions or other content on your comment page. Notify readers that all comments/content/questions will be reviewed by the Company's Chief Compliance Officer prior to posting. Comments that violate the Community Guidelines for Social Media will not be posted.

g. State clearly that the comments/opinions/content expressed by visitors to the site do not reflect the position/opinions/stance of the Company.

h. Identify yourself by name and title on business-related sites. For contact information, provide a link to the contact page of the Company's official website.

i. Federal law (Electronic Communications Privacy Act) makes clear the fact that the Company's computer system is the property of the employer, and employees have no reasonable expectation of privacy when using Company computer systems, sites, accounts, and devices. The Company intends to exercise its legal right to monitor all social media activity, use, and content. Be sure visitors to your sites understand that the comments/questions/opinions they post are public, not private.

j. Employees are prohibited from using any personal devices (desktops, laptops, smartphones, tablet PC, or other mobile devices) to access and manage Company-hosted social media sites without first securing permission from the Chief Compliance Officer.

### IV. Personal Use of Social Media

The Company understands that many employees operate personal social networking sites and engage in social networking for private, non-business-related reasons. Employees must adhere to the following rules when engaged in personal social networking:

a. During the workday, employees may use only personal accounts and private devices to engage in personal social networking. The use of Company accounts, systems, and devices for personal social networking is prohibited.

b. During otherwise productive working hours, employees are limited to no more than 20 minutes of personal social networking. In addition, employees are free to engage in personal social networking during the lunch hour, scheduled work breaks, and before and after normal business hours.

c. Employees must adhere to all Company policies at all times—at the office, at home, and elsewhere. Whether engaged in personal social networking during business hours or after hours, employees must adhere to all employment policies including but not limited to Social Media Policy, Blog Policy, Email Policy, Internet Policy, Confidentiality Policy, Computer Security Policy, Media Relations Policy, Privacy Policy, Investor Relations Policy, and Harassment and Discrimination Policy.

d. Employees are prohibited from posting or disseminating any confidential Company information including but not limited to internal email, Company financials, trade secrets, copyright-protected material, and intellectual property.

e. Employees are prohibited from posting or disseminating any confidential customer information including but not limited to credit card numbers, debit card numbers, Social Security numbers, birth dates, street addresses, full names, and phone numbers.

f. Employees should use their own personal email addresses on personal social media sites. Use of Company/business email addresses or the Company's URL is prohibited. Employees may not link from personal sites to any Company-hosted websites, blogs, or social media sites, including business sites written by employees.

g. You may identify yourself as a Company employee, strictly by name, title, and job description. Beyond that, you may not discuss the Company in any way. Employees may not post any business-related photos or videos of images including but not limited to Company uniforms, logos, offices, facilities, employees, executives, customers, job applicants, official Company documents, or products.

h. Be aware that privacy settings on social media are constantly in flux. Do not assume that private information is ever truly private. Think before you post.

i. If you become aware of the fact that another employee has violated the Company's Social Media Policy, or any Company employment policy, please notify the Chief Compliance Officer immediately. Your report will be kept in strict confidence.

## V. Acknowledgment and Signature

If you have any questions about this Social Media Policy, please address them to the Human Resources Director before signing the following agreement.

I have read the Company's Social Media Policy and agree to abide by it. I understand that a violation of any of the above rules, policies, and procedures may result in disciplinary action, up to and including my termination.

Employee Name (Printed): _____

Employee Signature: _____

Date: _____

*Source:* ©2012, The ePolicy Institute, www.epolicyinstitute.com, Executive Director Nancy Flynn. For informational purposes only. Individual policies should be developed with assistance from competent legal counsel.

## SAMPLE SOCIAL MEDIA POLICY, 3

The Company believes that social media—including but not limited to blogs, Facebook, MySpace, Twitter, YouTube, Wikis, LinkedIn, Flickr, and other platforms and sites—are valuable business tools that can help us communicate with and educate the market, position our organization and executives, and build our brand and business reach. We also are aware of the fact that employees engage in social networking, via our Company sites and your own personal accounts, while at work and after business hours.

This Social Media Policy is intended to guide employees' online use, content, and behavior when engaged in social networking on behalf of the Company or yourself, during working hours or on your own time, using our business resources or your own personal accounts and devices.

### Online Content Is a Reflection of Your Professionalism

When posting to business sites, you must make clear your employment status by citing your name, title, and role at the Company. You also must use your Company email address (not your personal email address) and cite the Company's web address on all business sites. The content you post on business sites may rise to the level of a business record. Please take your responsibilities as a writer seriously. Make sure all of your business-related posts, tweets, and other content is written in a professional, business-appropriate tone and style.

### Keep Personal Posts Personal

Use your personal email address, not your business email address, on your personal social networking sites and blogs. When posting after business hours on personal social networks, you may not identify yourself as an employee of the Company, refer to the Company, or discuss Company business in any way without first securing permission from the Chief Compliance Officer. If you are granted permission to cite your business affiliation or otherwise discuss the Company, be aware of the fact that your content will be monitored and reviewed by the Company to ensure compliance with all of our employment policies, rules, and guidelines.

### Be Honest

Never post false or misleading information in business or personal social media profiles. If you are one credit hour short of a masters degree in business administration, do not claim to hold an MBA in your Facebook profile. If you attended a continuing education seminar at Harvard, don't try to pass yourself off as Ivy League trained. If you are a management trainee, do not refer to yourself as a member of the Company's management team.

### Safeguard Customers' Privacy

Never mention, discuss, or otherwise refer to any customer of the Company—on business sites or personal sites—without first receiving authorization from the Chief Compliance Officer, as well as written permission from the customer. The disclosure of customers' personal information, whether accidental or intentional, could result in legal or regulatory action against the Company and you, the individual user.

### Be Accurate

Before posting any content to business or personal sites, be sure to double-check all facts, statistics, and other data. Use spell check and grammar check. Be sure your punctuation and other mechanics are correct. If you are authorized to refer to other people, make sure you get their names, titles, company names, and other details right.

### Keep Company Secrets Safe

Adhere at all times to the Company's Confidentiality Policy and Privacy Policy. Never disclose confidential, secret, or proprietary Company information. Confidential information includes but is not limited to Company financials, internal email messages and memos, Company business records, personnel files and records, customer lists, intellectual property, marketing plans, and strategic plans. The disclosure of Company financials or other confidential data information, whether accidental or intentional, could result in legal or regulatory action against the Company and you, the individual user.

### Keep Comments Lawful, Polite, and Professional

Employees must adhere to the Company's netiquette guidelines and content rules at all times. Avoid making comments that could trigger an argument, lead to a legal claim, or generate a negative impression of the Company and you. It is not necessarily your job to defend the Company against bloggers who post negative or defamatory comments about our people and products. Do not respond to negative posts about the Company without first securing permission from the Chief Compliance Officer.

### Think Before You Post

Social media content is public and has a long shelf life. Always think carefully before you post any text, photos, or videos. A seemingly innocent comment about the proposal you're working on could alert the competition to the Company's new business strategy. A cute photo of your kids vacationing at the beach could be good news to a house burglar. A post about your new puppy could give a data thief a clue as to your computer password.

### Be Productive, Have Fun, and Comply with Policy

Social networking creates tremendous opportunities for internal and external communication and collaboration. The Company encourages all employees to explore the world of social media as a means to communicate with customers, educate prospects, collaborate with colleagues, and build the reputation of the Company and yourself. To that end, we urge you to be productive, have fun, and comply with our Social Media Policy and all other employment policies, 24 hours a day, 365 days a year.

### NLRA Rules

The Company is covered by and compliant with the National Labor Relations Act (NLRA). The Company supports employees' legal right to engage in protected concerted activity and communication under Section 7 of the NLRA. This Social Media Policy will not be interpreted or applied in a manner that interferes with employees' protected concerted activity or communication. For additional information, see the Company's "Employee Rights Under the NLRA" poster.

### Disciplinary Action

Violation of the Company's Social Media Policy, or any other Company employment policy, will result in disciplinary action, up to and including termination, whether using a Company-hosted social media site or a personal social networking site or account.

### Acknowledgment and Signature

If you have any questions about this Social Media Policy, please address them to the Human Resources Director before signing the following agreement.

I have read the Company's Social Media Policy and agree to abide by it. I understand that a violation of any of the above rules, policies, and procedures may result in disciplinary action, up to and including my termination.

Employee Name (Printed): _____

Employee Signature: _____

Date: _____

*Source:* ©2012, The ePolicy Institute, www.epolicyinstitute.com, Executive Director Nancy Flynn. For informational purposes only. Individual policies should be developed with assistance from competent legal counsel.

## SAMPLE SOCIAL NETWORKING AND BLOG POLICY, 1

To help facilitate effective communication with employees, customers, prospects, suppliers, investors, the media, and public, (Organization) operates both external (facing out) and internal business blogs and also has a corporate presence on external (public) social media sites.

(Organization) provides this Social Networking and Blog Policy to help ensure that employees communicate and collaborate effectively and compliantly on (Organization's) external social media sites and business blogs, as well as on employees' personal blogs and personal social networking sites.

Please remember that blogs and social networking sites (external and internal) are nothing more that the latest avenues of electronic communication. All of (Organization's) long-standing employment policies and formal rules of appropriate business conduct apply, regardless of the technologies used for communication.

Employees are required to adhere to this Social Networking and Blog Policy at all times, whether using business blogs and corporate social networking accounts or personal blogs and private social networking accounts. Violation of (Organization's) Social Networking and Blog Policy may result in disciplinary action, up to and including termination.

1. Employees are required to adhere to all of (Organization's) employment policies at all times, whether blogging and social networking for business or personal reasons, via (Organization's) computer system and accounts or your own private accounts and personal devices. Included among the company policies with which employees must comply at all times are (Organization's) Computer, Email, Internet, Mobile Device, Ethics, Confidentiality, Security, Media Relations, Investor Relations, and Content Policies.

   Violation of this rule could trigger a lawsuit against or regulatory investigation of (Organization). For example, a blogger who violates (Organization's) Confidentiality and Investor Relations Policies by posting company financials in advance of their official release to regulators by the Investor Relations department could trigger a regulatory investigation of (Organization) by the SEC. Similarly, an employee who violates (Organization's) Content Policy by tweeting a defamatory comment about a customer could trigger a potentially costly lawsuit.

2. Some employees may be asked by management to write and post "official" business content on behalf of (Organization). Unless you are asked to serve as an authorized business blogger, networker, or tweeter, you must write in the first person (I, me, my, mine, myself) whenever your connection to (Organization) is apparent. In other words, make it clear that you are writing on your own behalf; you are not speaking as an authorized (Organization) spokesperson.

3. To clarify the fact that you are writing on behalf of yourself, not (Organization), you are required to incorporate this disclaimer statement in the "About Me" section (or elsewhere) on your blog or social networking profile: "The views, opinions, comments, and other content expressed and contained on this site are my own, not my employer's."

4. Unless authorized to do so, employees may not communicate about (Organization) on public blogs or external social networking sites. That means no mention of (Organization), our people and products, customers and services, business and brand, or any other company-related matter. This rule exists to protect your privacy, reputation, and career, as well as the company's assets, future, and credibility. Inappropriate or inaccurate information could result in lawsuits and regulatory investigations that could negatively impact both (Organization) and you.

5. Never use your business email address on personal blogs or public social networking sites. Instead, use your personal email address on personal blogs, personal websites,

and whenever you are expressing personal views. Using your business email address on personal blogs or public social networking sites is a violation of this Social Networking and Blog Policy, as well as (Organization's) Computer Security Policy and Anti-Spam Guidelines.

6. When posting content online, always be respectful of others, including (Organization's) employees, managers, executives, board members, job applicants, customers, prospective customers, suppliers, business partners, and the general public.

7. Personal blogging and personal social networking should never interfere with your work commitments. Employees' personal blogging and personal social networking is limited to 20 minutes a day during regular business hours (the time when employees are expected to focus on business-related tasks). In addition, employees are free to spend any portion of the lunch hour or other legitimate work breaks engaged in personal blogging and personal social networking via (Organization's) computer devices and Internet system and/ or employees' own, private mobile devices and personal Internet accounts.

8. The use of external social media sites or other outside websites for business-related purposes must be approved by (Organization's) Compliance Officer or Media Relations Director, depending upon the situation. For example, seek authorization from Media Relations before sharing business-related photos through Flickr. Contact the Compliance Officer before accepting an invitation to network with business associates via LinkedIn. When in doubt, seek guidance from your department head, who will direct you to the appropriate party for formal authorization.

9. The Company is covered by and compliant with the National Labor Relations Act (NLRA). The Company supports employees' legal right to engage in protected concerted activity and communication under Section 7 of the NLRA. This Social Networking and Blog Policy will not be interpreted

or applied in a manner that interferes with employees' protected concerted activity or communication. For additional information, see the Company's "Employee Rights Under the NLRA" poster.

10. If you have any questions, concerns, or doubts about what constitutes appropriate and compliant online content and use, contact the Compliance Officer or Human Resources Director for assistance. Do not post any content that may result in a violation of this Social Networking and Blog Policy or any other (Organization) employment policy.

**Acknowledgment and Signature**

If you have questions about the above Social Networking and Blog Policy, address them to the Human Resources Director before signing the following agreement.

I have read (Organization's) Social Networking and Blog Policy, and I agree to abide by it. I understand that a violation of any of the above rules, policies, and procedures may result in disciplinary action, up to and including my termination.

Employee Name (Printed): _____

Employee Signature: _____

Date: _____

*Source:* ©2012, The ePolicy Institute, www.epolicyinstitute.com, Executive Director Nancy Flynn. For informational purposes only. Individual policies should be developed with assistance from competent legal counsel.

## SAMPLE SOCIAL MEDIA AND BLOG POLICY, 2

Online communication and collaboration via social media sites is changing the ways in which employees work and engage with colleagues, customers, and other important business audiences. As an innovative organization, the company encourages employees to explore the benefits of social networking and blogging—both at the office during working hours and at home after hours. That said, whether or not an employee elects to have a presence on blogs or social networking sites is the decision of each individual employee. Employees who opt to participate in social networking and blogging are required to adhere to the company's Social Media and Blog Policy. Noncompliance with this policy, or any other company employment policy, may result in disciplinary action, up to and including termination.

1. Employees are required to adhere to the company's Social Media and Blog Policy—and all other company employment policies—24 hours a day, at work, at home, and on the road. Regardless of whether you are using company-owned computer resources or your own personal Internet account and devices, you must comply 100 percent with all of the company's employment policies, including but not limited to Social Media Policy, Internet Policy, Email Policy, Confidentiality Policy, Ethics Policy, Investor Relations Policy, Media Relations Policy, Government Affairs Policy, Netiquette Policy, and Writing Style Policy.

2. Each employee is personally responsible for the content you publish on blogs and other forms of social media. Bear in mind the fact that the comments and other content that you publish online will remain accessible to the public for a long time. Protect your family, friends, and reputation by keeping your private information private.

3. You must always identify yourself (by name and title or role at the company) whenever you discuss the company or any business-related matters.

4. Employees are required to write in the first person (I, me, mine, myself, and so on) at all times. You must make clear the fact that you are expressing your own opinions and thoughts in your posts; you are not writing as an authorized company representative. Use your own voice; bring your own personality to the forefront; say what is on your mind.

5. Any time you publish work-related comments or content to any external website (your own blog or someone else's, your own Twitter account or someone else's, your own Facebook page or someone else's, and so forth) you must insert this disclaimer: "The postings on this site are my own and don't necessarily represent the positions, strategies, plans, or opinions of my employer."

6. Employees must adhere to copyright law at all times. Never post copyright-protected material without the express permission of the copyright holder. It is illegal to take copyright-protected material from websites, articles, books, or other sources—and then post it on your site as though it were your own original content.

7. Always cite the original source of surveys, data, quotes, and other information that you incorporate into blog and social media posts.

8. Employees are prohibited from revealing the company's confidential, proprietary, or secret information. This includes, but is not limited to, intellectual property, trademark-protected information, company financials, internal email, personnel records, and any documents, data, and information that is intended solely for internal distribution.

    You must not comment on confidential financial information such as the company's future business performance, business plans, or prospects anywhere in world. This includes statements about an upcoming quarter or future periods or information about alliances. This rule applies to anyone, including conversations with Wall Street analysts, the media, or other third parties. If you feel there is a legitimate reason to publish or report on conversations that are meant to be private or internal to the company, you must first secure permission from the Chief Compliance Officer.

9. Employees are prohibited from revealing customers' private financial data or other personal information. This includes Social Security numbers, credit card numbers, debit card numbers, home addresses, and dates of birth.

10. You may not cite, reference, or otherwise mention the company's customers, prospective customers, business partners, suppliers, employees, job applicants, board members, investors, or other internal or external parties without the approval of the Company's Compliance Officer. If a reference is approved, be sure to incorporate a hyperlink to the individual, if possible.

11. When writing on a public site, you must show respect for your audience. Always use business-appropriate language. Never write posts that are insulting, obscene, defamatory, harassing, discriminatory, bullying, or otherwise offensive, unlawful, or inappropriate. Be considerate of other people's privacy, beliefs, and feelings. Steer clear of topics that may be viewed as objectionable or inflammatory, such as politics and religion.

12. If you hope to broaden your readership, do your homework. Find out who else is blogging or posting about your topic, and then cite them and link to them.

13. Be mindful of your "positioning" on blogs and social networking sites. If you identify yourself as an employee of the company, for example, be sure that your "About Me" profile and related content is consistent with how you wish to position yourself with colleagues, customers, and the company. Don't allow thoughtless comments or "funny" photos to undercut your professionalism. The lines between public and private, personal and professional are blurred in online social networks. By virtue of identifying yourself

as an employee of the company within a social network, you are now connected to your colleagues, managers, and customers. If you have recently joined the company, be sure to update your social profiles to reflect our corporate guidelines.

14. Take the high road at all times. Never pick fights with other posters. Always admit to—and correct—your own mistakes. Never alter or "correct" a previous post without explaining why you have done so. When you see misrepresentations made about the company by media, analysts, or other bloggers, you may certainly use your blog—or join someone else's—to point that out. Always do so with respect, stick to the facts, and identify your appropriate affiliation to the company.

Also, if you speak about a competitor, you must make sure that what you say is factual and does not disparage the competitor. Avoid unnecessary or unproductive arguments. Brawls may earn traffic, but nobody wins in the end. Don't try to settle scores or goad competitors or others into inflammatory debates. Here and in other areas of public discussion, make sure that what you are saying is factually correct.

15. Try to create value-added posts. Provide worthwhile information and thoughtful opinions, particularly if your affiliation with the company is made clear on the site. Blogs and social networks that are hosted on company-owned domains should be used in a way that adds value to the company's business. If it helps you, your coworkers, our clients, or our partners to do their jobs and solve problems; if it helps to improve knowledge or skills; if it contributes directly or indirectly to the improvement of the company's products, processes, and policies; if it builds a sense of community; or if it helps to promote the company's values, then it is adding value. Though not directly business-related, background information you choose to share about

yourself, such as information about your family or personal interests, may be useful in helping establish a relationship between you and your readers, but it is entirely your choice whether to share this information.

16. If you have any doubt about whether you ought to post a particular comment or content online, contact the Chief Compliance Officer or director of media relations.

17. Some bloggers and social networkers post anonymously, using pseudonyms or false screen names. The company discourages anonymity in blogs and other forms of online communications that relate to the company, our people, products, services, or any matter in which the company is engaged. We believe in transparency and honesty. If you are blogging, tweeting, or posting about the work you do for the company, we encourage you to use your real name, be clear about who you are, and identify that you work for the company. Honesty is valued in the blogosphere and social networking world. If you have a business or personal interest in the topic you are discussing, acknowledge it (in compliance with FTC endorsement guidelines). That said, be smart about protecting your privacy—and the privacy of your family and friends. Online content is permanent. Think twice before disclosing personal, potentially embarrassing, or otherwise harmful details.

18. It is against company policy for unauthorized employees to respond to media inquiries. Only the media relations director is authorized to speak with the press on the company's behalf. If a print reporter, broadcast producer, blogger, or other media representative contacts you online regarding any company-related matter, forward the request to the media relations department.

19. Protect the company's customers, business partners, and suppliers. Outside the company, never identify a client, partner, or supplier by name without permission and never discuss confidential details of a client engagement.

Internal social networking sites allow suppliers and business partners to participate, so be sensitive to whom will see your content. If clients haven't given explicit permission for their names to be used, think carefully about the content you're going to publish on any internal social media site and get the appropriate permission where necessary.

It is acceptable to discuss general details about types of projects and to use nonidentifying pseudonyms for a client (Client X), as long as the information provided does not make it easy for someone to identify the client or violate any nondisclosure or intellectual property agreements that may be in place with the client. Furthermore, your blog or online social networking site is not the place to conduct confidential business with a client.

20. Don't allow your online activities to interfere with your job or work commitments.

## Acknowledgment and Signature

If you have questions about this Social Media and Blog Policy, address them to the Human Resources Director before signing the following agreement.

I have read the Company's Social Media and Blog Policy, and agree to abide by it. I understand that a violation of any of the above rules, policies, and procedures may result in disciplinary action, up to and including my termination.

Employee Name (Printed): _____

Employee Signature: _____

Date: _____

*Source:* ©2012, The ePolicy Institute, www.epolicyinstitute.com, Executive Director Nancy Flynn. For informational purposes only. Individual policies should be developed with assistance from competent legal counsel.

## SAMPLE SOCIAL MEDIA AND BLOG POLICY, 3

This is the Company's official Social Media and Blog Policy. If you are a full-time or part-time employee, paid or unpaid intern, executive, board member, independent contractor, or freelance professional engaged in blogging or any other form of social networking on the Company Internet or outside of our system, this Social Media and Blog Policy applies to you. Failure to comply with this policy may result in disciplinary action, up to and including termination of your employment or contract.

### Social Media and Blog Rules

**Always Think Before You Post.** Your posts reflect your personality and your position within our organization. Keep your comments civil and polite, responsible and appropriate, whether you are posting for business purposes or personal reasons. In the age of social media, the lines between public and private, personal and professional are blurred. When you identify yourself as a Company employee, you create reader expectations regarding your knowledge about our business and expertise about our products and services. Be certain the content you create is consistent with our organization's mission, values, and standards. Keep in mind the fact that every post you publish is a reflection of your professionalism and the Company's credibility. Treat the social web with respect.

**Adhere to All Company Employment Policies.** Bloggers and social networkers are obligated to adhere at all times to all Company policies including, but not limited to, Social Media Policy, Mobile Device Policy, Privacy Policy, Confidentiality Policy, Computer Security Policy, Media Relations Policy, Investor Relations Policy, Online Writing Style Policy, and Corporate Code of Conduct.

**Focus on Your Expertise and Interests.** The social web offers employees the chance to share their unique perspectives on what's happening within our organization and around the globe. This is your opportunity to share your know-how with the world.

**Add Value to the Online Conversation.** If you are writing on behalf of the Company, please be sure your content provides value to our customers and prospects, employees and executives, suppliers and business partners, the general public and other readers. Try to post content that answers a question, solves a problem, helps people do their jobs, or creates greater awareness and understanding of our company's mission.

**Keep Company Business Under Wraps.** Never reveal Company secrets including, but not limited to, confidential data, company financials, internal email and other documents, intellectual property, customer lists, marketing plans, salary and benefits packages, or company secrets of any kind. Adhere to the Company's Confidentiality Policy, Media Relations Policy, Investor Relations Policy, Privacy Policy, and all other employment policies when engaged in social networking and blogging at work, home, or elsewhere.

**Investor Relations.** Employees are forbidden to post any content related to the Company's financials, including but not limited to revenues, earnings, sales, projections, future plans, inventories, strategies, share prices, executive salaries, performance bonuses, or severance packages.

**Keep Your Personal Business Private.** Never share private information that could potentially harm or embarrass your family, friends, or self. You never know who may be reading.

**Be Completely Honest.** The blogosphere and social media world are attuned to honesty—and dishonesty. If you have a vested interested in a topic, be sure to mention it. If you are writing about the Company, or on behalf of the Company, identify yourself by name, title, and role within the company.

**Litigation Rules.** Employees are prohibited from commenting on any lawsuits in which the Company currently is engaged, has been engaged in the past, or may one day in the future become engaged. Employees are prohibited from discussing, commenting on, or answering questions about legal claims, financial settlements, jury awards, legal strategies, or any other aspects of litigation involving the Company. Refer all litigation-related questions that may be posted on your business or personal blogs or social media sites to the Company's legal department.

**Keep Content Legal.** Employees are responsible for their business and personal blog and social media content including text, audio, photos, videos, and other images. Fraudulent, obscene, vulgar, abusive, harassing, profane, discriminatory, sexually suggestive, intimidating, misleading, defamatory, bullying, or otherwise offensive, objectionable, inappropriate, or illegal content is prohibited.

Jokes, disparaging remarks, and inappropriate comments related to ethnicity, race, color, religion, sex, age, disabilities, physique, sexual orientation, and sexual preference are prohibited by law and Company policy.

When blogging and networking online, employees must comply with all Company policies including but not limited to Social Media and Blog Policy, Sexual Harassment and Discrimination Policy, Ethics Policy, Confidentiality Policy, Online Writing Style Policy, and Netiquette Guidelines.

**Copyright Adherence.** Employees are not permitted to post, copy, transfer, rename, or edit copyright-protected material without permission of the copyright owner. Employees may not link to copyright-protected content without permission of the copyright holder. Copyright infringement may result in disciplinary action, up to and including termination, as well as legal action by the copyright holder.

**Respect Regulatory Rules.** That means no exposure of customers' personal financial data to unauthorized employees or outside parties. Private financial data includes credit card numbers, debit card numbers, Social Security numbers, dates of birth, mailing addresses, full names, and home phone numbers.

**Write as You Speak.** Be conversational, yet professional. Put a human face on your posts and the Company. Your written posts should reflect your normal speaking style and the tone you would use in business situations, when chatting with coworkers or explaining concepts to customers. Short, simple sentences are best. Make an effort to engage your readers by asking questions and initiating thought-provoking discussions.

**Media Inquiries.** Many reporters turn to blogs and social media, looking for story ideas and news sources. All business-related media inquiries should be routed to the Company's media relations director. Employees are not permitted to respond to media inquiries, conduct interviews, provide background material, or otherwise engage in business-related media relations activities without permission from the Company's media relations director.

**Privacy and Security.** All blog posts and social media content published on the Company's system are the property of the organization, and should be considered public information. The Company reserves the right to access and monitor all blog posts, comments, and archives on the Company's system as deemed necessary and appropriate. Blog and social media content is public, not private, communication. All posts and comments, including text and images, can be disclosed by the Company to law enforcement agencies, courts, regulators, or other third parties without prior consent of the employee who created, transmitted, acquired, or posted the information.

**Monitoring.** When using the Company's blogs, social media sites, or Internet system, employees have no reasonable expectation of privacy. The Company reserves the right to access and monitor all blog posts, comments, and archives on the Company's system as deemed necessary and appropriate. The Company also reserves the right to monitor the blogosphere and the Internet as a whole, including personal blogs, tweets, YouTube videos, Facebook posts, and other online content that employees may create and post on their own time, using their own personal accounts, via their own electronic devices. Blog and social media content is public, not private, communication. Violation of the Company's Social Media and Blog Policy—or any other Company policy, rule, guideline, or code—will result in disciplinary action, up to and including termination, regardless of whether the violation occurs on a Company-hosted site or the employee's own personal blog or social media site.

**Netiquette Rules.** In accordance with the Company's netiquette guidelines, employees must adhere to the rules of electronic etiquette when communicating online. In other words, be polite, polished, and professional. Write and post content that is 100 percent appropriate, legal, civil, and compliant with all Company policies.

**NLRA Rules.** The Company is covered by and compliant with the National Labor Relations Act (NLRA). The Company supports employees' legal right to engage in protected concerted activity and communication under Section 7 of the NLRA. This Social Media and Blog Policy will not be interpreted or applied in a manner that interferes with employees' protected concerted activity or communication. For additional information, see the Company's "Employee Rights Under the NLRA" poster.

**Policy Violations.** This Social Media and Blog Policy is designed to provide employees with a general idea of acceptable and appropriate use of Company-hosted and personal blogs and other social media sites. Any violation of this policy—or any Company rules, policies, and procedures—may result in disciplinary action, up to and including your termination.

**Acknowledgment and Signature.**

If you have any questions about this Social Media and Blog Policy, please address them to the Human Resources Director before signing the following agreement.

I have read the Company's Social Media and Blog Policy and agree to abide by it. I understand that a violation of any of the above rules, policies, and procedures may result in disciplinary action, up to and including my termination.

Employee Name (Printed): _____

Employee Signature: _____

Date: _____

*Source:* ©2012, The ePolicy Institute, www.epolicyinstitute.com, Executive Director Nancy Flynn. For informational purposes only. Individual policies should be developed with assistance from competent legal counsel.

## SAMPLE BLOG POLICY, 1

The Company provides employees with external blog access, primarily for business purposes. Employees using the Company's external blogs are responsible for behaving professionally, ethically, and responsibly in the blogosphere. To that end, the Company has established the following Blog Policy.

Employees are required to adhere to the Company's Blog Policy when at the office, at home, on the road for business, or anywhere else. The Company's Blog Policy governs use of the Company's business blog system for business or personal reasons. The Company's Blog Policy also governs any business or personal blogging employees may engage in at home via personal accounts and personal computer devices. In other words, employees are required to adhere to the Company's Blog Policy (and all Company employment policies) 24 hours a day, seven days a week, 365 days a year.

Violations of the Company's Blog Policy, whether they occur on the Company's external business blogs or the employee's own personal blogs, will result in disciplinary action, up to and including termination.

1. Employee-bloggers are required to write under their own names, whether using a Company-hosted business blog or a personal blog. Pseudonyms and anonymous postings by employees of the Company are prohibited—even if you are blogging after hours (at home or elsewhere) via personal accounts and personal computer devices.

2. When writing about the Company, employee-bloggers are required to identify themselves, by name and title, as employees of the Company, whether using a Company-hosted business blog or a personal blog.

3. Employee-bloggers must incorporate the following legal disclaimer into their business and personal blogs: "The opinions expressed on this blog are my own personal opinions. They do not reflect the opinions of my employer, the Company."

4. Employee-bloggers are prohibited from attacking, defaming, harassing, discriminating against, menacing, threatening, bullying, or otherwise exhibiting inappropriate or offensive behavior or attitudes toward coworkers, supervisors, executives, customers, vendors, shareholders, the media, other bloggers, or any other internal or external parties, whether using a Company-hosted business blog or a personal blog.

5. Employee-bloggers are prohibited from disclosing confidential, sensitive, proprietary, top-secret, or private information about the Company, our employees, executives, customers, partners, suppliers, or other third parties, whether using a Company-hosted business blog or a personal blog.

6. Employee-bloggers are prohibited from disclosing financial information about the Company without permission from the Investor Relations department, whether using a Company-hosted business blog or a personal blog. Financial information includes revenues, profits, forecasts, quarterly reports, annual reports, acquisition plans, merger plans, salary and benefits packages, and other Company-related financial information. See Company's Investor Relations Policy and Confidentiality Policy.

7. Employee-bloggers may discuss the Company's competitors, but must do so in a respectful, professional manner, whether using a Company-hosted business blog or a personal blog.

8. Employee-bloggers must adhere to the Company's Online Content Policy and Netiquette Policy, whether using a Company-hosted business blog or a personal blog. Prohibited content includes, but is not limited to:

    No obscene, profane, adult-oriented, pornographic, harassing, discriminatory, menacing, threatening, bullying, and otherwise offensive text, art, photos, videos, graphics, cartoons, and other content.

No harassment or discrimination based on race, color, religion, sex, sexual orientation, national origin, age, disability, or other status protected by federal law.

No disclosure of confidential Company, executive, or employee data, including but not limited to Social Security numbers, salary and benefits packages, and corporate financials.

No exposure of customers' personal financial data to unauthorized employees or outside parties. Private financial data includes, but is not limited to, credit card numbers, debit card numbers, Social Security numbers, dates of birth, mailing addresses, and so on. See Company's Confidentiality Policy.

No disclosure of patients' electronic protected health information (EPHI) to unauthorized employees or third parties. EPHI includes data related to patients' health status, medical care, treatment plans, and payment issues.

No rumors, gossip, or defamatory comments—about anyone within the Company or outside the organization.

No whining or complaining about the Company, customers, or business.

No posting of, or commenting on, internal email or other eyes-only information that is intended solely for internal distribution, communication, and use. See Company's Confidentiality Policy.

No jokes or "funny" text, cartoons, videos, photos, files, or art of any kind.

No obscene, off-color, pornographic, or otherwise inappropriate and offensive language, art, or other content.

9. Employee-bloggers are prohibited from posting copyright-protected material without the express written permission of the copyright owner, whether using a Company-hosted business blog or a personal blog. Copyright-protected material includes, but is not limited to, books, articles,

whitepapers, brochures, web pages, surveys, research documents, PowerPoint presentations, training materials, and other intellectual property.

10. Employee-bloggers may not post content or conduct activities that violate local, state, federal, or international laws. Among other laws, employees may not violate 15 U.S.C. 6501 et seq. ("Children's Online Privacy Protection Act of 1998"), whether using a Company-hosted business blog or a personal blog.

11. Employee-bloggers must comply with all of the Company's employment policies, including the Company's Blog Policy, Sexual Harassment and Discrimination Policy, Ethics Policy, Code of Conduct, Confidentiality Policy, Investor Relations Policy, Media Relations Policy, Mobile Device Policy, Content and Netiquette Policy, Record Retention Policy, Email Policy, Internet Policy, Computer Security Policy, and Social Media Policy, whether using a Company-hosted business blog or a personal blog.

12. The Company is covered by and compliant with the National Labor Relations Act (NLRA). The Company supports employees' legal right to engage in protected concerted activity and communication under Section 7 of the NLRA. This Blog Policy will not be interpreted or applied in a manner that interferes with employees' protected concerted activity or communication. For additional information, see the Company's "Employee Rights Under the NLRA" poster.

13. Violation of the Company's Blog Policy (or any other Company employment policy) will result in disciplinary action, up to and including termination, whether using a Company-hosted business blog or a personal blog.

### Acknowledgment and Signature

If you have questions about the above Blog Policy, address them to the Human Resources Director before signing the following agreement.

I have read the Company's Blog Policy, and agree to abide by it. I understand that a violation of any of the above rules, policies, and procedures may result in disciplinary action, up to and including my termination.

Employee Name (Printed): _____

Employee Signature: _____

Date: _____

## SAMPLE BLOG POLICY, 2

The Company provides employees with blog access for the benefit of the organization and customers. Employees using the company blog are responsible for maintaining the organization's public image and communicating with the blogosphere appropriately. To that end, the Company has established the following Blog Policy.

Employees are required to adhere to the Company's Blog Policy when at the office (or elsewhere) using the Company's business blog system for business or personal reasons. Employees also are expected to comply with the Company's Blog Policy when at home (or elsewhere) using a personal blog or a third-party blog for business or personal reasons.

Violations of the Company's Blog Policy, whether they occur on the Company's blog, the employee's own personal blog, or a third-party blog will result in disciplinary action, up to and including termination.

1. I will not use a pseudonym, fake name, or otherwise blog anonymously. I will identify myself by name as the writer of my business blogs and publisher of my personal blogs.
2. I will identify myself as an employee of the Company, including my title, in all business-related blog posts published on the Company's blog, my own personal blog, or third-party blogs.
3. I will post the Company's legal disclaimer on my Company-hosted business blogs and my own personal blogs. The Company's legal disclaimer reads: "The postings on this blog are my own and do not necessarily reflect the opinions, positions, or strategies of my employer, the Company."
4. I will abide by the Company's Blog Policy, Harassment and Discrimination Policy, Mobile Device Policy, Email Policy, Internet Policy, Confidentiality Policy, Privacy Policy, Media Relations Policy, Record Retention Policy, Code of Ethics, Netiquette Rules, and Language and Content Guidelines, as

well as all other employment rules and policies in all of my blog posts, business-related and personal.

5. I will treat my readers, as well as those who post comments on my business and personal blogs, with respect, civility, and professionalism.

6. I will reply to my readers' comments, questions, and messages in a timely and professional manner.

7. I will not engage in any form of spamming (comment spam or splogging) on my business and personal blogs or any external blogs. I understand that comment spam occurs when spammers use tools to automatically flood a blog with advertising in the form of bogus comments. I understand that splogging occurs when spammers use automated tools to create fake blogs that are populated with links to websites on which goods and services are sold.

8. I will write all blog posts in an honest, transparent, first-person style.

9. I will make every effort to ensure that my business and personal blog posts are 100 percent accurate and factual.

10. I will not post gossip, rumors, lies, falsehoods, defamatory comments, personal attacks, harassing, discriminatory, menacing, bullying, or otherwise inappropriate and offensive content that violates any of the Company's employment policies, rules, codes, or guidelines.

11. I will be mindful of the fact that my blog posts may create electronic business records, which will be retained by the Company for business, legal, and regulatory purposes.

12. I will not violate copyright law. I will secure permission of the copyright holder before publishing copyright-protected material. Whenever I use content that is not original to me, I will cite my sources and link to online references and source material.

13. I will adhere to the Company's Confidentiality Policy when engaged in business and personal blogging. I will not post content that violates the trade secrets, confidentiality,

or privacy of the Company, its employees, executives, customers, business partners, suppliers, or any other third parties.

14. I will strive to keep my business and personal blog posts well written, mechanically correct, factually accurate, original, readable, and appealing to my readers.

## Violations & Disciplinary Action

Employees who violate the Company's Blog Policy may face disciplinary action, up to and including termination.

## Acknowledgment and Signature

If you have any questions about this Blog Policy, please address them to the Human Resources Director before signing the following agreement.

I have read the Company's Blog Policy and agree to abide by it. I understand that a violation of any of the above rules, policies, and procedures may result in disciplinary action, up to and including my termination.

Employee Name (Printed): _____

Employee Signature: _____

Date: _____

*Source:* ©2012, The ePolicy Institute, www.epolicyinstitute.com, Executive Director Nancy Flynn. For informational purposes only. Individual policies should be developed with assistance from competent legal counsel.

## SAMPLE BLOG POLICY, 3

The Company provides employees with external blog access, primarily for business purposes. Employees using the Company's external blog are responsible for behaving professionally, ethically, and responsibly in the blogosphere. To that end, the Company has established the following Blog Policy.

Employees are required to adhere to the Company's Blog Policy when at the office, at home, or elsewhere. Employees are required to adhere to the Company's Blog Policy whether you are blogging for business or personal reasons via our Company system and tools or your own personal blog account and devices.

Violations of the Company's Blog Policy, whether they occur on the Company's blogs or the employee's own personal blogs, will result in disciplinary action, up to and including termination.

1. Employee-bloggers are required to write under their own names, whether using a Company-hosted business blog or a personal blog. Pseudonyms and anonymous postings are prohibited at all times.
2. Employee-bloggers are required to identify themselves, by name and title, as employees of the Company, whether using a Company-hosted business blog or a personal blog.
3. Employee-bloggers must incorporate the following legal disclaimer into their business and personal blogs: "The opinions expressed on this blog are my own personal opinions. They do not reflect the opinions of my employer, the Company."
4. Employee-bloggers are prohibited from attacking, defaming, harassing, discriminating against, menacing, threatening, bullying, or otherwise exhibiting inappropriate or offensive behavior or attitudes toward coworkers, supervisors, executives, customers, vendors, shareholders, the media, other bloggers, or other third parties, whether using a Company-hosted business blog or a personal blog.

5. Employee-bloggers are prohibited from disclosing confidential, sensitive, proprietary, top-secret, or private information about the Company, our employees, executives, customers, business partners, suppliers, or other third parties, whether using a Company-hosted business blog or a personal blog.

6. Employee-bloggers are prohibited from disclosing financial information about the Company without permission from the Investor Relations Director, whether using a Company-hosted business blog or personal blog. Financial information includes but is not limited to Company revenues, profits, forecasts, projections, salary and benefits packages, mergers, acquisitions, and other business-related financial information.

7. Employee-bloggers may discuss the Company's competitors, but must do so in a respectful and professional manner, whether using a Company-hosted business blog or a personal blog.

8. Employee-bloggers must adhere to the Company's written content and language guidelines, whether using a Company-hosted business blog or a personal blog. Prohibited content includes obscene, profane, adult-oriented, pornographic, harassing, discriminatory, menacing, threatening, defamatory, bullying, and otherwise offensive or unlawful text, art, photos, videos, graphics, cartoons, and other content.

9. Employee-bloggers are prohibited from posting copyright-protected material without the express written permission of the copyright owner, whether using a Company-hosted business blog or a personal blog.

10. Employee-bloggers may not post content or conduct activities that fail to conform with local, state, and federal laws, including, without limitation, 15 U.S.C. 6501 et seq. (the "Children's Online Privacy Protection Act of 1998"), whether using a Company-hosted business blog or a personal blog.

11. Employee-bloggers must comply with all of the Company's written rules and policies, including the Company's Blog Policy, Sexual Harassment and Discrimination Policy, Investor Relations Policy, Media Relations Policy, Privacy Policy, Computer Security Policy, Confidentiality Policy, Ethics Policy, Online Writing Style Policy, Internet Policy, Mobile Device Policy, and Email Policy, whether using a company-hosted business blog or a personal blog.

12. Violation of the Company's Blog Policy, or any other Company employment policy, will result in disciplinary action, up to and including termination, whether using a Company-hosted business blog or a personal blog.

### Acknowledgment and Signature

If you have any questions about this Blog Policy, please address them to the Human Resources Director before signing the following agreement.

I have read the Company's Blog Policy and agree to abide by it. I understand that a violation of any of the above rules, policies, and procedures may result in disciplinary action, up to and including my termination.

Employee Name (Printed): _____

Employee Signature: _____

Date: _____

*Source:* ©2012, The ePolicy Institute, www.epolicyinstitute.com, Executive Director Nancy Flynn. For informational purposes only. Individual policies should be developed with assistance from competent legal counsel.

**SAMPLE COMMUNITY GUIDELINES FOR BLOGS AND SOCIAL MEDIA, 1**

(Organization) welcomes the participation of our customers, prospects, investors, suppliers, business partners, and other interested parties who would like to share their experiences (positive and negative) with us, suggest ways in which we might improve our products and services, and participate in an open, public conversation with other members of our corporate family. To ensure that all online conversations that take place on (Organization) blogs and social networking sites are focused and friendly, civil and productive, we have established this policy for nonemployees who opt to post content on our sites. (Organization) reserves the right to revise this policy at any time at our sole discretion. Our most current policy is always available online at our corporate website.

1. Be aware that (Organization's) online community is moderated and managed by a trusted member of our staff. All comments are reviewed and approved by (Organization) prior to posting.
2. The purpose of our content review is to ensure that posted comments contribute to the online conversation in a positive and productive, respectful and lawful manner.
3. Comments that fail to live up to (Organization's) standards will not be posted. Prohibited comments include those that are deemed to be:

**Off Topic.** We will exclude comments that are unrelated to the conversation that is under way.

**Spam.** Comments that are focused on selling a product or service, or driving traffic to an external website for personal, political, or monetary gain will be excluded.

**Malicious or Hurtful Comments.** Personal attacks against anyone are prohibited. Also outlawed are bullying, threatening, menacing, disparaging, disrespectful, or otherwise demeaning comments. Gossip and rumors about people, products, and businesses are forbidden. Hateful, racist, sexist, and ethnically offensive or derogatory content is banned. Obscene, pornographic, and sexually explicit language is prohibited.

**Illegal.** All comments and conversations must adhere to local, state, and federal laws. Posters are prohibited from violating copyright law, revealing trade secrets, exposing confidential company or customer information, violating patients' privacy rights, or posting any content that otherwise violates federal or state laws or industry or government regulations. There is to be no harassment or discrimination on the grounds of race, color, religion, sex, sexual orientation, national origin, age, disability, or other status protected by U.S. federal law.

**Private, Personal, and Confidential Information.** Please do not provide any personal information about yourself, your family, your friends, your employer, and so on. Do not list home addresses, work addresses, telephone numbers. Do not discuss vacation or travel plans. Remember, the content you post on (Organization's) blogs and social media sites will be read by many people inside and outside the company. Keep your private information private!

**Age Requirements.** Please note that we do not accept comments from minors under age 18. Once you turn 18, we welcome your participation.

**Format.** We will not accept comments in HTML format. We will not post links to URLs (web addresses). Please contribute all comments in plain text only.

**Employee Participation.** (Organization) does not endorse comments made by employees, unless they have been authorized by management to post "official" content on behalf of the company. Otherwise, all statements and viewpoints expressed by unauthorized employees are strictly those of the individual writer, and do not constitute an official position of the company. Employees of (Organization) are required to disclose their employment status when submitting a comment or question to a blog or social media site hosted by the company. If management determines that an employee's comment is confidential, reveals "insider" information, or otherwise could negatively impact (Organization), then we reserve the right to exclude the comment.

**Thank you for your adherence to (Organization's) Community Guidelines for Blogs and Social Media.** We appreciate your efforts to keep the online conversation friendly and focused, civil and compliant.

*Source:* ©2012, The ePolicy Institute, www.epolicyinstitute.com, Executive Director Nancy Flynn. For informational purposes only. Individual policies should be developed with assistance from competent legal counsel.

**SAMPLE COMMUNITY GUIDELINES FOR BLOGS AND SOCIAL MEDIA, 2**

Our company has a thriving and engaged online community, and we actively encourage community members to comment on our business blogs and social media sites. Because we are dedicated to operating respectful, engaging, and informative sites, we have developed a community comment policy for all users.

We enforce our community comment policy 24 hours a day, seven days a week, 365 days a year through the hands-on involvement of authorized staff members and selected community moderators, supported by content management and moderation tools. If you wish to participate in our company's online community, we ask you to adhere to the following mandatory guidelines.

### Comments Must Be Polite and Add Value to the Conversation

All comments must be civil and should add value to the conversation. Comments that are rude, impolite, unkind, mean-spirited, or that otherwise make this online community a less civil environment will be excluded.

### Beware: Comments May Be Moderated

To help ensure a civil online community, the company's content management and moderation team may read comments before they are published. Approval times vary, depending on the amount of content that is pending approval at any given time. We review comments as quickly as possible. Thank you for your patience.

### Your Help Is Appreciated

As a member of this online community, you have the power and responsibility to help elevate the level of conversation—and exclude those who do not conform to the rules. On every comment, you can "fan and favorite" users who are posting great content, or you can flag comments for review by moderators. Flagging comments helps us act quickly to delete comments that don't comply with our community comment policy. We appreciate your help.

### Be Honest and Transparent

We rely on community members to be themselves and express their true opinions. Do not pretend to be someone else. Do not misrepresent yourself. Do not use your comments to spread false information. If you do, you face rejection of your comments and expulsion from our sites.

### Keep Our Community Free from Hostile, Hateful, or Harassing Behavior

Online bullying is a growing problem and will not be tolerated by our company or our sites. Our goal is to maintain a civil online community. We will not tolerate language or comments that are threatening, harassing, discriminatory, bullying, menacing, or in any way offensive or frightening to others. If a credible threat is made against an individual or group, the comment will be removed, and the commenter will be excluded. In addition, we may report the user and comment to law enforcement. If so, we will cooperate fully with any requests from law enforcement to review records, content, registrations, and other data.

### Safeguard Your Secrets and Protect Your Privacy

You never know who may be reading or replying to your online comments. Protect your privacy. Never post personal information (full name, address, date of birth, phone number). Never reveal financial data (credit card numbers, Social Security numbers, and so on). Never discuss employment information (name of your employer, facility where you work, salary details, and so on). Never write anything that could haunt you or harm your friends and loved ones (travel schedules, medical conditions, family secrets, and so on).

**Thank you for your adherence to our Community Guidelines for Blogs and Social Media.** We appreciate your efforts to keep the online conversation friendly and focused, civil and compliant.

*Source:* ©2012, The ePolicy Institute, www.epolicyinstitute.com, Executive Director Nancy Flynn. For informational purposes only. Individual policies should be developed with assistance from competent legal counsel.

## SAMPLE SOCIAL NETWORKING AND VIDEO-SHARING POLICY

The Company prohibits employees from accessing public social networking sites (Facebook, Twitter, and so on) and external video-sharing sites (YouTube, and so on) via the Company Internet system and Company-owned computer resources (including, but not limited to, desktops, laptops, BlackBerries, smartphones, tablets, and handheld and hands-free cell phones) during business hours (including, but not limited to, time spent at headquarters and branch offices or on the road for business reasons in cars, airplanes, airports, hotels, restaurants, client offices, prospects' offices, and suppliers' offices).

The Company recognizes, however, that some employees may, for personal reasons, choose to access, view, post, download, or upload content to external social networking sites and video sites on their own personal time via their own personal computer equipment and private Internet accounts. When accessing, transmitting, viewing, downloading, uploading, or posting content (including but not limited to text, photos, videos, and art of any kind) to external social networking or video sites, employees are responsible for behaving professionally, ethically, responsibly, and in accordance with all of the Company's employment rules and policies.

To that end, the Company has established the following Social Networking and Video-Sharing Policy, which all employees are obligated to comply with at all times—during business hours on Company time and after hours on employees' own personal time.

Violations of the Company's Social Networking and Video-Sharing Policy, whether they occur at work during business hours or on the employees' own time and own computer equipment and private accounts, will result in disciplinary action, up to and including termination.

1. Unauthorized employees are prohibited from mentioning the Company or identifying themselves as employees of the Company via text, photos, art, Company logos,

Company uniforms, Company letterhead, Company products, Company trademarks, or any other image, copy, or content, whether using a personal social media site, public video-sharing site, or Company-hosted social networking or video site.

2. Employees must incorporate the following disclaimer into their personal social networking pages and public video-sharing site posts: "The opinions expressed on this site [in this video] are my own personal opinions. They do not reflect the opinions of my employer, Company."

3. Employees are prohibited from attacking, defaming, harassing, discriminating against, menacing, threatening, bullying, or otherwise exhibiting inappropriate or offensive behavior, attitudes, opinion, or commentary toward or about coworkers, supervisors, executives, board members, customers, vendors, shareholders, the media, or other parties, whether using a personal social media account, public video-sharing site, or Company-hosted social networking or video-sharing site.

4. Employees are prohibited from disclosing confidential, sensitive, proprietary, top-secret, or private information about the Company, its employees, executives, customers, partners, suppliers, or other parties, whether using a personal social networking site, public video-sharing site, or a Company-hosted social networking or video-sharing site.

5. Employees are prohibited from using Company-provided or personal cell phones, BlackBerries, or smartphones to take, transmit, download, or upload to social networking or video-sharing sites any photos or videos of customers, prospects, suppliers, business partners, investors, job applicants, or any other third party without first securing the written permission of your subject and an authorized member of the Compliance Department, whether using a personal social networking site, public video-sharing site, or a Company-hosted social networking or video-sharing site.

6. Employees are prohibited from using Company-provided or personal cell phones, BlackBerries, or smartphones

to take, transmit, download, or upload any business- or company-related photos or videos to any social networking or video-sharing sites without first securing written permission from an authorized member of the Compliance Department, whether using a personal social networking site, public video-sharing site, or a Company-hosted social networking or video-sharing site.

Banned text, photos, and videos include, but are not limited to, the following: (1) "funny," embarrassing, or unprofessional images of Company employees, managers, executives, board members, or other internal parties; (2) Company buildings (internal or external images), offices (headquarters or remote locations), R&D facilities and operations, products and services that are proprietary, top-secret, in development, or trademark-protected; (3) confidential Company data, intellectual property, and internal documents, including but not limited to Company email, photos, and videos; (4) Company logos, signage, trademarks, business cards, letterhead, literature, or any other printed or electronic content that could be used to identify the company or employees, whether using a personal social networking site, public video-sharing site, or a Company-hosted social networking or video-sharing site.

7. Employees are prohibited from posting or otherwise disclosing financial information about the Company without permission from the Investor Relations Department, whether using a public social networking site, personal video-sharing site, or Company-hosted social networking or video-sharing site. Financial information includes, but is not limited to, revenues, profits, losses, forecasts, salary and benefits packages, merger and acquisition strategies, and all other Company-related financial information.

8. Employees must adhere 100 percent to the Company's content, language, and netiquette guidelines, whether using a Company-hosted social networking or video-sharing site or

a public social networking or video-sharing site. Prohibited content includes, but is not limited to, obscene, profane, adult-oriented, pornographic, harassing, discriminatory, menacing, threatening, bullying, and otherwise offensive text, art, photos, videos, graphics, cartoons, and other content, whether using a personal social networking site, public video-sharing site, or a Company-hosted social networking or video-sharing site.

In addition, employees are prohibited from writing, posting, or otherwise transmitting or distributing content that violates legally protected classes. In other words, no harassment or discrimination on the grounds of race, color, religion, sex, sexual orientation, national origin, age, disability, or other status protected by federal law.

9. Employees are prohibited from posting copyright-protected material without the express written permission of the copyright owner, whether using a personal social networking site, public video-sharing site, or a company-hosted social networking or video-sharing site. If you are unsure about what constitutes copyright-protected content, see the Glossary of Terms at the end of this Social Networking and Video-Sharing Policy or consult with the Compliance Officer.

10. Employees may not write, post, transmit, distribute, upload, download, copy, or print content—or otherwise conduct online activities—that violate any local, state, federal, or international laws. Included among other laws with which employees must comply is 15 U.S.C. 6501 et seq., the "Children's Online Privacy Protection Act of 1998." In other words, employees must behave in a lawful manner at all times, whether using a personal social networking site, public video-sharing site, or a Company-hosted social networking or video-sharing site.

11. Employees must comply with all of the Company's written employment policies, including the Social Networking and Video-Sharing Policy, Sexual Harassment and Discrimination

Policy, Ethics Policy, Code of Conduct, Confidentiality Policy, Computer Security Policy, Media Relations Policy, Investor Relations Policy, Public Relations Policy, Government Affairs Policy, Content and Netiquette Policy, Email Policy, Internet Policy, and Mobile Device Policy, whether using a personal social networking site, public video-sharing site, or a Company-hosted social networking or video-sharing site.

12. Violation of the Company's Social Networking and Video-Sharing Policy (or any other Company employment policy) will result in disciplinary action, up to and including termination, whether using a personal social networking site, public video-sharing site, or a Company-hosted social networking or video-sharing site.

### Acknowledgment and Signature

If you have questions about the Company's Social Networking and Video-Sharing Policy, address them to the Human Resources Director before signing the following agreement.

I have read the Company's Social Networking and Video-Sharing Policy, and agree to abide by it. I understand that a violation of any of the above rules, policies, and procedures may result in disciplinary action, up to and including my termination.

Employee Name (Printed): _____

Employee Signature: _____

Date: _____

*Source:* ©2012, The ePolicy Institute, www.epolicyinstitute.com, Executive Director Nancy Flynn. For informational purposes only. Individual policies should be developed with assistance from competent legal counsel.

## SAMPLE CELL PHONE AND TEXT MESSAGING POLICY

The Company provides employees with electronic communications tools, including cell phones with text messaging capabilities. This written policy governs employees' use of Company-provided cell phones and the organization's text messaging (texting) system, as well as employees' use of personal cell phones and texting accounts. This Cell Phone and Text Messaging Policy applies to cell phone and text messaging use at the Company's headquarters and district offices, as well as at remote locations including but not limited to Company-provided vehicles, employee-owned or leased vehicles, rental cars, employees' homes, clients' offices, suppliers' offices, hotels, trains, rental cars, airports, and airplanes.

The Company's Cell Phone and Text Messaging Policy applies to employees' use of cell phones, smartphones, BlackBerries, and other mobile handheld and hands-free phones, whether provided by the Company or owned by the employee or a third party.

The Company's Cell Phone and Text Messaging Policy applies to full-time employees, part-time employees, independent contractors, interns, consultants, agents, business partners, and other third parties working on behalf of, for the benefit of, or under the control of the Company.

Any employee or other user who violates the Company's Cell Phone and Text Messaging Policy is subject to disciplinary action, up to and including termination of employment, contracts, work agreements, or other arrangements the Company and the policy violator may have entered into.

1.  Cell phones and text messaging are made available for business purposes primarily. During business hours, employees may use Company-provided cell phones and the Company's texting system, as well as personal devices and private accounts, for personal use strictly in accordance with this policy.

2. Authorized personal use of cell phones and text messaging: employees may use Company-provided cell phones and texting for personal communication with spouses, children, domestic partners, teachers, babysitters, physicians, and emergency responders. Except for emergency situations, employees' personal use of cell phones to talk or text is limited to lunch breaks and authorized work breaks only. Employees may not use Company-provided or personal cell phones to engage in personal, non-business-related talk or text during otherwise productive business hours.

3. Any employee who needs to hold a personal conversation (voice or text) with persons other than spouses, children, domestic partners, teachers, babysitters, physicians, or emergency responders via a personal device or a Company-provided cell phone must first obtain permission from your immediate supervisor.

4. At no time may an employee use a Company-provided cell phone or other mobile device to operate a business, conduct an external job search, solicit money for personal gain, campaign for political causes or candidates, or promote or solicit funds for a religious or other personal cause.

5. During business hours and/or on Company property, employees are prohibited from using private accounts, personal cell phones, or other mobile devices to operate a business, conduct an external job search, solicit money for personal gain, campaign for political causes or candidates, or promote or solicit funds for a religious or other personal cause.

6. Employees are prohibited from using Company-provided cell phones to play online games, visit chat rooms, or engage in illegal activity, including but not limited to gambling and drug dealing.

7. Text messages and voice mail messages created, transmitted, acquired, and stored on the Company's system may rise to the level of business records. Electronic business

records are subject to the Company's Record Retention Policy, which governs the retention and disposition of text messages, email, social media posts, and all other forms of electronically stored information.

8. Employees have no reasonable expectation of privacy when using the Company's computer and texting systems. All text messages created, acquired, transmitted, and stored on the Company's system via Company-provided or personal cell phones, smartphones, BlackBerries, or other mobile devices are the property of the Company. The Company reserves the right to monitor all text messages created, acquired, transmitted, and stored via the Company's system. Employees have no reasonable expectation of privacy when it comes to business and personal use of the Company's computer and texting systems.

9. The Company reserves the right to retain, monitor, inspect, copy, review, and store at any time and without notice any use of the Company's computer, cell phone, and texting systems, as well as any and all data, files, information, software, and other content created, sent, received, downloaded, uploaded, accessed, or stored in connection with employee usage. The Company reserves the right to disclose text messages and other electronic content to regulators, the courts, law enforcement agencies, and other third parties without the employee's consent.

10. Company employees have the right to work in an environment that is free from hostility, harassment, discrimination, or bullying of any kind. When using Company-provided or personal cell phones, smartphones, BlackBerries, and other mobile devices, employees are required to adhere to the following content, language, and netiquette (electronic etiquette) rules:

    a) Obey the Company's electronic content and language guidelines. Whether conducting a cell phone conversation or texting, you must use a professional tone and businesslike language. You are prohibited from using language that is obscene, vulgar, abusive, harassing, profane, discriminatory, sexually suggestive, intimidating, misleading, defamatory, or otherwise offensive, objectionable, inappropriate, or illegal.

Jokes, disparaging remarks, and inappropriate comments related to ethnicity, race, color, religion, sex, age, disabilities, physique, sexual orientation, or sexual preference are prohibited.

b) Turn off cell phones, smartphone, BlackBerries, and other mobile devices (Company-provided or personal, handheld or hands-free) when driving any vehicle (Company-owned or personal) during business hours. Pull off the road to make a call, take a call, send a text message, or check voice and text messages.

c) Remember that a policy is a policy. Cell phone users and texters are expected to comply with all Company employment policies including Sexual Harassment and Discrimination Policy, Ethics Policy, Code of Conduct, Confidentiality Policy, Cell Phone and Texting Policy, Email Policy, Internet Policy, Social Media Policy, Blog Policy, and Computer Security Policy among others.

d) Adhere to the Company's rules regarding personal use of cell phones, smartphones, BlackBerries, and other electronic business communication tools during business hours. Regardless of whether you are using your own cell phone or a Company-provided phone, employees are required to adhere to the Company's personal use rules governing when, where, why, with whom, and for how long you may engage in personal, non-business-related talking and texting.

e) Never discuss Company business in any public setting in which you could be overheard. Not every location is right for a cell phone conversation. Find a secluded spot (hotel room, car, private office, and so forth) to conduct Company business via your cell phone.

f) Never mention passwords, user names, account numbers, financial data, customers, prospects, or other confidential or proprietary Company or personal information if there is any chance that your cell phone conversation could be overheard. An indiscreet one-sided conversation may be all a malicious party needs in order to gain access to valuable business or personal data.

g) Never assume that your cell phone conversation is "safe" just because you don't mention the Company by name. If you wear or carry an item that features the Company logo, your name, or the organization's business address, a third party may put two and two together and identify the Company by overhearing your indiscreet conversation.

h) Do not use Company-owned cell phone cameras or video recorders to take, transmit, download, upload, print, or copy photos or videos that are not directly related to Company business. Prohibited photos and videos include, but are not limited to, "funny," embarrassing, or unprofessional images (of anyone or anything), as well as photos or videos of Company buildings (internal and external), offices, facilities, operations, products, services, confidential data, and internal documents.

i) Never use a Company-owned or person cell phone camera or video recorder to take, transmit, download, upload, print, or copy photos or videos of coworkers, executives, customers, suppliers, or any other third party without getting the express permission of your subject and Company management.

j) Do not distract officemates by engaging in unnecessary cell phone chatter.

k) Turn off your cell phone during business-related meetings, seminars, conferences, luncheons, dinners, receptions, brainstorming sessions, and any other situation in which a ringing phone or tapping fingers are likely to disrupt proceedings or interrupt a speaker's or participant's train of thought.

## Violations

These guidelines are intended to provide Company employees with general examples of acceptable and unacceptable use of corporate and personal cell phone and text messaging tools, accounts, and systems. Employees are obligated to report violations of the Company's Cell Phone and Text Messaging Policy to the Human Resources Manager. Failure to report a coworker's cell phone or texting violation may result in disciplinary action against the witness, as well as the policy violator. Employees should remember that any violation of the Company's Cell Phone and Text Messaging Policy may result in disciplinary action, up to and including termination.

## Acknowledgment

If you have questions about the above Cell Phone and Text Messaging Policy, address them to the Chief Information Officer before signing the following agreement.

I have read the Company's Cell Phone and Text Messaging Policy, and agree to abide by it. I understand that a violation of any of the above rules, policies, and procedures may result in disciplinary action, up to and including my termination.

Employee Name (Printed): _____

Employee Signature: _____

Date: _____

*Source:* ©2012, The ePolicy Institute, www.epolicyinstitute.com, Executive Director Nancy Flynn. For informational purposes only. Individual policies should be developed with assistance from competent legal counsel.

## SAMPLE SMARTPHONE AND MOBILE DEVICE POLICY

The Company provides every employee with a smartphone, which is intended primarily for business use. Employees using company-provided smartphones are responsible for behaving professionally, ethically, and responsibly. To that end, the Company has established the following Smartphone and Mobile Device Policy, which employees are required to adhere to at all times. Whether at the office, at home, or elsewhere, employees must comply with the Company's Smartphone and Mobile Device Policy. Whether using your Company-provided smartphone for business or personal reasons, employees must comply with the Company's Smartphone and Mobile Device Policy. In other words, employees are expected to adhere to the Company's Smartphone and Mobile Device Policy 24 hours a day, 365 days a year. Violations of the Company's Smartphone and Mobile Device Policy, whether they occur on Company time or the employee's own personal time, will result in disciplinary action, up to and including termination. All Company employees are required to adhere to the following rules, policies, and procedures.

1. Adhere to the Company's electronic content rules and language guidelines at all times. Whether you are engaged in a phone conversation, sending a text message, or leaving a voicemail message, you must always use a professional tone and business-appropriate language.

   Whether you are talking, texting, emailing, or otherwise communicating via smartphone, never use language that is obscene, vulgar, abusive, harassing, profane, discriminatory, sexually suggestive, intimidating, misleading, defamatory, bullying, or otherwise offensive, objectionable, inappropriate, or illegal. Jokes, disparaging remarks, and inappropriate comments related to ethnicity, race, color, religion, sex, age, disabilities, physique, sexual orientation, and sexual preference are prohibited by law and Company policy.

2.  It is against Company policy (and illegal in many U.S. cities and states in which the Company does business, employs people, and operates facilities) for employees to talk or text while driving. Turn off all smartphones and other mobile devices (Company-provided and personal, hand-held and hands-free) when driving any vehicle (company-owned or personal) during business hours. Mobile devices include but are not limited to smartphones, cell phones, BlackBerries, laptops, and electronic tablets. Pull off the road and stop driving if you need to make a call, take a call, send a text message, or check voice or text messages.

3.  Remember that a policy is a policy. Smartphone users are expected to comply with all Company rules and policies including Harassment and Discrimination Policy, Ethics Policy, Confidentiality Policy, Content Rules and Language Guidelines, Email Policy, Internet Policy, Computer Security Policy, among others.

4.  Regardless of whether you are using a Company-provided smartphone or your own personal cell phone, smartphone, or electronic tablet, employees are required to adhere to the Company's personal use rules governing when, where, why, with whom, and for how long you may engage in personal, non-business-related talking and texting.

    Employees may engage in personal talking and texting during the workday strictly to communicate with children, spouses, domestic partners, immediate family members, physicians, teachers and school personnel, and childcare providers. Personal talking and texting is limited to no more than 20 minutes a day during business hours. Employees also are free to text and talk with children, spouses, domestic partners, immediate family members, physicians, teachers and school personnel, and childcare providers during the lunch hour and other authorized break times.

    Employees may not use Company systems, Company accounts, Company-provided smartphones, or other

Company-owned mobile devices to solicit for any purpose, campaign for political candidates, espouse political views, promote religious causes, advertise the sale of merchandise, or announce personal milestones (engagements, births, graduations, and so on) without first receiving approval from the Chief Compliance Officer.

5. Employees may use their own private cell phone accounts strictly for personal non-business-related communication. Employees may use their own personal devices (smartphones, BlackBerries, cell phones, tablet PCs) strictly for personal communication. All business-related communication (including but not limited to phone, text, email, web, and social media) must be conducted, composed, transmitted, acquired, and retained via Company systems, using Company-provided devices, including but not limited to desktops, laptops, tablets, smartphones, and other mobile devices. In addition, employees are obligated to comply with all Company policies including Email Policy, Social Media Policy, and Internet Policy when communicating via personal and Company-provided systems and devices.

6. In accordance with the Company's Data Security Policy, employees are required to provide the Chief Information Officer with a list of all current passwords for company-provided and personal smartphones used for business reasons. Only authorized personnel are permitted to use passwords to access another employee's electronic content without consent. Misuse of passwords, the sharing of passwords with nonemployees, the unauthorized use of another employee's password, or failure to provide the CIO with current passwords will result in disciplinary action, up to and including termination.

7. Privacy does not exist when using the Company's computer system, telecommunications system, smartphones, or other devices, including desktop computers, laptops, and mobile devices, among others. Confidential company,

customer, or personal information never should be sent via email or text without the understanding that it could be intercepted. This includes the transmission of the organization's intellectual property, customer financial information, Social Security numbers, employee health records, proprietary data and trade secrets, and other confidential material.

8. Do not use a smartphone or other mobile device to discuss Company business in any public setting in which your conversation could be overheard, or your messages read by prying eyes. Not every location is right for a business-related smartphone conversation. Always locate a secluded spot, such as a hotel room, car, private office, and so on, in which to conduct Company business via your smartphone.

9. Do not mention passwords, user names, account numbers, financial data, customers, prospects, or other confidential or proprietary Company or personal information if there is any chance that your phone conversation could be overheard. An indiscreet one-sided conversation may be all a malicious party needs in order to gain access to valuable business or personal data.

10. Don't assume that your public smartphone conversation is "safe" just because you don't mention the Company by name. If you wear or carry an item that features the Company logo, your name, or our business address, a third party may put two and two together and identify the Company, simply by overhearing your indiscreet conversation.

11. Employees are prohibited from using Company-provided smartphones or other mobile device to take, transmit, acquire, download, upload, print, or copy photos or videos that are not directly related to Company business. Prohibited photos and videos include, but are not limited to, "funny" or embarrassing images of any internal or external party, photos or videos of company buildings (internal and external), offices, facilities, operations, products, services, confidential data, and internal documents.

12. Do not use a Company-provided or personal smartphone or other mobile device to take, transmit, acquire, download, upload, print, or copy photos or videos of coworkers, executives, customers, suppliers, or any other third party without getting the express permission of your subject and Company management.

13. Adhere to the rules of netiquette, or electronic etiquette, at all times. Do not distract your officemates (or others) by engaging in unnecessary, loud, or otherwise excessive smartphone chatter or keyboard tapping.

14. Turn off all Company-provided and personal smartphones and other mobile devices during business-related meetings, seminars, conferences, luncheons, dinners, receptions, brainstorming sessions, and any other situation in which a ringing phone or tapping fingers are likely to disrupt proceedings or interrupt a speaker's or participant's train of thought. Don't assume that texting is any less annoying or distracting than talking. If a pressing business matter requires you to check or transmit text messages during a meeting or other business gathering, leave the room—briefly—to do so.

15. If you become aware of Smartphone and Mobile Device Policy violations by other employees, please report those violations to the Company's Human Resources Manager. This is particularly important if you witness an employee texting or talking while driving. Distracted driving is illegal in many jurisdictions, and it creates potentially costly liability risks for the Company. Your cooperation is appreciated, and your report will be kept strictly confidential. Failure to report a coworker's policy violation may result in disciplinary action against the witness, as well as the offender.

16. Bear in mind the fact that any violation of the Company's Smartphone and Mobile Device Policy (or any other employment policy, for that matter) may result in disciplinary action, up to and including termination.

**Acknowledgment and Signature**

If you have questions about the Company's Smartphone and Mobile Device Policy, please address them to the Human Resources Director before signing the following agreement.

I have read the Company's Smartphone and Mobile Device Policy, and I agree to abide by it. I understand that a violation of any of the above rules, policies, and procedures may result in disciplinary action, up to and including my termination.

Employee Name (Printed): _____

Employee Signature: _____

Date: _____

*Source:* ©2012, The ePolicy Institute, www.epolicyinstitute.com, Executive Director Nancy Flynn. For informational purposes only. Individual policies should be developed with assistance from competent legal counsel.

## SAMPLE EMAIL POLICY IN THE AGE OF SOCIAL MEDIA

(Organization) is pleased to make email available to authorized employees. The email system is intended primarily for business purposes. Personal use of (Organization's) email system is restricted to the terms outlined below. The email system is the property of (Organization). Employees accessing (Organization's) email system are required to adhere to the following policy and procedures. Violation of (Organization's) Email Policy may result in disciplinary action, up to and including termination.

1. (Organization's) Email Policy applies regardless of whether employees are using desktops, laptops, or mobile devices. The Email Policy applies 24 hours a day, seven days a week, 365 days a year. The Email Policy applies regardless of whether employees are using the company's email system and tools, their own email accounts and devices, or a third party's email system and tools.

2. All conversations, content, and other information created, transmitted, received, or archived in (Organization's) computer system belongs to the company. The federal Electronic Communications Privacy Act (ECPA) gives management the right to monitor, access, and disclose all employee email messages created, transmitted, or received via the company system. (Organization) intends to exercise our legal right to monitor employees' email activity. Employees should have no expectation of privacy when using the company's email system.

3. The email system is intended primarily for business use. Only under the following circumstances may employees use (Organization's) email system for personal reasons:

   a) Communication with children, spouses, domestic partners, immediate family members, physicians, teachers and school personnel, and childcare providers is permitted but must be limited to no more than 20 minutes a day during business hours. Employees also are free to email children, spouses, domestic partners, immediate family members, physicians, teachers and school personnel, and childcare providers during the lunch hour and other authorized break times.

b) Personal email communication that exceeds the time limits outlined in point 3a and/or which is conducted between the employee and an individual other than children, spouses, domestic partners, immediate family members, physicians, teachers and school personnel, and childcare providers is prohibited unless authorized by (Organization's) Human Resources Manager.

c) The use of (Organization's) email system to solicit for any purpose, campaign for a political candidate, espouse political views, promote a religious cause, advertise the sale of merchandise, or announce personal milestones (engagements, births, graduations, and the like) is strictly prohibited without the prior approval of the Human Resources Manager.

4. Employees may use their own private email accounts strictly for personal non-business-related communication. Employees may use their own personal BlackBerries, smartphones, cell phones, tablets, or other mobile devices strictly for personal email communication. All business-related email must be composed, transmitted, and acquired via the company's email system, using company-provided tools, including but not limited to desktops, laptops, tablets, and other mobile devices. Employee use of personal email accounts and personal devices must adhere to (Organization's) personal use rules (see point 3) and Mobile Device Policy.

5. Email passwords and other computer passwords are the property of (Organization). Employees are required to provide the Chief Information Officer with a list of all current passwords, including passwords for corporate email and (for data security reasons) passwords for personal

smartphones that are used for business reasons. Only authorized personnel are permitted to use passwords to access another employee's email without consent. Misuse of passwords, the sharing of passwords with non-employees, the unauthorized use of another employee's password, or failure to provide the CIO with current passwords will result in disciplinary action, up to and including termination.

6. Privacy does not exist when using (Organization's) email system, computer system, or devices including desktop computers, laptops, and mobile phones, among others. Confidential company, customer, or personal information never should be sent via email without the understanding that it could be intercepted. This includes the transmission of the organization's intellectual property, customer financial information, Social Security numbers, employee health records, proprietary data and trade secrets, or other confidential material. When sending confidential information (or any messages, for that matter), employees should use extreme caution to ensure that the intended recipient's email address is correct.

7. Email usage must conform to all of (Organization's) employment policies, including Record Retention Policy, Harassment and Discrimination Policy, Ethics Policy, Confidentiality Policy, Mobile Device Policy, Investor Relations Policy, and Media Relations Policy.

8. Email messages should be treated as formal business documents and must be written in accordance with (Organization's) Electronic Writing Style Policy and Netiquette Guidelines.

9. Employee email must comply 100 percent with the company's content rules, including but not limited to:

   No harassment or discrimination based on race, color, religion, sex, sexual orientation, national origin, age, disability, or other status protected by federal law.

No disclosure of confidential company, executive, or employee data, including but not limited to Social Security numbers, salary and benefits packages, and corporate financials.

No exposure of customers' personal financial data to unauthorized employees or outside parties. Private financial data includes credit card numbers, debit card numbers, Social Security numbers, dates of birth, mailing addresses, and so forth.

No disclosure of patients' electronic protected health information (EPHI) to unauthorized employees or third parties. EPHI includes data related to patients' health status, medical care, treatment plans, and payment issues.

No rumors, gossip, or defamatory comments—about anyone within the company or outside the organization.

No whining or complaining about the company, customers, or business.

No external distribution of internal email or other eyes-only data that is intended strictly for in-house readers.

No posting or disclosing company financials to external websites or outside parties.

No jokes or "funny" text, cartoons, videos, photos, files, or art of any kind.

No obscene, off-color, pornographic, or otherwise inappropriate and offensive language, art, or other content.

10. Employees are prohibited from sending organization-wide email messages to all employees or requesting email replies to organization-wide email without the permission of the Chief Information Officer.

11. Employees may not transmit company email or other internal documents to outside parties without permission of management.

12. Employees using email or other (Organization) computer systems to send, access, upload, or post content (text, photos, videos) to any social media site (including but not limited to Facebook, YouTube, Twitter, and external blogs) must do so in compliance with the rules set forth in (Organization's) Social Media Policy, Blog Policy, and Mobile Device Policy.

13. Employees are responsible for knowing and adhering to (Organization's) Record Retention Policy.

14. Email transmitted or accessed via mobile devices, including but not limited to, company-provided or personal BlackBerries, smartphones, cell phones, or tablets must adhere to (Organization's) Mobile Device Policy.

15. Text messaging is mobile email. Text messaging use, content, and records must adhere to (Organization's) Text Messaging Policy, Mobile Device Policy, and Record Retention Policy.

16. Instant messaging (IM) is turbocharged email. IM use, content, and records must adhere to (Organization's) IM Policy, Mobile Device Policy, and Record Retention Policy.

17. Violation of (Organization's) Email Policy will result in disciplinary action, up to and including termination.

**Employee Acknowledgment**

I have read (Organization's) Email Policy and agree to abide by it. I understand violation of any of the above rules, policies, and procedures may result in disciplinary action, up to and including my termination.

Employee Name (Printed): _____

Employee Signature: _____

Date: _____

*Source:* ©2012, The ePolicy Institute, www.epolicyinstitute.com, Executive Director Nancy Flynn. For informational purposes only. Individual policies should be developed with assistance from competent legal counsel.

## SAMPLE INTERNET POLICY IN THE AGE OF SOCIAL MEDIA

(Organization) provides employees with a network connection and Internet (web) access. This policy governs all use of (Organization's) network and Internet access at headquarters, remote offices, hotels, airports, employees' homes, and any other location.

(Organization's) network and Internet access are intended primarily for business use. Employees may access the Internet for personal use only during non-working hours, and strictly in compliance with the terms of this policy.

All information created, transmitted, acquired, viewed, downloaded, or uploaded via the organization's network and Internet is the property of (Organization). Employees should have no expectation of privacy regarding this information. The organization reserves the right to access, read, review, monitor, and copy all content, messages, and files on its computer and Internet systems at any time and without notice. When deemed necessary, the organization may disclose text, files, and images to law enforcement agencies or other third parties without the employee's consent.

No employee may use a password unless it has been disclosed in writing to (Organization's) Chief Information Officer.

Alternate Internet Service Provider (ISP) connections to (Organization's) internal network are not permitted unless authorized by the organization's Chief Information Officer (CIO) and properly protected by a firewall or other appropriate security device(s).

Files downloaded from the Internet may not be viewed or opened until scanned with up-to-date virus detection software. Employees are reminded that information obtained from the Internet is not always reliable and should be verified for accuracy before it is used.

## Prohibited Activities

Employees are prohibited from using (Organization's) network or Internet access for the following activities:

1. Downloading any software other than company-purchased and approved software, without the prior written approval of (Organization's) CIO. See the Software Usage Policy.
2. Disseminating or printing copyright-protected materials, including software, articles, books, whitepapers, web content, or any other content in violation of copyright laws.
3. Acquiring, sending, receiving, printing, or otherwise disseminating (Organization's) proprietary data, trade secrets, intellectual property, or other confidential company information in violation of (Organization) Confidentiality Policy or written confidentiality agreements between the company and individual employees.
4. Operating a business, usurping (Organization's) business opportunities, soliciting money for personal gain, or searching for jobs outside (Organization).
5. Making objectionable, harassing, discriminatory, hostile, disparaging, or otherwise offensive, inappropriate, or unlawful comments about internal or external parties based on race, color, religion, national origin, veteran status, ancestry, disability, age, sex, sexual orientation, or any other federally protracted class.
6. Acquiring, viewing, downloading, uploading, transmitting, soliciting, printing, or copying obscene, pornographic, off-color, sexually oriented, or otherwise offensive and objectionable messages or images.
7. Visiting or posting comments or other content on websites featuring pornography, terrorism, espionage, theft, drugs, or other unlawful or unethical activities or content. See (Organization's) Ethics Policy.
8. Gambling or engaging in any other criminal activity in violation of local, state, or federal law.

9. Participating in activities, viewing, writing, posting, transmitting, downloading, or uploading content that could damage (Organization's) professional reputation, credibility, and standing with customers and prospects, employees and prospective employees, the investment community, the media, government officials, the public, courts, regulators, or any other internal or external parties.

## Compliance and Violations

Managers are responsible for ensuring employee compliance with this policy. Employees who learn of policy violations are required to notify (Organization's) Human Resources Director. Employees who violate this policy or otherwise use (Organization's) network or Internet access for improper purposes will subject to discipline, up to and including termination.

## Acknowledgment

If you have questions about the above Internet Policy, address them to the Chief Information Officer before signing the following agreement.

I have read the Company's Internet Policy, and I agree to abide by it. I understand that a violation of any of the above rules, policies, and procedures may result in disciplinary action, up to and including my termination.

Employee Name (Printed): _____

Employee Signature: _____

Date: _____

*Source:* ©2012, The ePolicy Institute, www.epolicyinstitute.com, Executive Director Nancy Flynn. For informational purposes only. Individual policies should be developed with assistance from competent legal counsel.

## SAMPLE SEXUAL HARASSMENT POLICY IN AGE OF SOCIAL MEDIA

Sex discrimination and sexual harassment are against the law. It is the policy of the Company to adhere to the federal and state laws that prohibit sexual harassment. The Company also is committed to maintaining a working environment that is free from sexual harassment, intimidation, coercion, and discrimination.

The Company will not tolerate the sexual harassment of any employee by another employee. The Company will not tolerate the sexual harassment of a client, supplier, business partner, or other third party by an employee. This Sexual Harassment Policy applies to all employees, regardless of rank, title, position, or tenure with the company.

Employees should treat their coworkers, subordinates, and supervisors with respect at all times. If the investigation of a complaint produces evidence that sexual harassment has occurred, appropriate disciplinary action, up to and including termination, will be taken.

Company employees are prohibited from engaging in the following inappropriate activities:

1. Using the Company's blogs, social media sites, Internet system, email system, or any other Company-hosted electronic business communication tool to write, post, acquire, transmit, download, forward, copy, print, or otherwise communicate off-color jokes that have a sexual connotation. This includes the deliberate and/or careless telling of jokes in the presence of employees (and nonemployees) who may be offended by the jokes.
2. Using the Company's blogs, social media sites, Internet system, email system, or any other Company-hosted electronic business communication tool to write, post, acquire, transmit, download, forward, copy, print, or otherwise communicate gossip, rumors, defamatory comments, or other

objectionable material that is related (or unrelated) to your job and the business of the Company.

3. Using the Company's blogs, social media sites, Internet system, email system, or any other Company-hosted electronic business communication tool to write, post, acquire, transmit, download, forward, copy, print, or otherwise communicate content (including but not limited to text, photos, videos, art, cartoons) that is obscene, off-color, adult-oriented, harassing, menacing, threatening, discriminatory, or objectionable in any way.

4. Using the Company's blogs, social media sites, Internet system, email system, or any other Company-hosted electronic business communication tool to make unwelcome suggestions or invitations to social engagements to coworkers and nonemployees.

5. Making unwelcome physical contact (touching) or invading another's physical space (getting too close to coworkers and nonemployees).

6. Using the Company's blogs, social media sites, Internet system, email system, or any other Company-hosted electronic business communication tool to state or imply that an employee's job security, job assignment, conditions of employment, or opportunity for advancement may depend upon the employee's granting sexual favors to another employee and/or a manager, supervisor, executive, or officer of the Company.

7. Taking any action related to an employee's job status based on the employee's granting and/or refusing sexual or social favors.

### Reporting Suspected Violations

The Company encourages employees to help keep the work environment free from sexual harassment. Employees who feel they have been subjected to sexual harassment in any form, or who believe they have witnessed sexual harassment, should contact the Human Resources Director. No retaliation of any kind will take place against an employee who reports an incident or a suspicion of sexual harassment.

### Acknowledgment and Signature

If you have any questions about this Sexual Harassment Policy, please address them to the Human Resources Director before signing the following agreement.

I have read the Company's Sexual Harassment Policy and agree to abide by it. I understand that a violation of any of the above rules, policies, and procedures may result in disciplinary action, up to and including my termination.

Employee Name (Printed): _____

Employee Signature: _____

Date: _____

*Source:* ©2012, The ePolicy Institute, www.epolicyinstitute.com, Executive Director Nancy Flynn. For informational purposes only. Individual policies should be developed with assistance from competent legal counsel.

## SAMPLE ELECTRONIC BUSINESS COMMUNICATION CODE OF CONDUCT

The Company provides employees with social media, blog, Internet, and email access for the benefit of the organization and our customers. Employees using social media, blogs, the Internet, and email are responsible for maintaining the organization's public image and using the Internet appropriately. To that end, the Company has established the following Electronic Business Communication Code of Conduct.

### Acceptable Social Media, Blog, Internet, and Email Use

Employees' online activity and electronic communication are intended primarily for business purposes. Employees are to use social media, blogs, the Internet, and email in an effective, ethical, and lawful manner, in accordance with the Company's Social Media Policy, Blog Policy, Internet Policy, Email Policy, and all other Company employment policies, rules, guidelines, and codes.

### Unacceptable Social Media, Blog, Internet, and Email Use

Employees may not use Company-hosted social media, blogs, Internet, or email systems for personal gain, the advancement of individual views, or solicitation of non-company business. Employees are prohibited from using social media, blogs, the Internet, and email to disrupt business operations, sabotage the organization, or interfere with employee productivity.

### Appropriate Content

Employees are responsible for the content of all text, audio, video, photos, or other content or images they write, post, transmit, acquire, download, copy, or print via social media, blogs, the Internet, and email. Fraudulent, harassing, menacing, obscene, bullying, or otherwise objectionable, illegal, or inappropriate content is prohibited.

Electronic content, including but not limited to social media posts and email messages, must include the employee's name. No messages may be written, posted, or transmitted anonymously, under an assumed name, or under the name or email address of another employee. Employees may not attempt to obscure the origin of posts, messages, or other online content.

Information published on blogs, social media sites, or elsewhere on the Internet should not violate or infringe upon the rights of others.

### Copyright Adherence

Materials that are copyrighted may not be posted, transmitted, copied, or otherwise used electronically by employees. Employees are not permitted to copy, transfer, rename, or edit copyrighted material without permission from the owner. Copyright infringement may result in disciplinary action, up to and including termination, as well as legal action by the copyright owner.

### Privacy and Security

All content written, posted, transmitted, acquired, or otherwise accessed via the organization's Internet system is the property of the organization and should be considered public information. The Company reserves the legal right to access and monitor all posts, messages, data, files, and other electronically stored information on the organization's computer system as deemed necessary and appropriate. Social media, blog, and other Internet postings are public, not private, communication. All electronic communications, including text and images, can be disclosed to law enforcement or other third parties without prior consent of the employee who created, posted, sent, received, uploaded, downloaded, stored, or published the information.

### Harassment and Discrimination

The organization prohibits the writing, posting, transmitting, downloading, accessing, acquiring, copying, filing, or printing of electronic content that is in any way harassing or discriminatory. Employees are prohibited from writing, posting, transmitting, downloading, accessing, acquiring, copying, and printing derogatory or inflammatory remarks about race, religion, national origin, physical attributes, sex, age, sexual preference, sexual orientation, or any other protected class.

### Violations and Disciplinary Action

Employees who violate the organization's Electronic Business Communication Code of Conduct may face disciplinary action, up to and including termination.

### Acknowledgment and Signature

If you have any questions about this Electronic Business Communication Code of Conduct, please address them to the Human Resources Director before signing the following agreement.

I have read the Company's Electronic Business Communication Code of Conduct and agree to abide by it. I understand that a violation of any of the above rules, policies, and procedures may result in disciplinary action, up to and including my termination.

Employee Name (Printed): _____

Employee Signature: _____

Date: _____

*Source:* ©2012, The ePolicy Institute, www.epolicyinstitute.com, Executive Director Nancy Flynn. For informational purposes only. Individual policies should be developed with assistance from competent legal counsel.

# GLOSSARY OF SOCIAL MEDIA, LEGAL, REGULATORY, AND TECHNOLOGY TERMS

15

**Amended Federal Rules of Civil Procedure (FRCP)** In December 2006, the United States Federal Court System announced amendments to the Federal Rules of Civil Procedure (FRCP). The amended rules govern the discovery of "Electronically Stored Information" (ESI), which refers to email, blog posts, public and private social networking content, videos, photos, and all other data that can be stored electronically. Enforced by the United States Supreme Court, the revised rules make it clear that all ESI is subject to e-discovery (may be used as evidence for or against your company) in civil lawsuits filed in federal court. As of 2011, discussions about possible e-discovery changes to the FRCP were under way by a subcommittee of the Judicial Conference of the United States. Official changes to U.S. federal e-discovery guidelines are not likely until 2013 at the earliest.

**Archive**   The use of technology (software, hardware, or cloud technology) to automatically store email, blog posts, social media content, text messages, and other forms of electronically stored information that warrant retention for legal, regulatory, or organizational reasons. Best practices call for the use of archiving technology that automatically captures and stores data in one central location; protects against malicious intruders intent on altering, deleting, or stealing your files; facilitates immediate access to archived data; and guarantees your ability to produce legally compliant, reliable electronic evidence in the event of a lawsuit or regulatory investigation.

**@Username**   Part of the language of Twitter, @Username enables you to make a public reply to a message that someone else has tweeted. Provides an effective way to start and maintain an ongoing, back-and-forth conversation.

**Attachment**   A computer file sent with a tweet, email message, instant message, or text message. The attachment could contain a photo, word processing document, spreadsheet, database, video, or graphic element. Attachments that are transmitted outside a company's firewall and security system, on the public web and social media sites via personal mobile devices, consumer-grade IM clients, or personal email accounts, put confidential company information and private consumer data at risk of theft, interception, and tampering.

**Authenticity**   In order for electronic business records or electronically stored information to be considered legally valid, the author and content must be verified as original and authentic. A legally reliable electronic document must, in other words, be what it claims to be.

**Backup**    A backup system is no substitute for automatic archiving technology. Designed solely for the recovery of critical data in the event of a man-made or natural disaster, backup is nothing more than the mass storage of electronic information in a known location. An archive, on the other hand, is a strategic record management tool that not only preserves social media posts, email, and other data, but also facilitates the speedy search and reliable retrieval of the specific records you need, exactly when you need them.

**Blawg**    A blog written by a lawyer or focused on legal issues.

**Blog**    Short for weblog, a blog is a self-published online journal that contains written content, links, and photos, which are regularly updated. Blogs enable anyone with a computer and Internet access to publish their thoughts, ideas, and opinions for anyone else to read and comment upon. Some blogs are business-related, while others are purely personal. Some highly influential blogs boast enormous public readerships, while other blogs are intended strictly for a limited audience of friends and family.

**Blogger**    Someone who either operates a blog or posts content on a business, public, or personal blog. Bloggers may be professional writers, retained by organizations to write the type of professional, compelling content that attracts readers and followers. Or they may be amateur writers, posting about issues, events, and topics of interest to them personally.

**Bloggerati**    The bloggerati are the most prominent writers in the blogosphere. The term is adapted from "literati."

**Blogosphere**    The universe, or community, of bloggers.

**Blogroll**    A blogger's compilation of links to recommended external sites, including other blogs, social networking sites, and websites. Typically posted on a blog's homepage, the blogroll contributes to the sense of community within the blogosphere by encouraging links among sites.

**Blogstorm**    Also known as a "cybersmear," a blogstorm is an attack in the blogosphere, which may be aimed at businesses or individuals.

A blogstorm typically occurs when one influential writer uses a high-profile blog to alert readers to a disturbing issue or problematic situation, and then other bloggers pile on, posting comments and writing blogs designed to fan the flames.

**Brand Bloggers**   Devotees who blog exclusively about their favorite brands on their own dedicated blogs, at their own expense, and on their own time. Brand bloggers' posts may be positive or negative.

**Breach Notification Laws**   The law takes data theft—and corporate compliance with security laws and procedures—seriously. In the United States, 47 states, the District of Columbia, and the United States Virgin Islands had enacted breach notification laws as of 2011, requiring companies to notify customers and other affected parties in the event of a data security breach. In May 2011, President Barack Obama proposed the implementation of a federal breach notification law.

**Business-Critical Email**   Email that rises to the level of a business record, as opposed to personal messages and other insignificant, non-business-related email. Business-critical email must be strategically retained, reliably archived, and quickly produced for legal, regulatory, and business management purposes. Insignificant, non-record messages, on the other hand, may be purged from the system.

**Business Record**   Business records provide evidence of business-related activities, events, and transactions. Organizations are obligated to retain business record social networking content, blog posts, email, IM, and other electronic information for their ongoing business, legal, regulatory, compliance, operational, or historical value.

**Categories**   Categories facilitate the archiving of blog entries. If a reader only wants to read posts related to one specific category ("social media policy," for example), the reader can review all of the blogger's "social media policy" posts, bypassing all unrelated posts.

**Chat**   Some social media discussion sites are structured in a chat format. Chats take place within a chat room and are conducted in real time, just like instant messaging and text messaging. Everyone who is logged into the chat room can participate in the live conversation, which may be either a planned event or a spontaneous gathering. Chat conversations, like forums and threads, may be retained and archived.

**Citizen Journalists**   Bloggers who offer an alternative to the mainstream media (MSM).

**Comments**   Many blogs include a comment feature, which allows readers to easily and automatically respond to posts, ask questions, or inject their own points of view. Considered a vital element of a blog by blogging enthusiasts, many organizations fail to edit comments before they are posted. Unedited comments can open an organization to claims of defamation, copyright infringement, and trade secret theft, among other risks.

**Comment Spam**   Blogs often provide comment sections to allow customers and other readers to add their own opinions and reactions to posts. Blog spammers use tools to automatically flood a blog with advertising in the form of bogus comments. Anything that's been spammed about in email is probably being spammed in the blogosphere. This is a growing and serious problem for bloggers and blog platforms.

**Communications Decency Act of 1996**   The United States federal law that protects blog hosts, as neutral carriers of Internet content, from liability for anything posted on the blogs they host.

**Connections**   Where Twitter has followers and Facebook has friends, LinkedIn has connections. On LinkedIn, connections are the business people or professional contacts you meet and communicate with. On LinkedIn, once you accept someone as a connection, that person can view all of your other connections, or contacts. Consequently, it's advisable to limit your connections to people you know and trust personally, as well as referrals from trusted sources.

**Content**   Any written text, photos, videos, or art that is created, transmitted, acquired, posted, downloaded, uploaded, printed, copied, attached, published, or stored online. Content includes but is not limited to email messages, text messages, blog posts, tweets, Facebook profiles, web pages, whitepapers, articles, attachments, photos, and

YouTube videos. When it comes to e-discovery and electronic evidence, it is the content that counts, not the devices, sites, or accounts that are used to produce, transmit, acquire, post, publish, or store the content.

**Content Syndication**   Syndication is the process through which bloggers make content available for posting on other blogs or external sites.

**Copyright**   The exclusive right granted to authors under the United States Copyright Act to copy, adapt, distribute, rent, publicly perform, or publicly display their works of authorship, such as literary works, databases, musical works, sound recordings, photographs and other still images, and motion pictures and other audiovisual works. The Library of Congress registers copyrights, which last the life of the author plus fifty years.

**Corporate Evangelists and Customer Evangelists**   Companies identify loyal customers (superfans) who already are actively blogging about the organization, and then develop them into "customer evangelists" or "corporate evangelists" who use their own blogs to write positive posts about the organization, its products and services. Typically, an organization turns superfans into evangelists by showering them with personal attention, and then motivating them to spread the "good word" about the company in the blogosphere.

**Cybersmearing**   Using blogs and other social networking sites to publish posts that criticize, attack, embarrass, or defame organizations and individuals. The ability to blog, tweet, and post anonymously makes it relatively easy to cybersmear others. Increasingly, companies are filing cybersmear lawsuits in an effort to force Internet service providers to reveal the identities of anonymous bloggers and posters. The U.S. courts, however, have not been consistent in their rulings when it comes to online attacks.

**DAX Index**   The Deutscher Aktien 30 Index (known as the DAX 30 or DAX Index) is the German stock market index that tracks the top-30 high-cap companies listed on the German Frankfurt Stock

Exchange. Among the companies listed on the DAX 30, are BMW, Adidas, Volkswagen, Daimler, and Siemens.

**Defamation**   A false statement of fact (versus opinion) that harms the reputation of a living person or entity. When a defamatory statement appears in writing (on blogs, Twitter, or Facebook, for example) it's called "libel." Defamatory statements that are made orally (on YouTube videos, for example) are called "slander."

**Deleted File**   Email messages or other electronically stored information that has been purged from the electronic media on which it resided.

**Deletion Schedule**   The systematic disposal of email, social media content, and other electronically stored information according to written rules and timelines that specify when business records have reached the end of their lifecycles and may be purged from the system.

**Delicious**   See "social bookmarking sites."

**Destructive Retention Policy**   The practice of retaining email for a limited time, and then deleting it permanently from the company network. When it comes to destructive retention, preservation periods can range from months to years. Seven years is a commonly applied corporate retention period for companies that practice destructive retention.

**Digg**   See "social bookmarking sites."

**Digital Millennium Copyright Act**   If an organization publishes reader comments on business blogs—and that content is protected by another third party's copyright—the organization could be held liable for copyright infringement, unless it has secured "safe harbor" protection from liability through the Digital Millennium Copyright Act (DMCA). To qualify, the organization must designate a DMCA agent with the Library of Congress and comply with all DMCA policies, procedures, and requirements. No organization should post third-party comments until DMCA registration has been completed and approved by a legal expert.

**Dooced**   To lose your job for blogging. Typically employee-bloggers are dooced because of the negative or unflattering comments they have posted about their employers' people, products, or services. The term dooced was coined by blogger Heather B. Armstrong, who in 2002 was fired for writing about her job and colleagues on her personal blog.

**Doximity**   Increasingly, medical professionals seeking security and privacy are choosing to network via private social networks like Doximity, a physician-only site connecting physicians, medical students, and medical residents. Medical professionals can communicate about patient care and cases and exchange HIPAA-secure messages, without the risks associated with Facebook, LinkedIn, or other public social networking sites.

**Electronic Communications Privacy Act (ECPA)**   The federal Electronic Communications Privacy Act of 1986 gives U.S. employers the legal right to monitor all employee computer activity and transmissions. The ECPA makes clear the fact that the organization's computer system is the property of the employer, and employees have absolutely no reasonable expectation of privacy when using company computer systems, tools, and technologies.

Courts in the U.S. have consistently ruled that employees should assume their computer activity is being watched—even if they have not been formally notified of monitoring. The courts generally support the position that informed employees neither would nor should assume that their email transmissions or other forms of electronic content are their own. Even in cases in which employers have told workers that incoming and outgoing email is not being monitored, the courts have ruled that employees still should not expect privacy when using a company system.

**Electronic Discovery (E-Discovery)**   The process of collecting and producing electronic evidence (including but not limited to email messages and attachments, blog posts, tweets, YouTube videos, and text messages) for litigation. Discovery prevents all parties to a lawsuit from being surprised by unexpected information, helps familiarize each side with facts and evidence (electronic and otherwise) prior to the proceeding, and helps prevent spoliation (destruction of evidence) claims.

**Electronic Protected Health Information**    U.S. health care companies that are regulated by the Health Insurance Portability and Accountability Act (HIPAA) are legally required to safeguard social media content, email messages, and other electronic records that contain electronic protected health information (EPHI) related to patients' health status, medical care, treatment plans, or payment issues. HIPAA retention rules require the preservation of patient billing records and authorizations for six years, while preserving patients' electronic conversations and other data for the life of the patient.

**Electronically Stored Information (ESI)**    In December 2006, the U.S. federal court system revised the Federal Rules of Civil Procedure (FRCP), governing the discovery of "Electronically Stored Information" (ESI). Referring to all data that can be stored electronically, ESI includes but is not limited to email messages and attachments, instant messenger chat, text messages, blog posts, tweets, Facebook profiles, history of web surfing, YouTube videos, voicemail, and all other forms of created, retained, acquired, or archived electronic data. Mindful of new and emerging technologies, ESI is intended to cover all current types of computer-based information plus future technology developments, as well.

**Encryption**    The process of scrambling text and other digital information to ensure privacy. Encrypted content can only be unscrambled and read by a person with the ability to decrypt. The scrambling process is called "encrypting," and the unscrambling process is "decrypting."

**Enterprise-Grade Social Networking**    Concerns about security, privacy, confidentiality, productivity, and other issues have led some organizations to establish and use private enterprise-grade social networking sites. Private enterprise-grade social media tools like Yammer, for example, allow employees to communicate and collaborate with colleagues within a secure internal network, rather than using a less-secure public site, such as Facebook, on the public Internet.

**Entry**    See also "post." The commentary written on a blog. Some bloggers write multiple entries every day. Most entries are relatively short. Entries often include external links and offer readers the opportunity to comment.

**Facebook**    The world's largest social networking site, Facebook announced in 2011 that it had 800 million active users worldwide. Facebook encourages people to introduce themselves to the online community, make "friends," share information, participate in the electronic conversation, and build business-related and personal relationships.

**Federal Trade Commission (FTC) Endorsement Guidelines for Bloggers**    In 2009, the United States Federal Trade Commission issued revised endorsement guidelines that have an impact on personal and business blogging. The FTC endorsement guidelines require bloggers to disclose any material connections between themselves and the products or services they discuss in their blog posts. Product, service, or company endorsements must be honest and cannot be deceptive. Failure to comply with FTC endorsement guidelines could create liability concerns for the blogger and advertiser.

**Filtering**    The act of scanning and blocking electronic content and messages that may violate the organization's content policy or the content-related regulations of government and industry. The recommended approach is to draft written rules and policy first, and then use a policy-based content filtering technology solution (software, an appliance tool, or cloud technology) to enforce your written guidelines.

**FINRA**    The Financial Industry Regulatory Authority (FINRA) is the largest independent regulator for all securities firms doing business in the United States. FINRA touches virtually every aspect of the securities business including enforcing rules governing electronic use, content, and business records.

**Firewall**    A technology solution that automatically examines network traffic and either blocks or allows it to pass based upon predefined rules and security policies. Firewalls typically sit between a private internal network and the Internet and are one of the most common tools for protecting internal networks and users from harmful content and intrusion. When employees use private mobile devices and accounts, personal email accounts, or consumer-grade IM tools to communicate, their messages travel across public networks, outside the organization's firewall. As a result, the organization is open to security breaches, and messages may be intercepted by thieves or other malicious outsiders.

**First Amendment**    The First Amendment to the United States Constitution prohibits the government from abridging the freedom of speech. Since the First Amendment only restricts government control of speech, private employers are free to fire at will in most states, provided the termination does not discriminate against protected classes, retaliate for whistle-blowing or union organizing, or violate National Labor Relations Board (NLRB) rules.

**Flickr**    A photo-sharing site that is available for personal use only. In addition to photos, Flickr also accepts brief videos that do not exceed ninety seconds in length. Flickr does not accept commercial photos or videos. Product photos, advertisements, logos, and other business-related images are banned. If you want to use Flickr for business reasons, you need to take a creative, rather than a commercial, approach.

**Followers**    Where Facebook has friends and LinkedIn has connections, Twitter has followers.

On Twitter, followers are the people who read, or follow, another tweeter's 140-character messages, or tweets, and engage in back-and-forth conversations.

**Forums**    Some discussion sites are structured as forums. A forum is an online resource that facilitates Q&A. In a forum, one participant posts a question and then awaits responses from other forum members. Unlike chats, which take place in real time, there can be a lag time of minutes, hours, or days between the time a question is posted and an answer appears. Forums sometimes go on for weeks, months, or years. Just like chat and threads, forum posts may be retained and archived.

**Freedom of Information Act (FOIA)**    The United States Freedom of Information Act (FOIA) is the law that ensures public access to government records. Upon written request by any individual or media member, agencies of the United States federal government are required to disclose requested records, unless they can be lawfully withheld from disclosure under one of nine specific exemptions in the FOIA. The right of access to records under the FOIA is enforceable in federal court. On the state level, FOIA laws are known as open records laws or state sunshine laws.

**Friend**   Where Twitter has followers and LinkedIn has connections, Facebook has friends.

On Facebook, friends are the people you talk and share information with. The ultimate networking site, Facebook encourages strangers to introduce themselves, in hopes of becoming "friends."

**Gramm-Leach-Bliley Act (GLBA)**   Requires U.S. financial institutions to protect the privacy of customers and their nonpublic personal information. Under GLBA, financial services firms are legally obligated to safeguard social networking content, email messages and attachments, and other forms of electronic data containing customers' private information (Social Security numbers, credit card numbers, debit card numbers, birthdates, and home addresses, for example).

**Health Information Technology for Economic and Clinical Health (HITECH) Act**   On February 17, 2009, President Barack Obama signed into law the American Recovery and Reinvestment Act (ARRA), a $787 billion economic stimulus package designed, in part, to promote the adoption, privacy, and security of electronic health records (EHRs). Title XIII of ARRA, the Health Information Technology for Economic and Clinical Health (HITECH) Act directs $19.2 billion to subsidize the "meaningful use" of health information technology by physicians and hospitals.

**Health Insurance Portability and Accountability Act (HIPAA)**   U.S. health care companies are legally required by HIPAA to safeguard social media content, email messages, and other electronic records that contain electronic protected health information (EPHI) related to patients' health status, medical care, treatment plans, and payment issues. HIPAA retention rules require the preservation of patient billing records and authorizations for six years, while preserving patients' electronic conversations and other data for the life of the patient.

**Hidden Reader**   An unintended reader of online content. Includes persons to whom your intended reader links, forwards, or copies your original post or message. Also may include your intended reader's employer, court personnel, regulators, law enforcement agencies, and the media, among others. (Also see "unintended reader.")

**Intended Reader**   The friends, followers, and contacts with whom bloggers, tweeters, and other social networkers converse online.

**Instant Messaging**   A combination of the telephone, which facilitates conversations with multiple people in real time, and email, which combines the speed of online communication with a written record of your conversation. Instant messaging (IM) is turbocharged email, offering all the risks, features, capabilities, and compliance requirements as email, at lightning speed.

**Intellectual Property (IP)**   IP includes but is not limited to brand names, logos, trade names, trade secrets, employee names and data, advertisements, customer lists, strategic plans, and copyright-protected content. Just like other kinds of property, intellectual property needs to be protected from unauthorized use. There are four ways to protect different types of intellectual property: patents, trademarks, copyrights, and trade secrets.

**Libel**   Defamation is defined as a false statement of fact, versus an opinion. When a defamatory statement appears in writing (such as a tweet), it's known as "libel." A defamatory statement that is made orally (on YouTube, for example) is "slander." An employer may be held liable for defamatory statements made by an employee, if the employee possesses "apparent authority" from the company to speak on its behalf.

**Litigation Hold**   The process of identifying and preserving blog posts, social networking content, email, electronic business records, and other electronically stored information that may be relevant to current or pending litigation or regulatory investigations. Once a lawsuit is filed, or if you anticipate a claim will one day be filed, you must stop deleting relevant email and other electronic evidence. Failure to preserve electronic documents can lead to charges of "spoliation" or destruction of evidence.

**Links**  Successful bloggers strive to increase traffic and readership by incorporating incoming and outgoing links into their sites. Bloggers enhance the relevance of their blogs, and provide readers with a service, by including outgoing links to sites that contain relevant content or otherwise are likely to appeal to readers. High-quality content (a timely or controversial topic, compelling writing, and high search-engine rankings) helps motivate bloggers to create links into a site.

**LinkedIn**  LinkedIn is an invitation-only business networking site that relies heavily on the power of personal referrals. Unlike Facebook and other social networking sites that create opportunities for strangers to meet and become "friends," LinkedIn is designed for professional networking with people, or "connections," you already know.

**Microblogging**  Microblogging is like blogging, only shorter. Twitter is a microblogging site that limits messages to 140 characters, or tweets.

**Mobile Blogging**  Using smartphones, tablet computers, and other mobile devices to blog. Some mobile bloggers report that they have adjusted their blogging style, writing shorter and more spontaneous posts to accommodate the space limitations and immediacy of mobile tools.

**Mobile Device**  A smartphone, cell phone, BlackBerry, iPhone, iPad, or tablet PC that is equipped with Internet access is known as a "mobile device." Mobile devices facilitate on-the-go talking and texting, blogging and social networking, Internet surfing, and other forms of electronic communication.

**MSM**  Mainstream media. Through blogs, citizen journalists offer an alternative to the mainstream media.

**National Labor Relations Act**  Enacted by Congress in 1935 to protect the rights of employees and employers, encourage collective bargaining, and curtail private sector labor and management practices that can harm workers, businesses, and the economy.

**National Labor Relations Board (NLRB)** An independent federal agency, the National Labor Relations Board (NLRB) is designed to protect private sector employees' rights to join together, with or without a union, to improve working conditions and wages.

**Netiquette** Etiquette rules governing electronic content and use. Netiquette rules apply to blogs, social networking, email, text messaging, and all other forms of electronic communication, business or personal.

**Newsvine** See "social bookmarking sites."

**Nixle** A microblogging site that is designed specifically for use by government agencies. Nixle sends quick text messages and email messages (local traffic updates, emergency information and alerts, and other advisories) via users' smartphones and other mobile devices.

**Open Records Laws** (See also "state sunshine laws.") The state-level equivalent of the Freedom of Information Act (FOIA), open records laws govern public access to the records of state, county, and local government agencies, school systems, municipalities, and other public entities. Open records laws are also known as state sunshine laws.

**Page** The specific portion of a social media site on which content is displayed and managed by an individual or, in the case of corporate social networking sites, individuals with administrative rights.

**PeerCase** Increasingly, medical professionals are seeking the security and privacy offered by private social networks like PeerCase, a mobile and Internet-based private oncology network that brings together the collective experience and expertise of the worldwide oncology community. Professionals can communicate about patient care and cases in a HIPAA-secure environment, without the risks associated with Facebook, LinkedIn, or other public social networking sites.

**Permalink** Contraction of "permanent link." The permalink creates a unique web address for every posting on a blog. Bloggers link to one another's posts, which typically remain accessible forever via the permalink (unlike web pages, which are subject to change).

**Personal Data** Users' personal, non-business-related data includes but is not limited to names, addresses, birth dates, employment history, Social Security numbers, credit card numbers, debit card numbers, bank account information, nationality, and religious affiliation.

**Photoblog** A blog that primarily contains photos, which are regularly updated and posted chronologically, just like text postings.

**Plagiarism** Under U.S. law, plagiarism is an act of fraud or literary theft. Plagiarism involves stealing someone else's work, ideas, or words, and then passing that material off as your own, without crediting the original source.

**Podcast** Blog radio shows and audio or video recordings that are posted on a blog and broadcast over the Internet, or syndicated via Really Simple Syndication (see "RSS") to iPods, MP3 players, cell phones, and other mobile devices.

**Policy Portal Solution** A policy portal technology solution gives organizations greater visibility into policies, easing policy implementation, aggregation, and management. The Prevalent Policy Portal and Prevalent Policy Store, for example, allow employers to purchase and test ePolicy Institute policy templates and other policies against IT resources and procedures in order to determine policy effectiveness, remediate problems, and increase compliance.

**Post** See also "entry." The commentary written on a blog or social networking site. Some bloggers and social networkers post multiple times per day. Most posts are relatively short. Posts often include text, photos, links to external sites, and offer readers the opportunity to comment.

**Profile** Biographical "about me" information that users post on social networking sites and blogs. Your profile gives visitors to your site their first glimpse into your experience and expertise, personality, and positioning. Typically, a profile includes a current photo, enabling you to put a face on your name, and assuring readers that you are legitimate.

**Proprietary Information** Proprietary information is confidential, secret, or sensitive information that is owned by a company and affords the organization some sort of competitive advantage. Proprietary information often is critical to the success of an organization.

**Protected Classes**   A term used in United States anti-discrimination law. Persons cannot be discriminated against based on these protected classes: race, color, religion, national origin, age, sex, familial status, disability, veteran status, genetic information, gender identity (some jurisdictions), or sexual orientation (some jurisdictions).

**Protected Concerted Activity**   Section 7 of the National Labor Relations Act gives employees the right to engage in concerted activities for the purpose of collective bargaining or other mutual aid protection. Protected concerted activities and communications involve two or more employees, discussing or dealing with wages, hours, or conditions of employment.

**Reddit**   See "social bookmarking sites."

**Reputation Management**   Thanks to social media, the rules of engagement between the business community and the public have changed. The social web has leveled the playing field between corporations that traditionally controlled their own messages and individuals who have no qualms about maligning managers, embarrassing executives, and criticizing companies on Facebook, Twitter, YouTube, the blogosphere, or other social networking sites. A proactive social media reputation management plan can help you respond immediately to online attacks from individuals or coalitions. Best practices call for the development and implementation of a reputation management plan to help minimize damage to your organization's brand and business, reputation and revenues, should you come under fire in the blogosphere or on social networking sites.

**ReTweet (RT)**   ReTweeting allows you to share interesting tweets that someone else has posted. To ReTweet, simply copy a message you have received and lead it with RT@username. Doing so will share that particular message, link, or related information with your entire list of Twitter followers.

**Respondeat Superior** *Respondeat superior* (and the related legal concept of vicarious liability) is the legal term that is used when an organization is held legally (and financially) responsible for the unlawful, offensive, or otherwise inappropriate actions of its employees. Vicarious liability applies, regardless of whether the offending employee's violation was accidental or intentional. It also may apply regardless of whether the employee commits the offense at the office using company-owned resources, at home using private devices and accounts, or on the road using either business or personal tools and technologies. In other words, thanks to vicarious liability, an employer might be held legally responsible for the obscene, harassing, discriminatory, or otherwise illegal or objectionable blog posts, tweets, or Facebook comments of a rogue employee—on the organization's business blogs and social networking sites or possibly on the employee's personal, home-based blog and social media accounts.

**RSS (Really Simple Syndication or Rich Site Summary)**   A file format that allows anyone to "syndicate" their online content, so other social networking sites and blogs can automatically receive and reproduce posts and links back to the originating site.

**RSS Feed**   Through an RSS feed, RSS notifies readers that their favorite social networking sites and blogs have been updated with new content. Great for trend watching and a time saver for readers, the RSS feed eliminates the need to visit social networking sites or blogs for new information on selected topics. Instead, the RSS feed automatically brings updates to readers.

**Sarbanes-Oxley Act (SOX)**   Designed by the Securities and Exchange Commission (SEC) to thwart fraud in public companies, SOX requires regulated companies to implement internal controls for gathering, processing, and reporting accurate and reliable financial information. Effective content management is fundamental to SOX compliance. Data security breaches, including but not limited to the accidental or intentional posting of confidential content on social media sites, intercepted email messages, corrupted files, stolen or altered data, and lost or misplaced mobile devices, can put an organization at risk of SOX noncompliance.

**SEC**    The United States Securities and Exchange Commission (SEC) is a federal regulatory agency that exists to protect investors, maintain fair and efficient markets, and facilitate capital formation.

**Sermo**    Increasingly, medical professionals are seeking the security and privacy offered by private social networks like Sermo, a physician-only site offering the benefits of clinical collaboration and conversations with professional colleagues in a secure online environment. Professionals can communicate about patient care and cases in a HIPAA-secure environment, without the risks associated with Facebook, LinkedIn, or other public social networking sites.

**Slander**    Defamation is defined as a false statement of fact, versus an opinion. When a defamatory statement is made orally (on YouTube, for example) it is known as "slander." A defamatory statement that appears in writing, such as a tweet, is "libel." An employer may be held liable for defamatory statements made by an employee, if the employee possesses "apparent authority" from the company to speak on its behalf.

**Smartphone**    A mobile phone, such as the BlackBerry, iPhone, or Droid, that offers advanced capabilities including wireless access to the Internet, social media, blogs, email, IM, phone, and voicemail, among others features.

**Social Bookmarking Sites**    Social bookmarking is a method for Internet users to organize, store, manage, and search for links to content online. In a social bookmarking system, users save links to content that they want to remember or share with others in their social community. The content itself isn't shared, just the links (or bookmarks) that reference the content. Descriptions may be added to social bookmarks, providing users with an overview of content before they download it. Social bookmarking sites like Digg, Delicious, StumbleUpon,

Newsvine, and Reddit often offer community members the ability to rate links and comments on bookmarks. That's what makes these sites "social."

**Social Media**   A category of Internet-based resources that facilitate user participation and user-generated content. Social media include but are not limited to social networking sites (Facebook and MySpace), microblogging sites (Twitter and Nixle), photo- and video-sharing sites (Flickr and YouTube), wikis (Wikipedia), blogs (The Huffington Post and TMZ), and social bookmarking or news aggregation sites (Digg and Reddit).

**Social Networks**   Social networks are online platforms where users create profiles, post content, share information, and socialize with others.

**Socialtext**   An enterprise-grade social media software solution for business. Increasingly, organizations are discovering that, for business purposes, effective social networking does not necessarily involve participation on free public sites like Facebook or Twitter. Many organizations prefer the security of internal social media tools like Socialtext, which offer all of the benefits of in-house social networking—minus all the risks to confidentiality, privacy, and productivity that are inherent in public social networking.

**Splog**   Spam blogs. Spam blogs do not provide any real content for users. Sploggers use automated tools to create fake blogs that are full of links to specific websites (generally sites selling goods and services). The goal of splogging is to boost search engine results and send traffic to the linked sites.

**Spoliation**   A legal term, spoliation refers to the destruction of evidence, intentional or otherwise.

**Squidoo**   A publishing platform and social community that allows the user to create an unlimited number of pages, which are called "lenses." Each Squidoo lens focuses on one specific topic and serves as an online "flier," on which the user shares information or expertise related to business, hobbies, or personal interests. Those who create lenses are known as "lensmasters"; readers and commenters are called "Squids."

**State Rules of Civil Procedure**    Civil procedure refers to the rules and judicial practices under which courts conduct civil trials, including workplace lawsuits. In the United States, federal courts follow the Federal Rules of Civil Procedure (FRCP), and state courts adhere to their own state rules of civil procedure. Some states' rules of civil procedure mirror the FRCP; others do not.

**State Sunshine Laws**    (See also "open records laws.") State sunshine laws are the state laws that govern public access to the records of state, county, and local government agencies, school systems, municipalities, and other public entities. State sunshine laws are also known as open records laws. Collectively, state sunshine laws are referred to as FOIA laws, after the federal Freedom of Information Act.

**StumbleUpon**    See "social bookmarking sites."

**Tablet**    A tablet personal computer (PC) is a tablet-sized computer operated primarily by a touch screen. Tablets are not intended to run the type of general PC operating systems or applications that run on desktops or laptops. Tablets are designed to be used for accessing the web, viewing videos, and social networking—essentially, oversized smartphones.

**Tchotchke**    A trinket or knickknack featuring a company name or logo. Baseball caps, coffee mugs, golf balls, mouse pads, and pens are popular corporate tchotchkes.

**Techmeme**    News aggregation site focusing on technology news. Techmeme.com arranges links to tech stories from hundreds of blogs and news sites onto a single page. Story selection is accomplished via computer algorithm combined with human editorial input.

**Threads**    Some discussion sites are structured as threads. Like email conversations, threads are contextual and are formed by a long string of comments and replies. The comment sections of blogs are threads.

Thread content may stay focused on one, original topic. Or, it may veer off onto other related (or unrelated) topics. Like chat and forum content, threads may be retained and archived.

**Trade Secrets**   A trade secret is confidential, closely guarded business information (including, for example, sales methods, distribution systems, advertising strategies, merger or acquisition plans, customer lists, or manufacturing methods) that provides an organization with a competitive edge over the competition. The formula for Coca-Cola, for example, is a famous trade secret.

**Tweets**   The 140-character messages that are posted on Twitter.

**Twitter**   Twitter is a microblogging site that limits messages, or tweets, to 140 characters. Readers who follow a writer's tweets are called "followers."

**Uniform Free Trade Secrets Act**   Adopted by forty-six states, the District of Columbia, and the U.S. Virgin Islands, as of 2011, this act prevents third parties (social networkers and bloggers, for example) from knowingly exposing confidential information (customer's private data or a company's trade secrets, for example) provided by people who are bound by confidentiality agreements (employees, for example).

**Unintended Reader**   Includes persons to whom your intended reader links, syndicates, forwards, or copies your original message. Also may include your intended reader's employer, court personnel, regulators, law enforcement, and the media among others. (See also "hidden reader.")

**URL Block**   Employers sometimes use a content filtering solution (software, hardware appliance, or cloud technology) to block employee access to external blogs, public social networking sites, or other websites that are deemed to be risky for legal or regulatory reasons or otherwise inappropriate.

**Vicarious Liability**   Under the legal principle known as vicarious liability, an employer may be held legally (and financially) responsible for employees' accidental or intentional misconduct including, for example, inappropriate, offensive, or unlawful social networking, blog, email, or Internet content or use.

**Video Blog**   Also known as a "vlog." Refers to the distribution of videos via blogs.

**Video-Sharing Site**   Video-sharing sites give employees direct access to the public. Thanks to YouTube and other video-sharing sites, anyone whose smartphone, cell phone, tablet PC, or other mobile device is equipped with a video recorder can capture and upload potentially embarrassing or otherwise damaging videos of company executives and employees, facilities and trade secrets—in a snap. Like other social networking sites, video-sharing sites increase the risk of confidentiality breaches and information leaks when employees and ex-employees shoot and post unauthorized videos of a company's people, products, and proprietary information.

**Video Snacking**   Employees who surf the web for personal reasons during their lunch breaks often are engaged in what's called "video snacking." A common practice within some organizations, unrestricted personal lunchtime surfing is an increasingly risky proposition for employers. Video snacking opens the organization to bandwidth waste and other risks as employees download and file large, non-business-related videos. Systems can be damaged and security breached as spyware, viruses, and other malicious intruders enter the company system via infected content. Employee productivity may be diminished as video snackers, hungry for more content, stretch the lunch hour into the afternoon.

**Vlog**   Video blog. Distributing videos via blogs.

**Web 2.0**   Web 2.0 is the term used to describe interactive, Internet-based communication and collaboration tools and technologies. Web 2.0 allows for the creation and exchange of user-generated content and is all about conversation, collaboration, and customization. Examples of web 2.0 applications are social networking sites, blogs, video-sharing sites, photo-sharing sites, and wikis, to name a few.

**Web Diary**  A web diary is a blog.

**Wiki**  Reported to be an acronym for "what I know is," a wiki is a website with pages that any reader can contribute content to or edit. Readers are encouraged to add pages, edit content, or comment on other writers' remarks. The term "wiki" is adapted from the Hawaiian phrase "wiki wiki," which means quick. Wikis primarily are used in the business arena as an internal collaboration platform for employees.

**Wikipedia**  A wiki, Wikipedia is an online encyclopedia that allows any user to post or edit entries.

**Worm**  A type of "person-created" malicious code or computer virus that replicates itself on a computer, using up more and more of the computer's memory and system resources until the computer becomes sluggish or even inoperable.

**Yammer**  A private enterprise-grade social networking site. Yammer allows employees to communicate and collaborate within a secure internal network, rather than using a less-secure public site, such as Facebook, on the public Internet.

**YouTube**  The "granddaddy" of video-sharing sites. YouTube offers users the ability to upload, tag, describe, share, find, watch, and comment on videos. YouTube has embraced, and been embraced by, the business community. Many organizations use YouTube to educate consumers about services, deliver how-to advice, build brand awareness, communicate a position, deliver a message, or promote people, products, and businesses. It's not unusual for popular YouTube videos to "go viral," attracting millions of viewers in the process.

# NOTES

## INTRODUCTION

1. Facebook, "Statistics," Aug. 2011. http://www.facebook.com/press/info.php?statistics.
2. T. Henneman, "Companies Making Friends with Social Media," Oct. 2010. http://www.workforce.com/section/software-technology/feature/companies-making-friends.
3. "One Blog Created 'Every Second,'" *BBC News,* August 2, 2005.
4. Panda Security, "First Annual Social Media Risk Index for Small to Medium Sized Businesses," September 2010. http://press.pandasecurity.com/usa/wp-content/uploads/2010/09/1st-Annual-Social-Media-Risk-Index.pdf. See also: "DataBank: Social Gauge," *SC Magazine,* Nov. 2010, p. 7.
5. T. Henneman, "Companies Making Friends with Social Media," Oct. 2010. http://www.workforce.com/section/software-technology/feature/companies-making-friends.

## CHAPTER ONE

1. Clearswift, "Web 2.0 in the Workplace Today," Report 1 in a series of 3, April 2010.
2. Ibid.

3. Facebook, "Statistics," Aug. 2011. http://www.facebook.com/press/info.php?statistics.

4. Clearswift, "Web 2.0 in the Workplace Today," Report 1 in a series of 3, April 2010.

5. American Management Association and The ePolicy Institute, "2009 Electronic Business Communication Policies and Procedures Survey," July 2009. http://www.epolicyinstitute.com.

6. Nucleus Research, "Facebook: Measuring the Cost to Business of Social Networking," *Research Note,* July 2009.

7. American Management Association and The ePolicy Institute, "2009 Electronic Business Communication Policies and Procedures Survey."

8. Ibid.

9. J. Blau, "Proposed Law Targets Companies Snooping on Social Networking Sites," *Deutsche Welle,* Aug. 24, 2010. http://www.dw-world.de.

## CHAPTER TWO

1. G. Yohe, "A Web 2.0 Warning," Oct. 2, 2009. http://www.hreonline.com/HRE/story.jsp?storyId=260328725.

2. N. Flynn, *Blog Rules,* New York: Amacom, 2006.

3. American Management Association and The ePolicy Institute, "2009 Electronic Business Communication Policies and Procedures Survey," July 2009. http://www.epolicyinstitute.com.

4. Thérèse Miller, Esq., Shook, Hardy & Bacon, LLP. Phone interview with Nancy Flynn, April 18, 2011.

5. Proofpoint, "Outbound Email and Data Loss Prevention in Today's Enterprise, 2010," June and July 2010. http://www.proofpoint.com/outbound.

6. Ibid.

7. *Tiburzi v. Holmes Transport, Inc.,* No. 4:08 CV 1151 DDN (E.D. Mo. 01/11/2010).

8. *Bustos v. Dyke Industries, Inc.,* Miami-Dade Case No.01–13370, 2001. See also: J. Vegosen and D. Dunn, "Employer Liability for Texting While Driving," Bloomberg Law Reports, 2010. http://www.fvldlaw.com/C014EC/assets/files/News/2010_Emp_liab_for_text_driving.pdf.

9. American Management Association and The ePolicy Institute, "2009 Electronic Business Communication Policies and Procedures Survey."

## CHAPTER THREE

1. E. Koblentz, "Committee Ponders EDD Changes to Federal Rules of Civil Procedure," *Law Technology News,* July 22, 2011. http://www.law.com/jsp/lawtechnologynews/PubArticleLTN.jsp?id=1202504322877&slreturn=1&hbxlogin=1.

2. *Zubulake v. UBS Warburg,* 02 Civ. 1243 (S.D.N.Y., Oct 22, 2003). See also: N. Flynn, *The e-Policy Handbook,* New York: Amacom, 2009.

3. *Qualcomm Inc. v. Broadcom Corp.,* No. 05cv1958-B (BLM) (S.D. Cal. Apr 2, 2010).

4. *Kipperman v. Onex Corp.,* 411 BR 805, (Dist. Court, ND Georgia, May 2009).

5. "Judge: Ky. Man Can See His Wife's E-Mail," *Associated Press,* Nov. 20, 2007.

6. State ex. rel. Mun. Const. Equip. Operators' Labor Council v. City of Cleveland, 2010 Ohio 2108 (8th Dist. Ct. of App.)

7. N. Flynn, *The e-Policy Handbook,* New York: Amacom, 2009.

## CHAPTER FOUR

1. Fulbright & Jaworski LLP, "Fulbright's Seventh Annual Litigation Trends Survey Report," 2010. http://www.fulbright.com/litigationtrends.

2. T. Molloy, "Reg FD and Social Media-Coloring Within the Lines," June 9, 2011. http://exchanges.nyx.com. See also: M. Kozubek, "Disclosure Dilemmas: Social Media Increase Possible Risk of Releasing Material Information," *Inside Counsel,* January 2010.

3. U.S. Securities and Exchange Commission, "Final Rule: Selective Disclosure and Insider Trading," Aug. 21, 2000. http://www.sec.gov/rules/final/33-7881.htm.

4. A. Ray, "Social Media Disasters (or How Not Having a Social Media Strategy Can Hurt)," June 21, 2008. http://socialmediatoday.com/index.php?q=SMC/37982. See also "Social Networking: Safely Manage the Paradigm Shift and Leverage Its Full Potential," Symantec .cloud/MessagesLabs Whitepaper, 2009. http://www.symanteccloud.com/en/gb/index.aspx.

5. FINRA, "FINRA Issues Guidance to Firms, Brokers on Communications with Public Through Social Networking Web Sites," FINRA News Release, Jan. 25, 2010. http://www.finra.org.

6. Smith, C. "Despite Huge Investment, Goldman Blocks Employees from Facebook," Jan. 3, 2011. http://www.huffingtonpost.com/2011/01/03/goldman-employees-blocked-from-facebook_n_803731.html.

7. N. Lewis, "UCLA Health System Pays $865,000 Over Privacy Charges," July 8, 2011. http://www.informationweek.com/news/healthcare/security-privacy/231001236.

8. S. Yin, "Hospital Worker Fired Over Facebook Comments About Patient," *FierceHealthcare,* Aug. 1, 2010. http://www.fiercehealthcare.com/story/hospital-worker-fired-over-facebook-comments-about-patient/2010–08–01.

9. J. Shafer, "The FTC's Mad Power Grab," Oct. 7, 2009. http://www.slate.com/id/2231808/.

## CHAPTER FIVE

1. S. Lawton, "IT's New Problem," *SC Magazine, 18,* Nov. 2010.

2. D. Beaulieu, "Nurses' Jobs at Risk for Allegedly Posting Patient Info on Facebook," June 8, 2010. http://www.fiercehealthcare.com.

3. "Social Insecurity: What Millions of Online Users Don't Know Can Hurt Them," *Consumer Reports,* June 2010. http://www.consumerreports.org/cro/magazine-archive/2010/june/electronics-computers/social-insecurity/overview/index.htm.

4. D. Backhouse, and others, "Court Compels Production of Personal Emails from Company Systems Citing Lack of Reasonable Privacy Expectation," June 9, 2011. http://www.lexology.com/library/detail.aspx?g=d3fe45eb-282c-4338–9908–1a10401519f4.

5. Womble Carlyle Sandridge & Rice PLLC, "Leahy Introduces Legislation Regarding Email Privacy," June 16, 2011. http://www.lexology.com/library/detail.aspx?g=1884b7cb-a3d7–4af9–8962-cb9ed2eb757a.

6. American Management Association and The ePolicy Institute, "2009 Electronic Business Communication Policies and Procedures Survey," July 2009. http://www.epolicyinstitute.com.

7. B. Quinn, "Virgin Sacks 13 Over Facebook 'Chav' Remarks," *The Guardian,* Nov. 1, 2008. http://www.guardian.co.uk/business/2008/nov/01/virgin-atlantic-facebook.

8. L. Czekaj, "Workers Fired Over Internet Postings," *Ottawa Sun,* Jan. 17, 2007. http://cnews.canoe.ca/CNEWS/Canada/2007/01/17/3394584-sun.html.

9. "Mike Bacsik Twitter Tirade: Ex-Pitcher Sends Racist Tirade," April 26, 2010. http://www.huffingtonpost.com/2010/04/26/mike-bacsik-twitter-tirad_n_552532.html?view=screen.

10. D. Bauder, "CNN Fires Middle Eastern Editor Over Tweet," *Associated Press,* July 8, 2010. http://www.huffingtonpost.com/huff-wires/20100708/us-tv-cnn-editor-fired/.

11. "Conn. Ambulance Co. Settles Facebook Firing Case with Labor Board," IBTimes.com, http://www.ibtimes.com/articles/113197/20110216/conn-ambulance-co-settles-facebook-firing-lawsuit-with-labor-board.htm. February 16, 2011. See also: E. Woollacott, "Ambulance Company Settles Over Facebook Firing," TG Daily, February 8, 2011. http://www.tgdaily.com/business-and-law-features/53992-ambulance-company-settles-over-facebook-firing. Also: Tim Kennedy, kennedy.tim1@gmail.com. "Facebook Settlement." Private email message to Nancy Flynn, nancy@epolicyinstitute.com, February 23, 2011.

12. American Management Association and The ePolicy Institute, "2009 Electronic Business Communication Policies and Procedures Survey," July 2009. http://www.epolicyinstitute.com.

13. Wikipedia, "Protected Class," July 13, 2011. http://en.wikipedia.org/wiki/Protected_class.

14. A. Hall, "Top German Firms Ban Facebook and Twitter from Workplace Over Industrial Espionage Fears." *Mail Online,* Oct. 25, 2010. http://www.dailymail.co.uk/sciencetech/article-1323591/Top-German-firms-ban-Facebook-Twitter-workplace-industrial-espionage-fears.html. See also: J. Blau, "Proposed Law Targets Companies Snooping on Social Networking Sites," *Deutsche Welle,* Aug. 24, 2010. http://www.dw-world.de.

15. "Data Protection Act, Switzerland," April 5, 2007. http://www.dataprotection.eu/pmwiki/pmwiki.php?n=Main.CH.

16. N. Flynn, *The e-Policy Handbook,* New York: Amacom, 2009. See also: "Data Protection Act 1998," 1998. http://www.legislation.gov.uk/ukpga/1998/29/contents.

17. Symantec, "What You Need to Know Before Embracing Social Networking," March 4, 2011. http://www.symantec.com/business/resources/articles/article.jsp?aid=20110204_what_you_need_to_know.

18. Proofpoint, "Outbound Email and Data Loss Prevention in Today's Enterprise, 2010," June and July 2010. http://www.proofpoint.com/outbound.

19. H. Anderson, "Obama Offers Breach Notification Bill: Federal Law Would Supersede State Laws," May 12, 2011. http://www.bankinfosecurity.com/articles.php?art_id=3637&search_keyword=Obama+Offers+Breach+Notification+Bill&search_method=exact.

20. T. Lewin, "Ohio State Says Hackers Breached Data on 760,000," *The New York Times,* Dec. 16, 2010. http://www.nytimes.com/2010/12/17/education/17colleges.html.

21. N. Flynn, "Economic Stimulus Package and Health Care" and "Compliance Rules for Healthcare Companies," Symantec.cloud/ MessageLabs and The ePolicy Institute white papers, 2010. http://www .symanteccloud.com/search.aspx?YLehNjYOUS3Pk/o5TsWxargu-W9YB8 +uRDym4OmBCzuw=.

22. N. Flynn, "Compliance Rules for Financial Firms and Institutions: Rules and Tools, Policies and Best Practices." Symantec.cloud/MessageLabs and The ePolicy Institute white paper, 2010. http://www.syman-teccloud.com/search.aspx?YLehNjYOUS3Pk/o5TsWxarguW9YB8 +uRDym4OmBCzuw=.

23. "Huge Data Breach at NYC Hospital, Backup Tapes Were Not Encrypted," Alertsec Xpress Data Security Blog, Feb 18, 2011. http:// www.alertsec.com.

24. "Four in Five Docs Could Have Smartphones by 2010." *Fierce MobileHealthcare,* Oct. 6, 2009. http://www.fiercemobilehealthcare.com /story/four-five-docs-could-have-smartphones-2012/2009-10-06.

25. N. Versel, "Docs Say Social Media Helps Care, But Hospitals Should Look Before They Leap." *FierceHealthIT,* April 19, 2010. http://www .fiercehealthit.com/story/docs-say-social-media-helps-care-hospitals-should-look-they-leap/2010-04-19.

26. A. Hall, "Top German Firms Ban Facebook and Twitter from Workplace Over Industrial Espionage Fears," *Mail Online,* Oct. 25, 2010. http:// www.dailymail.co.uk/sciencetech/article-1323591/Top-German-firms-ban-Facebook-Twitter-workplace-industrial-espionage-fears.html.

## CHAPTER SIX

1. Wikipedia, "Blogger," August 27, 2011. http://en.wikipedia.org/wiki/ Blogger_%28service%29. See also: Facebook, "Facebook Timeline," 2010. http://www.facebook.com/press/info.php?timeline. See also: Wikipedia, "Twitter," August 26, 2011. http://en.wikipedia.org/wiki/ Twitter.

2. S. Baker and H. Green, "Blogs Will Change Your Business," *BusinessWeek Online,* May 2, 2005, http://www.businessweek.com.

3. J. Sobel, "State of the Blogosphere 2010 Introduction," *Technorati,* Nov. 3, 2010. http://technorati.com/blogging/article/state-of-the-blogosphere-2010-introduction/.

4. Proofpoint, "Outbound Email and Data Loss Prevention in Today's Enterprise, 2010," June and July 2010. http://www.proofpoint.com/ outbound.

5. N. Flynn, *Blog Rules,* New York: Amacom, 2006.

6. Ibid.

7. Ibid.

8. Federal Trade Commission, "FTC Publishes Final Guides Governing Endorsements, Testimonials," Oct. 5, 2009. http://www.ftc.gov/opa/2009/10/endortest.shtm.

9. J. Sobel, "State of the Blogosphere 2010 Introduction."

## CHAPTER SEVEN

1. ZoomSafer. "Distracted Driving: Understanding Your Corporate Risk and Liability." http://www.slideshare.net/ZoomSafer/distract. See also C.J. Driscoll and Associates. "U.S. Mobile Resource Management Systems Market Study." http://www.cjdriscoll.com/US_Mobile_Resource_Management_Systems_Market_Study.htm.

2. A. Smith, "Smartphone Adoption and Usage," Pew Internet & American Life Project, July 11, 2011. http://www.pewinternet.org/Reports/2011/Smartphones.aspx.

3. Proofpoint, "Outbound Email and Data Loss Prevention in Today's Enterprise, 2010," June and July 2010. http://www.proofpoint.com/outbound.

4. R. Cheng, "So You Want to Use Your iPhone for Work? Uh-oh," *The Wall Street Journal,* April 25, 2011, p. R1.

5. Ibid.

6. Ibid.

7. American Management Association and The ePolicy Institute, "2009 Electronic Business Communication Policies and Procedures Survey," July 2009. http://www.epolicyinstitute.com.

8. CareerBuilder News Release. "More Than Half of Workers Admit to Checking Their Smart Phones While Driving, Finds New CareerBuilder Survey," March 10, 2010. http://www.careerbuilder.com/share/aboutus/pressreleasesdetail.aspx?id=pr558&sd=3/10/2010&ed=12/31/2010&siteid=cbpr&sc_cmp1=cb_pr558_&cbRecursionCnt=2&cbsid=35b19caeb97b40bdb1618299a3639045−334150388−wg-6.

9. M. Madden, "Adults Text While Driving Too!" Pew Internet & American Life Project, June 18, 2010. http://pewresearch.org/pubs/1633/adults-texting-talking-on-cellphone-while-driving-like-teens.

10. J. Sobel, "State of the Blogosphere 2010 Introduction," Nov. 3, 2010. http://technorati.com/blogging/article/state-of-the-blogosphere-2010-introduction/.

11. Facebook, "Statistics," Aug. 2011. http://www.facebook.com/press/info.php?statistics.

12. Distraction.gov website, "Statistics and Facts About Distracted Driving," October 2011. http://distraction.gov/stats-and-facts/index.html.

13. Virginia Tech news release, "New Data from Virginia Tech Transportation Institute Provides Insight Into Cell Phone Use and Driving Distraction," July 29, 2009. http://www.vtnews.vt.edu/articles/2009/07/2009-571.html.

14. *Tiburzi v. Holmes Transport, Inc.,* No. 4:08 CV 1151 DDN, (E.D. MO, January 11, 2010).

15. *Bustos v. Dyke Industries Inc.,* Miami-Dade Case No.01–13370 (2001). See also: J. Vegosen and D. Dunn, "Employer Liability for Texting While Driving," *Bloomberg Law Reports,* 2010. http://www.fvldlaw.com/C014EC/assets/files/News/2010_Emp_liab_for_text_driving.pdf.

16. *Huggins v. FedEx Ground Package System, Inc.,* 592 F. 3rd 853 (8th Cir. 2010). See also: Vegosen and D. Dunn, "Employer Liability for Texting While Driving."

17. *Jeewarat v. Warner Bros. Entertainment, Inc.,* 177 Cal. App. 4th 427,437 (Cal. Ct. App. 2009). See also: Vegosen, and Dunn, "Employer Liability for Texting While Driving."

18. The White House, "Executive Order: Federal Leadership on Reducing Text Messaging While Driving," Oct. 1, 2009. http://www.whitehouse.gov/the_press_office/Executive-Order-Federal-Leadership-on-Reducing-Text-Messaging-while-Driving. See also: The Library of Congress, "Bill Text: 112th Congress (2011–2012), H.R.2333.IH," June 2011. http://thomas.loc.gov/cgi-bin/query/z?c112:h2333:.

19. Governors Highway Safety Association, "Cell Phone and Texting Laws," Sept. 2011. http://www.ghsa.org/html/stateinfo/laws/cellphone_laws.html.

20. Vegosen and Dunn, "Employer Liability for Texting While Driving."

21. American Management Association and The ePolicy Institute, "2009 Electronic Business Communication Policies and Procedures Survey."

22. Ibid.

## CHAPTER NINE

1. M. Madden, "Older Adults and Social Media," Pew Internet & American Life Project, Aug 27, 2010. http://www.pewinternet.org/Reports/2010/Older-Adults-and-Social-Media.aspx.

## CHAPTER TEN

1. Time, "Lexicon: Video Snacking," *Briefing Column,* Jan 21, 2008. See also N. Flynn, *The e-Policy Handbook,* New York: Amacom, 2009.
2. American Management Association and The ePolicy Institute. "2009 Electronic Business Communication Policies and Procedures Survey," July 2009. http://www.epolicyinstitute.com.

## CHAPTER ELEVEN

1. McAfee, "Web 2.0: A Complex Balancing Act," July 2010. http://www .mcafee.com/us/resources/reports/rp-first-global-study-web-2.0-usage.pdf.
2. Proofpoint, "Outbound Email and Data Loss Prevention in Today's Enterprise, 2010." http://www.proofpoint.com/outbound.
3. M. Pounds, "Risque Business," SunSentinal.com, Aug. 20, 2009. http://articles.sun-sentinel.com/2009−08−20/business/0908190255_ 1_sexual-harassment-text-messages-e-mail.
4. The Columbus Dispatch, "Delaware County Jail Director Resigns," Nov. 20, 2009. http://www.dispatch.com/content/stories/local/2009/11/20/ Delaware-County-jail-chief-resigns.html.
5. The Huffington Post, "Waiter Jon-Barrett Ingels Fired For Twittering About Hung Star Jane Adams," March 18, 2010. http://www.huffington-post.com/2009/10/06/jane-adams-waiter-jon-bar_n_310783.html.
6. Twitter Blog, "Measuring Tweets," Feb. 22, 2010. http://blog.twitter. com/2010/02/measuring-tweets.html.
7. A. Witt, "Blog Interrupted," *The Washington Post,* April 15, 2004. See also: R. Leiby, "The Hill's Sex Diarist Reveals All (Well, Some)," The *Washington Post,* May 23, 2004.
8. D. Willis, "Bloggers Beware," *Asbury Park Press,* Sept. 26, 2005.
9. T. Decker, "Bigoted Videos Investigated," *The Columbus Dispatch,* Aug. 29, 2007.
10. American Management Association and The ePolicy Institute, "2009 Electronic Business Communication Policies and Procedures Survey," July 2009. http://www.epolicyinstitute.com.

## CHAPTER TWELVE

1. American Management Association and The ePolicy Institute, "2009 Electronic Business Communication Policies and Procedures Survey," July 2009. http://www.epolicyinstitute.com.

## CHAPTER THIRTEEN

1. "DataBank: Social Gauge," *SC Magazine,* Nov. 2010, p. 7. See also: McAfee, "Web 2.0: A Complex Balancing Act," July 2010. http://www.mcafee.com/us/resources/reports/rp-first-global-study-web-2.0-usage.pdf.

2. Facebook, "Statistics," Aug. 2011. http://www.facebook.com/press/info.php?statistics. See also: Wikipedia, "Twitter," August 26, 2011. http://en.wikipedia.org/wiki/Twitter See also: YouTube, "Press Room," Sept. 2011. http://www.youtube.com/t/press.

3. D. Lyons, "Attack of the Blogs," *Forbes,* Nov. 14, 2005.

4. Ibid. See also: T. Miller, "Social Media & Web 2.0 as Evidence," PowerPoint presentation at ARMA International Greater Columbus Ohio Chapter, 2011 Annual Spring Seminar, Columbus, May 2011.

5. "DataBank: Social Gauge," SC Magazine, Nov. 2010, p. 6. See also Burson-Marsteller, "The Global Social Media Check-Up," 2010. http://www.burson-marsteller.com/Innovation_and_insights/blogs_and_pod-casts/BM_Blog/Documents/Burson-Marsteller%202010%20Global%20Social%20Media%20Check-up%20white%20paper.pdf.

6. Cornell University Law School, Sept. 2011. http://www.law.cornell.edu/uscode/47/usc_sec_47_00000230——000-.html. See also: T. Miller, "Social Media & Web 2.0 as Evidence."

7. Facebook, "Statistics." See also: J. Sobel, "State of the Blogosphere 2010 Introduction," Nov. 3, 2010. http://technorati.com/blogging/article/state-of-the-blogosphere-2010-introduction/.

8. L. Stick, "Why I Co-opted BP's Twitter Presence," The Huffington Post, June 3, 2010. http://www.huffingtonpost.com/leroy-stick/why-i-co-opted-bps-twitte_b_599283.html.

9. L. Gaines-Ross, "Reputation Warfare," *Harvard Business Review,* December 2010, 5.

10. N. Flynn, *Blog Rules,* New York: Amacom, 2006.

# INDEX

## A

"About Me" section, 250, 255–256, 328–329

Acceptable use policies (AUPs): best practices for blog, 87; description of, 2; e-discovery of, 37; helping to manage vicarious liability, 13–14, 24, 25; media policy audit questionnaire on, 153–154; mobile device use, 108–109, 118; prohibiting anonymous blogging and posting, 223; reputation management through use of, 221–222; social media policy audit of your, 139–162; testing your know-how about, 4; tips for blogging, 87, 95–99. *See also* Best practices; Sample policies; Social media policies

Accident-related liability, 23, 25, 114–118

Acknowledgment form requirement, 208–209

Action plan. *See* Social media action plan

Age Discrimination in Employment Act, 20

Amended Federal Rules of Civil Procedure (FRCP), 313–314. *See also* Federal Rules of Civil Procedure (FRCP)

American Management Association, 7, 19, 23, 68, 73, 114, 118, 172, 211

American Medical Response (AMR), 71–72

American Recovery and Reinvestment Act (ARRA), 324

Americans with Disabilities Act, 20

Anonymous blogging, 101

Anti-Defamation League, 188

Archive: categories of, 316; definition of, 314

ArcMail Technology, 44

Armstrong, Heather B., 320

Associated Press, 69

Attachment, 314

Audits. *See* Social media policy audits

Authenticity, 314

Automatic archiving system, 34

## B

Backup system: definition of, 315; ESI stored using, 33; "virtual shredding" of tape, 33–34

Banning sites: German workplace practice of, 80; growing challenge of, 169–170. *See also* Blocking sites

Best practices: automatic archiving of ESI, 34; blog policies, 87, 95–99, 102–105; company privacy and security, 66, 80–81; compliance management, 8; compliance with international privacy laws, 14, 76, 113; a comprehensive legal review of policy as, 231–232; content management rules, 198–199; effective records management team and record retention policy, 45–47; effective social media policies, 87, 166, 180–181; employee privacy protection, 68; financial services industry regulatory compliance, 59; know the state rules affecting your company, 39; knowing international privacy/monitoring laws, 76; legal compliance, 23–25; management of third-party comments, 95–99; management of vicarious liability risk, 13–14; mobile devices use, 25, 110–114, 119–120; policy is essential to compliance management, 8; policy training, 212–213, 222; private social networks, 60–61, 327, 331, 336; records management and e-discovery compliance, 47–49, 327; Regulation FD